CW01211035

Proof of Life

Also by Jennifer Pastiloff

On Being Human

Jennifer Pastiloff

Proof of Life

Let Go, Let Love, and Stop
Looking for Permission
to Live Your Life

DUTTON

An imprint of Penguin Random House LLC
1745 Broadway, New York, NY 10019
penguinrandomhouse.com

Copyright © 2025 by Jennifer Pastiloff

Penguin Random House values and supports copyright. Copyright fuels creativity, encourages diverse voices, promotes free speech, and creates a vibrant culture. Thank you for buying an authorized edition of this book and for complying with copyright laws by not reproducing, scanning, or distributing any part of it in any form without permission. You are supporting writers and allowing Penguin Random House to continue to publish books for every reader. Please note that no part of this book may be used or reproduced in any manner for the purpose of training artificial intelligence technologies or systems.

DUTTON and the D colophon are registered trademarks
of Penguin Random House LLC.

BOOK DESIGN BY KATY RIEGEL

LIBRARY OF CONGRESS CATALOGING-IN-PUBLICATION DATA
has been applied for.

ISBN 9780593474075 (hardcover)
ISBN 9780593474082 (ebook)

Printed in the United States of America
1 3 5 7 9 10 8 6 4 2

The authorized representative in the EU for product safety and compliance is Penguin Random House Ireland, Morrison Chambers, 32 Nassau Street, Dublin D02 YH68, Ireland, https://eu-contact.penguin.ie.

This one is for my sister, Rachel: my I Got You Person *since the late seventies and the person who taught me that it's okay to choose ourselves*

Instructions for When You Feel Lonely

Open the window and scream.
When no one screams back
don't go *See?*
as if silence is evidence
that you are alone in the world.
You can't use that quiet as proof
of your forsakenness.
Look for evidence somewhere else.
Carve your name with a tiny fork in a secret spot.
Something to touch
when you need to remember
that you are here.
Then, begin to sing and sing,
until birds land on the sill and flowers begin to bloom,
until your voice goes hoarse and you piss yourself with delight
at how off-key you are, at made-up lyrics,
at positively absolutely nothing at all,
the best kind of delight.
Then sing even louder,
until someone sings back.
And even then, don't stop.

Contents

INTRODUCTION:	Do It Before You Run Out of Light	1
	Poem: *Proof of Life*	21
	Glossary of Terms in *Proof of Life*	22
CHAPTER ONE:	You Get to Have This	29
	Poem: *Changing Lanes*	49
CHAPTER TWO:	You Are Never Lost	51
	Poem: *Show-Off*	77
CHAPTER THREE:	The Era of *Because I Want to Do It This Way*	79
	Poem: *Kinds of Afraid*	88
CHAPTER FOUR:	Leaving *The Land of Fine*	90
	Poem: *Shame*	125
CHAPTER FIVE:	Shame Loss	127
	Poem: *Altering Time*	149
CHAPTER SIX:	You Are Right on Time	152
	Poem: *How to Get Connected*	171

CHAPTER SEVEN:	*Love* Is a Verb	173
	Poem: The Coal Town Bus Route from Lewisburg to Philadelphia	194
CHAPTER EIGHT:	The Will to Grow Must Outweigh the Need to Stay Safe	196
	Poem: To Be Spoken in a Whisper	224
CHAPTER NINE:	Chasing Goats, Finding Compassion, and Ending That Lonely Life of Self-Abandonment	227
	Poem: Perspective	246
CHAPTER TEN:	Suppose	248
	Poem: When We Really Look	271
CHAPTER ELEVEN:	Find a Way In	272
	Poem: Afterbirth	293
CHAPTER TWELVE:	Keep Bending	295
	Poem: It's All Ours	314
EPILOGUE:	Eat the Cake	316
	Acknowledgments	321

INTRODUCTION

Do It Before You Run Out of Light

THERE'S AN EXPRESSION mistakenly attributed to John Lennon: *Life is what happens when you are busy making other plans.** Life happened while I was busy trying to write this book.

Except, it didn't just *happen*. It didn't even *blow up*.

My whole life blew up, I'd say, like it was some passive thing that I had no choice in.

I blew it up, and despite what I initially believed (and what some other people told me) I neither wrecked nor destroyed my life.

I expanded it.

I've got to tell you, it can feel like the same thing.

YOU GET TO *have this* is a thing I now say pretty regularly. I believe it, too. But for most of my life, I did not believe I deserved anything.

I did deserve some things, of course. Guilt, feeling bad, punishment, things being taken away from me, et cetera. But as far as love, joy, ease, contentment, or any kind of feeling good? Nope. Ever since

---

* Allen Saunders is the author of the quote.

I was eight years old, I'd held tight to the fact that I was a bad person. A monster, as it were.

For reference, here's how my monster got made: The last thing that my favorite person, my entire universe—my father—said to me was *You're being bad and making me not feel good.*

Then he dropped dead.

I took on that badness as a permanent uniform. Starting that July, between the second and third grades, I imagined horns and fangs and scales when I looked in the mirror. I knew I had to pay for what I did, for the rest of my life.

I eventually did take off that uniform of badness and accept all I'd denied myself, even when it felt like I was wearing someone else's life without my old uniform on. I wasn't.

What I'm saying is that if I could do what I believed to be impossible, you can, too.

Oh, and it isn't impossible.

⸻

I UNEXPECTEDLY BOUGHT a house, then left my husband. *After* I bought the house. Neither planned; both complicated. Equally as complicated and unplanned was my falling madly and unexpectedly in love with someone else, then becoming engaged to that person while still disentangling myself from my long and very precarious marriage, which included custody of our small child and, perhaps most damning—at least for a person in California who wants to exit a long marriage—my being the breadwinner.

I started writing poetry again, then teaching poetry workshops to hundreds of people. I switched antidepressants, after years of taking Prozac, and became a prolific painter, despite not even being able to draw a stick figure. Then there was the incredible blow that was my mother's new diagnosis: Alzheimer's.

It all happened while I was *supposed* to be working on *this* book.

Some other awful *s* words of note in addition to *supposed*: should, shame, stupid, sorry.

WHEN I FIRST broke up my family unit, while it still felt as if I'd taken a wrecking ball to things rather than having created expansiveness, my old *bad* uniform unretired itself. I'd keep waking with the phrase *should is an asshole** on my tongue, as if my subconscious knew I needed it and had been trying to put the words back in me while I slept.

Before bed I'd ruminate—do not do this, but if you insist on it, before bed is the absolute worst time to ruminate—on all my *should*s and *should have*s and *should have not*s.

I'd mull over how I should be earning more money so I could afford to get legally divorced, how I should have known better than to think I deserved to be happy, and how I should have definitely *not* fallen in love at the same time I was exiting my marriage. This, as far as the *Imaginary Time Gods (ITG)* are concerned, is a huge no-no. The *Imaginary Time Gods* aren't real, but this doesn't stop most of us from adhering to their guidelines or listening to their drivel. We'll discuss these bogus gods more in the coming pages.

I'd try to swat it away like that mosquito who ignores everyone except me,† and same as that damn mosquito, *should is an asshole* kept coming back until I paid attention to it.

---

* Should is an asshole, and that is a fact. Scientifically proven by me.
† And no, I do not find the mosquito love flattering or cute when people say *It's because you're so sweet*. That is straight up mosquito bypassing.

It had been years since I'd waitressed at the Newsroom Café, the trendy West Hollywood restaurant where I'd for years served veggie burgers and watermelon margaritas to celebrities and Very Important Movie Producers. I fell in love with yoga and how much it helped with my depression, and, although begrudgingly at first, I became a yoga teacher. *Begrudgingly* because, although I loved how it felt to practice yoga, I had no desire to become an instructor. Until finally (also begrudgingly, but ultimately thankfully) I went on antidepressants and was able to see how teaching could be possibly an exit route out of the Newsroom.

It was. I used yoga as a way out of my dirty, ketchup-stained apron for good by mixing the only things (I thought) I knew how to do and creating a kind of weird stew of yoga, writing, sharing, and listening. That weird stew grew; it simmered and became workshops I traveled the world with.

I started giving keynote speeches, where I'd use my beloved sticky notes in lieu of PowerPoint presentations and wear whatever I felt like wearing onstage.

I gave talks on authenticity and connection, on how we're all recovering from something, on invisible disabilities and mental health, and on being human. In other words, I gave speeches on *making* and *being* your own weird stew.

My weird stew workshops were unique each time, but they remained constant in their focus on paying attention to your feelings, needs, and wants, as well as finding the voice to express those feelings, needs, and wants. The whole time that I was leading these sold-out workshops—I was excellent at tending to other people's hearts—I in no way was in touch with my own feelings, needs, wants, or heart. The shoemaker's son always goes barefoot. It was something like that.

In the lead-up to the eruption of my life, everything seemed fine. On the face of things, at least. Which is like saying *But you seem so happy on social media.*

If we want to transform anything, it is essential to go beyond the face of things or how they *seem* to appear. Especially with regard to ourselves.

We can't stop at the surface if we want to unearth or explore anything. How would we be able to grow or expand if we did? How can there ever be a shot at challenging our thoughts and beliefs, or the *Bullshit Stories* we've held on to, if we are not willing to look deeper?

I was willing. I went subterranean deep by allowing for change in my life, despite a lifetime of unequivocally believing that change equals death. It is not an exaggeration to say I would have done anything to avoid it. At all costs.

I left the little apartment I had lived in for twenty years, and with some real nerve (which I inherited from my mother), I bought my first home on a freakish whim. After decades of being emotionally constipated and not being able to cry or access how I felt, I began to feel my feelings again, as well as rediscover my sexuality after I left my marriage. I was wildly alive for the first time ever.

And, as is often the case, I was simultaneously wildly sad.

Grief was right there next to joy. A mourning in conjunction with excitement. Anguish pressed up and into elation. The bliss of new love and feeling my feelings again and the incredible bursts of creativity I was experiencing were side by side with the ache of my mother's Alzheimer's diagnosis, facing the terror of the unknown, and the guilt over breaking apart the little family I'd built. And this was just the tip of the lifeberg.*

At the end of that upheaval of a year, I looked around and couldn't find anything to show for it all, except the infinite paintings I'd done in lieu of literally anything else.

I hadn't done *the next big thing*, whatever those words I kept scolding myself with even meant. I hadn't even done *the next little thing*. I canceled retreats when it felt like too much was on my plate; I lost my income; I didn't file my taxes; I didn't start paying back a loan I'd taken out during the pandemic. I was still living with my husband in the exact dynamic we were in before I'd left him. I hadn't even properly filed for divorce.

I panicked. And not for the first time in my life, I asked myself *What have you done?*

You have done love. My own words came back at me, like they were taunting me for memeing them to death.

I'd forgotten something I naively didn't know could be forgotten. I'm hell-bent on not doing that again, which is why I repeat *May I remember* so frequently.

See, I didn't need any verification showing that I'd spent the year being productive so I'd be permitted to continue existing in the world.

What I'd forgotten was that we do not need to prove to anyone that we matter.

We need no proof to show that we're worthy. Ever.

---

* *Iceberg + life = lifeberg.* (I feel it's also probably the last name of someone in my family.)

YOU EXISTING AS you want to exist is not selfish. Honoring your authenticity is not showing off, as the patriarchy (and, at times, our *Inner Assholes*) would have us believe.

I ended that internal strife when I gave myself—because no one else could give it to me—permission to live a life in which I feel fully alive.

Will you do the same?

⚡

RECENTLY, I CURLED up next to my lover—a word that makes me squirm, yet no other feels germane. He was fast asleep and I put my hand on his chest, slid my fingers into the slots between his shirt buttons, touched his chest hair. Listening to this man I love snore is one of my great pleasures. Knowing he's lying there next to me, holding on to my arm that's draped across his body, and the comfort all of that brings.

What an important task: knowing what brings us comfort. We all get to have comfort, to experience that exhale feeling of relief.

In one of my workshops called "Shame Loss," someone said she was taught that you show people you love them by putting all your needs and wants aside.

How many of us were also taught this? How were you taught to show love? What about receiving it? How do we show ourselves? How do you show yourself love?

Until pretty recently, I would have stared blankly had you asked me that last one. *I got nothin'*, I'd have said in response to *How do you show yourself love?*

I learned that, contrary to my *Inner Asshole*'s faux wisdom, loving our own selves is not impractical or far-fetched, nor is it out of the realm of what is possible.

You show yourself love by not putting aside your needs and wants. Simple, and not always easy.

If We Dissect It, Can We Learn from Our Past?

What do we do when our lives come—or fall—apart? Do we crawl on the floor to get a closer look at our past strewn all over the linoleum? A cadaver made of our memories.

Do we search our catalog of mistakes—most of which turned out to be blessings—for data confirming that someone did this *to* us, instead of us having painfully cut the pieces from our own bodies? Will it give us insight if we follow the curves of our life and study them? Maybe. The kind of sight it *definitely* provides is what I am interested in: Heartsight.

ANGEL'S TRUMPETS IS a stunning, bell-looking flowering plant with a gorgeous scent. In fact, the one outside my office window intoxicates me so much that I'd follow it to the end of the earth and back, just to listen to anything it had to say. That's what *Heartsight* is. The listening to our own selves in this way.

⸻

YOU CAN LESSEN your chances of hurt, shame, loss, and sorrow by not allowing love in or out. No one is going to stop you. Although I do imagine it's a lonely way to go through life.

It is impossible to protect yourself from everything. Unless you are dead.

You are not dead.

YOU KNOW IT exists even though you may not have known what it was or had a word for it. We've all had it guide us in ways that bypass vision, logic, brain messaging, sense. Even when it steered us to a love that didn't work out as we'd hoped, it was not *wrong* because love is never wasted.

Heartsight is what allows you to remember your past aliveness, what it felt like to be awake and wide open. If you've never felt those things, it's what allows you to imagine them. Even the feeling of being heartbroken is a kind of aliveness. The dead don't have broken hearts, after all.

Heartsight will bring you back to life.

Recently, I misheard my friend when she said the word *realize*. I heard *re-alive*. There's nothing to study or obsess over with our *Heartsight*. It's simply a remembering and what I've decided *re-alive* means.

Heartsight is what allows you to re-alive.

⸎

SO MANY SEEMINGLY impossible things were happening around me, yet I was trying to repudiate them as if they were not happening—the same way I saw others deny what was possible in their own lives, even as what they were denying was very obviously occurring. I became aware that I was doing the exact thing I'd witnessed folks do in my workshops. I was trying to negate what was right in front of me, just like I'd coached people to *stop* doing. (Hi, Pot. It's me, Kettle.)

I had no choice* but to write about it if I wanted to work through it. I wrote to remind myself—as well as anyone who needed it—how easy it is to cling to old, familiar stories or live in denial, and certainly not because we need reminding how easy it is to fall back into old patterns. But because we do need reminders to use kid gloves on ourselves because of how easy it can be.

I'd try to convince myself by emphatically saying things like *This cannot really be happening because it is not permitted to be happening. You are not allowed to have this, so whatever it is that you think is occurring most certainly is not. Turn around and walk away and go back to your place. You know your place. This is not it.*

I clung to what I knew. Those old *Bullshit Stories* of *You don't get to have this* and *You are bad and do not deserve to feel good.*

I had to keep assuring myself that we can hold more than one thing at once. Even when what we are holding appears to be contradictory or paradoxical, and that we do not have to keep carrying old beliefs we decided on when we were younger.

Writing this book demanded that I tell the truth† to you, and to myself. The latter was hard and uncomfortable but ultimately the most generous thing I have ever done for myself.

The following pages offer tools and support, not only to help you get to know yourself but also to fully *be* yourself. Unapologetically. I wrote them with great love, which I hope you feel as you read and

---

* I did have other choices. We always do. I could have gone back to sleep, the way I had been for a long time. This was the only time it felt like there was no other choice though.

† By *truth*, I mean *my* truth because, look, you can ask both my sister and me what happened in our childhood and we will have different stories, as if neither of us was really there and yet both of us were there, at the same time.

that it settles into you like it belongs to you. Because it does. Love, I mean.

May you be willing to let go of the belief that life is something to be tolerated and that choosing and *being* yourself is not permissible.

No matter what you have been told, no matter what you think—you can't believe everything you think anyway—you *are* deserving and worthy of the life you want. You *are* deserving and worthy. That's the whole sentence. No qualifiers or exceptions come after. That's it.

⁂

MAYBE YOU'VE SPENT God knows how many years climbing the corporate ladder, just to realize that not only have you not climbed anywhere besides out of your overflowing inbox filled with Zoom invites, but also that you don't want to spend another second climbing a hallucinatory ladder. Maybe you've stayed at a soul-sucking job but are too afraid to leave for all the reasons we are ever too afraid to leave. Maybe you've painstakingly admitted you are a writer at last and have begun your book. Maybe you've gone back to school at fifty or seventy or twenty-two. Maybe your beloved passed away, and the thought of even opening the cupboard and seeing their coffee mug brings you to your knees. Maybe you're tired of being single and ready to break out the dating apps or sign up for a hip-hop class to meet people, even though dating apps scare you and you have two left feet. Maybe you've had your heart broken. Maybe you did the breaking, to save your own heart for once. Maybe you've just entered recovery and are navigating the world as a sober person, or maybe you've relapsed and are beginning again. Maybe you're recovering from a heart attack or adjusting to life after a double mastectomy or some kind of cancer that kicked your ass. Maybe your best friend broke up with you for a reason you'll never understand, even though you have tried very hard to. Maybe you ended a friendship because you finally get what boundaries mean despite growing up with nary a one. Maybe you are in the process of transitioning and using your beautiful new name out in the world. Maybe you lost a child, gave birth, became a solo parent, or took in your brother's kids who were left orphans. Maybe your kids are out of the house and *empty nester* is your new moniker, which alternately makes you weep with missing them and has you jumping on the bed like a toddler, flinging yourself in the air with glee at the thought of your new freedom.

THERE ARE ENDLESS *maybe*s of what may be going on in your life, but one thing is certain. This next phase is: *The Era of You*, and may this book be your companion as you enter it.

YOU ABSOLUTELY AND wholeheartedly get to choose yourself, even if others don't approve. Even if others don't choose you. Especially then, *you* must choose you.

If you feel like I am speaking directly to you, it's because I am. You can stop wondering if I *found you out*. Thankfully, I found me out, too.

I am speaking into your soul with both a spotlight and a megaphone. Especially if you, too, walk around with a *Bullshit Story* that says you don't get to have *it*. As far as *it* goes, it can be anything—love, ease, freedom, joy, leaving, a promotion, choosing you. And on and on.

So many think they don't get to rest, or feel guilty for it. They feel they need to constantly be producing, and that they must be able to show for what they produced.

When my son, Charlie, was little, he asked me if the trees stay awake at night or if they sleep. My friend overheard his sweet and profound question. (She had just published her first book, at the age of sixty-five no less. Take that, idiotic *Imaginary Time Gods!*)

She answered him.

Charlie, dear, why they sleep, of course. Holding up the sky is very tiring.

WE DO GET to rest. To just *be*. No caveats.

The list of what we tell ourselves we don't get to have is as endless as it is ridiculous.

I am talking to you and to myself, without an intermediary.

I see you, and I got you. And not just you either. After a lifetime, I finally got me, too.

How to Use This Book

This book contains parts of my story. Some I chose to keep just for me, which is something we all get to do. Also, it can never be the complete story because as long as we are living and breathing, our story is not finished. Sharing and listening to each other with compassion is one of the most fundamental tenets—and one of the greatest privileges—of being human.

I invite you to consider, with as little judgment and shame as possible: *What am I not allowing myself to have?*

This will lead to more questions. Questions like: *What am I not allowing myself to say? To feel? What am I not allowing myself to do?*

Who am I not allowing myself to be? In what ways have I not allowed myself to truly know myself? In what ways am I hiding?

BEFORE YOU END up in *TLOO* (or *The Land of Overwhelm*) from pondering answers that arise, from chastising yourself for so-called wasted time, or from going hoarse from telling yourself it's too late, let me reiterate something: No matter what you've been led to believe, you *are* right on time. Anything that suggests otherwise is a flat-out *Bullshit Story*.

It's common to be uneasy when asking hard questions because of the fear of what we may find. If we choose to go deeper, we know we'll have to ask ourselves *Now what?* If we don't want to feel like a big fraud, we know we'll have to take some kind of action, no matter how minuscule; therefore, we'll often decide to stay superficial or barely scratch the surface to avoid that uncomfortableness. That's what I did. For a very long time.

It's critical to face whatever arises with as much unflinching honesty as possible and, most important, not look away, like I did. For years, I stayed with easy questions, or asked none at all. I did little investigating, thereby allowing for complacency and what I perceived as safety.

YOUR DISCOVERIES MIGHT rattle you. They should. I hate the word *should*, but if what you find isn't rattling you a little, you probably aren't going deep enough with the snake* to unclog the drain.

---

* I know diddly squat about plumbing, but apparently a drain snake is the answer to resolving quite a lot of issues. Consider that we all have plumbing issues, and I am not just talking constipation (raises hand) but rather the upkeep of our fantastically intricate human machinelike selves.

They might make you go *Holy mother of salt-and-vinegar chips, I am not allowing myself to have what I want. For the love of sleeping in, I don't even allow myself to want, period. I don't allow hunger. Desire? Well, who gets to have that? I'm not allowing myself to say that I need something different. I'm not allowing myself to leave, or to change. I'm not allowing myself to do what lights me up. I don't even* know *what lights me up. Wait, I get to be lit up?*

I am not allowing myself to be my full, gloriously weird and magic self.*

LET THIS BOOK be like that friend who reminds you that you are lovable, when you need reminding.

Let it be like that friend who needs no plan, who just shows up and sits there, or unpacks your boxes when you're too depressed to get out of bed. The friend who understands you. The one you don't have to use words with, who picks up the phone, who calls to tell you a funny story only you'd get. The one who doesn't judge, who gives you space to be you, without pretense. The friend who brings out the best in you and who has your back, no matter what. The one who doesn't leave, even when you swear *No, really, I'm fine.* They stay because they just know. Let it be like that friend who's an *I Got You Person*.

Being an *I Got You Person* is integral to everything I am and I don't want you to be confused when I refer to *I Got You People*, so let me introduce that indispensable magic before we go any farther. There is more on them in depth in chapter seven, but briefly, here's what it means:

---

* Of course, your answers will be different because all of our personal details vary, but the gist is the same, in that so many of us have not allowed ourselves to just be ourselves, without apology, simply because we didn't believe we got to.

- We remind each other when we forget that we always get to begin again.
- We help each other see what we can't see for ourselves.
- We hold each other up when holding up is needed, even if the holdee is in denial and doesn't believe they get to be held up.
- We show up.
- We say what is true, kind, and necessary.
- We are just there. *We are here* never even needs to be spoken.

WHAT FOLLOWS ARE questions, prompts, stories, memories, poems, exercises, and what I call *daily practices*. They are *daily-ish* for me, so I renamed them *daily-ish practices*, in the same vein as my yoga classes are yoga-ish. I am Jew-ish, rather than Jewish. Just like how I can be fearless-ish, but I am not fearless.

The verb *allow* is one of the most important words of my life, so each chapter contains sections called ALLOW. These are designed as invitations for you to lovingly (and hopefully playfully) discover where you've been holding back or what you've been denying, and places for you to explore and to query include *What am I allowing in? What am I not?* and *Am I willing?*

The idea of "simply allowing" may feel easier said than done. Except it's not. You just have to get out of the way.

How much of whatever you're not allowing is courtesy of your *Inner Assholes* or one of *Shame's Minions*? After that, ask yourself *Now what?*

Then, begin the allowing.

The exercises and prompts in the book are meant to orient you toward breath and a space of openness and reflection. They are all the things that worked in helping me to survive, and then to thrive, during the hardest time of my life.*

I call it all *The School of Whatever Works*, or *TSOWW* for short.

To clarify, it was the hardest *and* the most beautiful time of my life. Life is never just one thing: There's always a plot twist. Always an *and*.

⸫

I'VE SPENT THE past seventeen years leading workshops to tens of thousands people all over, which I've distilled into this book. Reading it will be like attending my workshop. You might cry and laugh and discover and get angry and feel seen and understood and have all sorts of surprising emotions and memories come up. Whether or not you have attended any of my events doesn't matter either. (Although I would always love to hug you, so let's try to make that happen?)

This book offers you a way in—many ways in—to curate your own private workshop, which you'll end up self-generating from intimately coexisting with this book, but it'll be a different kind of ride than my other workshops. You can take this one with you wherever you go, like a pocket workshop ride that you can get on and off as you please and repeat as often as you want.

Before you begin, I have an ask: Would you be willing to try your damnedest to commit to choosing curiosity over fear?

---

* The hardest time I have ever gone through besides my dad dying when I was eight years old, which I don't know if I even remember anymore or have just talked and written about it so much that I think I do. Memory is quite a thing, isn't it?

Relentlessly practice this commitment. Especially when responding to an ALLOW section, even if shame tries to coerce you into a dark closet. Just be like *Yo, I am not playing Spin the Bottle with you in the closet, Shame. I'm out here with Curiosity, who's way more interesting and kind.**

If fear tells you it's too scary to look inward, go buy it a cup of coffee, then go show it how it's done. Like a boss.

What happens when someone consistently denies to themselves who they really are or what they want? Life appears to just keep happening *to* them. Because they are not in the driver's seat life takes the wheel, and they let it, not realizing they have a choice. They mistakenly think they have no agency, eventually giving up hope of going in a different direction. They then let everyone else decide who they are, what they want, and where they should be. They take what they can get, believing they don't get to do, have, or be anything different.

I wrote this book so that we remember. We might forget again. That's okay, because we're human. Check out this list of unassailable facts (although it took me decades to accept them), and tattoo in your brain the following: *I can begin again.*

- We all need help.
- No one can do it all alone.
- You get to feel your feelings; this will not kill you.
- Change also will not kill you, even though it may feel like that at times.
- Your people are there. Look for them. Find them. Stay open.

---

* Remember that if you apologize to Shame, you'll owe five bucks to the Sorry Bank.

- It's not too late. For anything. That's the *Imaginary Time Gods* talking.
- It's not pointless. And even if it is, so what? What's so wrong with a circle?
- You get to have peace. It is your birthright (not stress, as some will have you believe).
- Rest is a nonnegotiable, and you no longer need to buy into the lie that it must be earned.
- Your want is enough. *I want to* is enough of a reason, and you owe no one any explanation.

I was the only one who could give myself permission and yet I waited for it like I was at some bus stop, waiting for a bus called Permission.

I kept waiting.

The bus never came. (Because there was never any stinking bus.) I just forgot I was the one I'd been waiting for.

I met legions of other people like me. Also on tenterhooks, seeking confirmation, validation, or any stamp of approval from *outside* themselves. There was no shortage of folks who also kept waiting for that stupid bus to let them on. I recognized those who were also spending their most precious resources, attention, and energy trying to prove they were worthy enough to have a life they loved. To add insult to injury, they were spending those resources on trying to prove it to only one person. Themselves.

One of the unassailable facts I need to reiterate in case you skimmed over it: As long as you are breathing, you get to begin again.

You're not too late, too behind, too early, too fat, too old, or too stuck. You are not too *anything*. You do not have to procure proof that you are worthy, nor do you have to *earn* the right to rest or to be fully yourself.

You do have to choose it. This means no more waiting for imaginary buses, or for anyone else to give you permission.

This Is *The Era of You*

You ~~get to~~ must become your own permission slip.

I hope this book helps you locate, or create, the courage you need for that.

WILL YOU WRITE something down real quick?

Side note: I am partial to sticky notes; they're like my ride or dies. They're all over my house, I use them in workshops and retreats, I put them in my son's lunchbox as love notes, and they are my version of PowerPoint when I give keynotes. They're cute and colorful, sure, but the best thing about them is that you can stick them anywhere. You can move them, stick them where the sun doesn't shine, crumple them, or throw them away. They can serve as little reminders that nothing is permanent. Especially not *stuckness*.

Like sticky notes, we, too, are malleable. We get to change and unstick ourselves from old stories and beliefs. (Obviously, we also get to be cute and colorful.)

What I'm saying is: *May we be more like sticky notes.*

Now, go grab a sticky note. (Or anything else will suffice if you don't have any.) Write in big, bold letters. Put the note where you'll see it frequently.

Feel free to replace the *we* with an *I*. Whatever works.

Our collective sticky note:

> *We do not have to prove that we deserve*
> *to be wildly alive ever again.*
>
> *We do not need to crush what lights us up ever again.*
>
> *We do not have to try to talk ourselves*
> *out of feeling good ever again.*

Wait. One more:

> *We are our own proof of life.*

Proof of Life

I have nothing to show for it, my friend says like she's dying
and some estate agent needs evidence to show she had value.
The listing invisible, the agent a pest, the whole thing: a scam.
Still, she bows in shame, has nothing tangible to prove her worth.
I tell her she doesn't need to show shit, but she doesn't buy it.
Can you remember how someone you love smells after they're gone?
How happy you were that one summer?
How pain eventually forgets how bad it hurts?
I remind her it's impossible to show what's invisible.

When we were young, it was called Show and Tell, I say to my friend
who wishes she was young
more than she wishes she wasn't dying.
There's no "Tell" anymore. It's just Show and Show.
Show you're relevant. Show you're deserving. Show you matter.
That these commands aren't real
is no deterrent to our obedience.
No wonder we feel like we're dying.
I try and convince her it's a sham,
she tries to convince me that unless
you can show proof that you matter, you don't.
I dump my purse's contents.
Guess I don't matter, all I have is this.
To show how I matter I hold up my proof:
one expired license, a LEGO man, three nickels,
dirt from the bottom of my bag that I tell her is holy,
a lone hearing aid, used Band-Aid, Lexapro,
a key I thought was lost that wasn't.

Glossary of Terms in
Proof of Life

- BASEMENT DOOR (noun): A subdivision of *The Land of Denial*, this is the thing that blocks you from being able to clearly see what you have shoved down into the basement. It's the barrier to being honest with yourself. If it swings open, it renders one unable to continue pretending.
- BEAUTY HUNTING (verb): A spiritual practice, aka *May I get my head out of my ass* practice. As often as you can, look around for five beautiful things, then name them. Five is an accessible

number, but you can choose any amount. The key to this mindfulness practice is to identify what is beautiful *now*—not yesterday, not tomorrow. This causes you to pay attention to *now*. It'll also cause you to get your head out of your ass. (It works for me.)

- BULLSHIT STORY (noun): Part of the whole being human thing. Things you believe to be true that are, in actuality, not true. Can be endlessly rewritten (and must be). Your *I Got You People* can help remind you that you are indeed fall-in-lovable and that you no longer have to carry your *Bullshit Stories*. Examples of *Bullshit Stories* include: *I am unlovable*; *I am a bad person*; *I will never be or have enough*. See also: *I Got You People*.
- DAILY-ISH PRACTICES (noun; may also be *daily*, sans *-ish*): Daily (or something like that) habits and practices that facilitate our being aligned with who we say we are or want to become—whatever that means for each of us personally.
- DOING LOVE (verb): There are infinite ways to say *I love you*. There are as many ways to *be* and to *do* love as there are stars. It's choosing softness, being of service, acting with compassion and empathy, and choosing curiosity over fear.
- FALL-IN-LOVABLE (adjective): You. When you allow yourself to be fully seen as you are. Not only do you let someone in to see *you*, but you also see them back, fully, which makes you even more *fall-in-lovable*.
- FEARLESS-ISH (adjective): Not to be without fear (unless they are a total psycho, everyone has some fear), but to be afraid and do it anyway. Or not. It's acknowledging *I am afraid*, instead of pretending it's not there.
- HEARTSIGHT (noun): A thing we all have but may have forsaken. It's the part of us that *just knows*. The part of us that

guides us toward love and reminds us that we *are* love. It brings *you* back to *you*. Always. *Heartsight* is the voice saying *You are not lost. You are here.* Listen to it. Like you've never listened before in your life.

- HERE I AM–NESS (noun; may also be used as adjective): How you show up when you go *Here I am!* The sharing of yourself without dimming your light to fit in to someone else's narrative of *should*. Should is an asshole, FYI.
- HUMAN (adjective): The weird ways of people. Paradoxical, hypocritical, beautiful, messy, lovely, hideous, unpredictable, predictable, makers of mountains from molehills, brave, fearful, et al., ad infinitum. Too many to list.
- I GOT YOU EFFECT OR IGYE (noun): An example of cause and effect. Like the butterfly effect but without butterflies. Also, an example of *Just Because It Feels Good*.
- I GOT YOU PEOPLE (noun): A group of people who . . .

  - Remind each other that we always get to begin again.
  - Help each other see what we can't see for ourselves.
  - Hold each other up when holding up is needed, even if the holdee is in denial and doesn't believe they get to be held up.
  - Show up.
  - Say what is true, kind, and necessary.
  - Are just there. *We are here* never even needs to be spoken.

- IMAGINARY TIME GODS OR ITG (noun): A (not real) group of people/wannabe gods. Soul-crushing (nonexistent) entities that dictate when we should be doing what we do, by what age, and for how long. The *ITG* demand that we follow their clock, wait an appropriate amount of time between relationships, experience (and show) joy after someone we loved has died, change our minds, announce pregnancy or miscarriages, go to (and finish) schooling by a certain age, find a spouse/partner by a certain age, own a home by a certain age, produce things at regular intervals (it doesn't matter what, as long as we are *very busy being productive*), prove we are relevant at regular intervals, listen to their lies about aging, and believe them when they tell us we are too late or too far behind.

- INNER ASSHOLE OR IA (noun): We all have one. It tries to keep us small, ultimately thinking it's protecting us. Alas, it's our job to not let this be the boss of us.
- OFF THE HOOK BOOK (noun): Any kind of journal or notebook, on which you write *Off the Hook Book* on the front. Or the back. You get to let yourself off the hook for being human (even though it needs no off-the-hook-letting, which one day we will hopefully understand).
- PROOF THAT YOU ARE WORTHY (noun): A person. You. Go look in the mirror. *You* are the proof.
- SHAME'S MINIONS (noun): Any of Shame's disguises that try to wreak havoc within.
- SHAME LOSS (noun): Actively choosing to put down shame that is no longer yours to carry, and perhaps never was, so that you may awaken the parts of yourself that were buried under it and reclaim any abandoned parts of you. The refusal to hide in shame, in this moment. Whatever you find that works to help name the shame, find community, and then alchemize it into something that opens you up instead of stifles you. This practice

can shape-shift all the time. *See also: The School of Whatever Works.*

- **SORRY BANK** (noun): A place to deposit your five *sorry dollars* for an unnecessary sorry over something that in no way required a sorry.* Do apologize when an apology is truly called for. The art of the apology is a beautiful thing.

- **THE LAND OF DENIAL OR TLOD** (noun; bad place): The place where we don't notice things, even if they're right in front of us or inside us.

- **THE SCHOOL OF WHATEVER WORKS OR TSOWW** (noun): Whatever you find in your life that works in helping you stay in alignment, feel good about yourself, be creative, expand, heal—you name it. As long as you are not intentionally harming yourself or another, anything goes.

- **THEM/THEY** (noun): Group of (elusive) people. No one really knows who *they* are, in this context. *They* have a lot to say. And so many opinions. And *they* are everywhere, especially in our heads.

- **THERE** (noun): Elusive place where we think things will be better and where we will be happier. We never get *there*. If we do, we only realize it after we are no longer *there* anymore.

- **THIS** (noun; as in *You get to have this*): *This* can mean anything. Whatever you've denied yourself, or anything your *IA* told you that you did not get to have. Examples: *I do not get to be happy; I do not get to rest; I do not get to leave; I do not get to feel good*

---

* This may feel hard for you to discern at first. *Does this require a sorry? Does this? And this?* Eventually it will become easy like Sunday morning to know when an apology is actually what needs to be said, rather than *Thank you* or *No* or *I'm crying and my snot is dripping down my chin—do you happen to have a tissue?* or *May I have more salad dressing?*

about myself. The *this* in each of those would be happiness, rest, leaving, and feeling good about yourself. You get to have those. They are your birthright. Your *this* is whatever your *this* is, and you get to have that, too.

- WEIRDO (noun): Term of endearment, spoken lovingly. High praise. The highest. We are all weird unicorns.

CHAPTER ONE

You Get to Have This

THERE I WAS. Saying one thing and living another. Trudging through my days, *Bullshit Stories* tethered tightly to me. The ones that said I had nothing to show for myself or my life, that I did not deserve love, and that I certainly did not get to be happy. I was in my forties and still trying to convince the world (the *world* meaning only myself) that I was not bad, and the world (meaning only myself) was not having any of it. Not be convinced, I let myself stay shackled to those stories and took whatever I could beg, borrow, or steal.

Who was I to ask for—or even want—anything different?

The School of the Seven Bells

I was almost pickpocketed. Twice. First in Rome and then again in Paris. *Almost*, because neither of my pickpockets were very good thieves.

There used to be a school for pickpockets. The School of the Seven Bells is said to be based in Colombia. There are exams, it being a school and all. One test required the hopeful pickpocket to try to pickpocket the teacher, whose suit pockets had seven hidden bells sewn inside. The goal was to pick the mark clean without ringing any of the bells.

DO YOU EVER think about what you have taken? Beliefs that you took to be true when they weren't? Shame that wasn't yours? What about mediocrity, misery, and even abuse because you believed it was all you deserved?

I find old notes in handwriting that is no longer mine, written in the margins of poems I wrote decades ago. My handwriting has gotten illegible over time. The letters run into each other as if they don't know where they end and the next begins. I have forgotten how to do this basic thing. *Now dot the i, cross the t, and let your fingers find the rhythm.*

If, like me, you (mostly) don't listen to yourself (except when you're being hard on yourself), if you listen better and pay more attention when someone else says something, let me be that someone else saying something. What I am saying is: *You get to have this.* You don't have to beg, or borrow, or steal. *You get to have this* (whatever your *this* is).

THE MOST MEMORABLE time I was almost pickpocketed was in Paris. By the Seine, I scooped down to pick up a ring glimmering in the sun, even though it was hideous. It was a huge ring, and with my unusually small (but wide) hands, it looked almost as big as my whole hand, like I had a third hand, just filthy and more copper-toned. I don't even like copper, but I was thrilled at my luck of finding something. It didn't matter what. I had that rush of excitement we can get when we find something, as if suddenly anything might be possible.

If I found this, what else can I find? inevitably bubbles up, however briefly, before we go back to disbelieving in our own good fortune.

A man ran over and began speaking in a language I didn't understand as he tried to grab the ring from me. I held on tight as if it had always been mine. I lied and told him I'd dropped it. He yelled at me, in English.

You must pay me for the ring! It is mine! he claimed, his arms flailing wildly.

I gave him the ring, which couldn't have been worth more than a few dollars.

I was miffed at how quickly I succumbed to lying and possessiveness, just for the sake of *having*.

The intricacies of thievery, with its endless possible outcomes, including forgetting what is ours, who we are, and what we get to have.

HAVE YOU THOUGHT about what you want? I'm talking middle-of-the-night radically honest *want of all wants* that you can only whisper into crouched darkness. Have you ever tried bringing it into the light? What happens when you name it? I urge you to see what happens for yourself.

I refused to acknowledge what I wanted, even in my most private moments of solitude and darkest of dark hours. Were I to admit what was so (such as my profound hearing loss), or what I really wanted, I knew I'd then have to do something about it. Or else face that I'd surrendered into complacency.

Instead, I chose *not* to name what I wanted so I could stay feeling safe. Albeit, this was a false sense of safety, which was also a choice. I convinced myself that never changing, and that sameness and consistency, would equal safety. If I could count on it being the same as it always was (nothing ever is, so this was a ridiculous way to lie to myself), then no one would suddenly leave or drop dead.

What it really meant was a lack of growth.

It also meant feeling like an imposter for not being self-expressed and having a longing for something that I did not know I wanted. An ignored longing becomes an itch you can never alleviate because you can't figure out where it's coming from, and each time you think you've got it, it moves.

If you keep naming it though, you'll start to feel comfortable with the words. Like you have the right to hold them in your mouth, which you do. Naming what we are afraid to is a kind of sorcery; you'll suddenly notice what you've named all around you. Eventually, it will become impossible to deny and it begins to feel real, which was the thing I was most afraid of. Because then what? Now what?

If you are willing to investigate what things you might want, which could you live without? Which are you already without?

I carried an ancient belief that I did not get to have what I wanted and had trained myself to not even notice I was going without. It was easy to go without, I thought.

Don't mistake me; my life was fine. I would not dare whisper to even the washing machine what it was that I hungered for: a deep connection with a partner, a true sense of *home*, big love, intimacy.

I'm still discovering what I want. There are so many things to want in this life, but the beginning and the end is love. If you have trouble remembering what love looks like (and we all do because besides us, love is the supreme shape-shifter) here are a few images to jog your memory:

- The friend who stood suddenly in your garage that day just to give you a hug when she knew you needed it more than anything.
- The coffee that's there by your bedside when you wake every morning, which could just as easily be a note saying *I love you*, and how you drink it even though it's cold by the time you wake because the person who placed it there let you sleep.
- The way your mother seemingly one day fell in love with birds and you accepted the bird lady part of her as if it were always there, and maybe it was, because that kind of delight over small-winged things, over anything, is contagious.

Love can be so many things, but one thing about it is unfaltering: No one can take it away from you. Love is what you are, and I can't say that I know the beginning from the end or what either means anymore, but I do know this.

Not only is love what is worth having, it also is what we all inherently get to have. It's our birthright.

But Mommy, We Can't Be Two Things at Once

Bear with this time jump. Although I haven't shared much yet about the dissolution of my marriage, this interlude is important. It was the moment I knew I had to embody *I get to have this*.

Robert, my then husband, and I had been separated for only a few months. Charlie and I were sitting in bed watching a movie when he began to cry. I hugged him and asked what was wrong, even though I had a hunch he was struggling with what was happening between his dad and me. A couple days earlier, he had an outburst in the car, moaning things about his daddy and me that I couldn't make out because he was in the back and I couldn't read his lips. It's frustrating that I can't understand anything coming from the back or passenger seats when I am in the car with *other* people, but when it's your own child and they are upset, go ahead and just cue a panic attack.

I begged him to wait until I stopped driving, but to no avail.

Why can't Mommy and Daddy be at the house at the same time? I don't want you to get divorced, he cried while we were watching the movie that night.

We had said nothing about divorce to him, but he has the emotional intelligence of an old wise grandma (probably channeling my Bubbie).

I wondered what he believed *divorce* meant? At the time, we were flip-flopping the house and apartment, or *nesting,* as it's commonly called. The child stays put, and the parents shuffle. I held my son as he cried in my bed, and a minute later, he asked if we could put the movie back on. He was upset but not inconsolable.

Even when we had been in the house at the same time, Robert and I were rarely in the same room together. I had never allowed myself to really consider *how* we were existing. We were more like roommates.

It occurred to me how it must have already seemed to Charlie like Mommy and Daddy didn't live together. It apparently seemed that way to everyone else.

The morning after he'd shed those tears, he was his normal, cheerful self. Nothing delights me more than the fact that my son came into the world with a joyful disposition, because sometimes, the apple does fall far.

We cuddled and did our silly morning dances.

I said *Charlie, remember how you were upset? You kept asking why Daddy and I can't be here at the same time? Well, sometimes mommies and daddies* do better *as friends. Daddy and I are really good friends. We are happier that way.*

He looked at me, confused.

But Mommy, he said, *you can't be two things at once.*

There it was.

I decided to gift my son with the possibilities of what we get to have in life, if we are willing to allow for them. This meant I had to walk my talk.

His best friend's parents were divorced and couldn't be in the same room together. The police were involved, and there was fighting and restraining orders. Charlie had intimated that Robert and I were going to divorce, so he associated the word with all he knew of it: what he'd seen and experienced at his friend's house. I was blown away by his ability to communicate that.

He explained that he did not think you could be divorced and also friends.

Oh, honey. You absolutely can be two things at once. In fact, you can be way more than two things at once. So much of life is about holding more than one thing at a time, I said into his hair as I kissed him.

Nothing is more important to me than having the courage to be who I say I am. I want to model to my child that I live what comes out of my mouth, as best as I can.

I wish we all learned at a young age that life isn't binary and that it's never just one thing. That there's always an *and*.

I explained this all before school, which made him late, but I like to ignore the *Imaginary Time Gods* and will often choose cuddling with him over being on time to school. Come arrest me, Mom Police. I'll even make you coffee.

Doing It Anyway

At my Italy retreat in 2023, Stephanie Monds joined us. She is one of my *I Got You People*, through and through. Stephanie is a writer who has fought to see herself as one. Does that sound familiar? Even if it isn't about being a writer, necessarily?

She has been in a cycle of poverty for her entire life. Being the primary breadwinner, she often had to travel to find work as a nurse, sometimes living states away from her family, which was exhausting and unsustainable. She didn't allow herself to grieve—something I understand and perhaps you do, too. She found other coping mechanisms instead, so that she could return to work as soon as possible to continue supporting her family. She believed that she couldn't afford to grieve, in any sense. I get it, and even though it's rarely true that we don't get to grieve, I understood what she meant in every part of me.

AT THE RETREAT in Italy, Stephanie stood and told us about the early days of grieving the loss of her daughter. *If someone would've just held my hand instead of repeating all the usual shitty things people say to a person who's grieving, it would've meant the world to me. They said things like "Well, at least you have your other children." Or "I remember how hard it was when my granny died." Or "God's got her now." And of course, the standard: "She's with the angels at last."*

On the rare occasions I'd snap out of my state of catatonia, all I wanted to say was "Fuck you, the horse you rode in on, your God, and your damn angels." But I didn't. I'd just nod my head and force a fake smile.

I hated everyone, especially myself, for feeling that way.

Before the retreat, as I boarded my flight, Stephanie had sent me a text.

She'd never left the country and was petrified.

I'm just a ball of nerves. I'm bringing some of Avah's ashes. I may do a small ceremony for her. She's the reason I met you. The reason I'm going to Italy. It's only right to leave a piece of her there.

It took so much to get her to say yes to the trip. Some of the things it took:

- Releasing irrational fears about traveling, leaving the country, flying, and getting lost.
- Letting go of any belief suggesting she wasn't worthy.
- Putting down the guilt she carried for leaving and for Avah dying.
- Putting down her imposter syndrome and her *Bullshit Story* that she didn't belong in Italy with us.
- Allowing herself to accept funds that were raised for her, without shame and without making it mean something other than that she was supported and loved.

She did what it takes to say *I get to have this*, and she boarded her flight with the extreme prowess it took to bring her daughter's ashes along, in her suitcase.

As she often says, *Ain't that some shit?*

Being *fearless-ish* is not being without fear. It's saying what Steph said—*I am a ball of nerves. I am scared. And I am doing it anyway.*

In Praise of the Ordinary

One ordinary day, I asked myself *What am I trying to get right, and for whom?*

I was horrified by the answer.

I don't know what or whom exactly I was trying to get it right for, but it was never, ever for me.*

Pause and ask yourself: *What am I trying to get right, and for whom?*

I LEARN BY repetition. Except when I don't. When I repeat the same behaviors and still refuse to see what is plain as day until, for whatever reason (and oftentimes there is no discernible reason), I stop refusing to see what is right in front of me and my invisible blinders come off. I'll be in the kitchen eating hummus with the refrigerator door open going *Holy shit! Look what I found!*

Everyone around me shaking their head, muttering *Um, it's been there all along.*

Well, whatever. I didn't see it.

Them: *You just chose not to see it. It's as plain as day.*

That's a really dumb expression, by the way.

But they weren't wrong.

I DECIDED I wanted to live in a state where fear of _____ (put whatever you want in that blank, like fear of rejection, of not being enough, or of sucking) isn't the boss. A state that demands we stop

---

* It was never, ever for me. It was never, ever for me. Three times because I am a fan of repetition, in poetry especially.

letting the invisible yet ever-present *them* determine how we spend our attention and energy. One that invites us to get messy rather than get it right.

A state of being where our self-worth is not determined by anyone or anything outside us.

There's a quote I love by the artist Robert Henri: *The object isn't to make art, it's to be in that wonderful state which makes art inevitable.*

I wanted to live in a place that makes art inevitable, so I began to use creativity as a way in to the life I said I wanted. I started writing poems again. I painted like a fiend. I let go of any notions* of *Will this make me worthy?* Of *good* and *bad.* Of *Will it sell? Will they like me?* and *Am I doing it right?*

Making art doesn't have to mean you are an artist by profession or that you can draw a stick figure or write a *New Yorker*–worthy poem. It means you are tapped in to the divine creative spirit, which is in every one of us. It means you stop allowing *them* to interrupt your connection to that divinity. (*Them* can also be your own *Inner Asshole.*)

Do not fret if you've not only been doing it all for *them* but also waiting for *them* to give you permission. What do you think I was doing all those years I waited for that bus that wasn't coming? Or searched under plates while waiting tables for instructions from someone that would tell me what to do, how to live, who I was, and if I was worth loving?

All that time it was in me all along. I just had to be willing to play. I finally am.

Are you?

---

* As best as I was able. Come on, now.

DO THIS WEIRDO thing:

- Go to the garbage. Under a tin can of smoked trout,[*] there will be a sticky note upon which you wrote *I am willing to be bad* before you threw it away after admitting you were *not* willing.
- Dig out that fish-stinking paper.
- Wipe off the old coffee grounds, and give yourself the gift of writing a rubbish poem or drawing a terrible drawing.
- Let *What am I trying to get right, and for whom?* become your lens. For everything. Use it as a guidepost. Who doesn't need guideposts and North Stars?
- This poem, or whatever you create, can be a list of names of people you forgot you slept with; an ode to the boy who, when you said *I love you*, only stared back; a few stanzas on how to stop feeling like you want to die; a meditation on peaches, pleasure, and the lie of productivity; a meditation on the benefits of staring out the window and doing nothing; or a meandering run-on sentence on the uselessness of the words *good, bad, should, never, always,* and *perfect*. It can be anything as long as you are willing to let it be true, and also suck.

If not, you will, once again, be at the mercy of that dictator in your head.

There will now be new monikers for eras of your life.[†] Here's the

---

[*] That was my garbage bin. Yours will contain your garbage, which may or may not include a tin of smoked trout from Trader Joe's, which has possibly been discounted. And you may be a tea drinker and, therefore, will not have coffee grounds in there, but Lord, there's something dramatic that feels powerful about that imagery so I suggest going to get some. You'll see.

[†] Feel free to come up with your own.

first one: *The Era of You.* There will be more, including but certainly not limited to the following:

- Celebrating the Ordinary and the Mundane
- The Revolt Against the Need to Achieve
- The Rise of Fucking Shit Up
- The Era of *Because I Want to Do It This Way*
- The Generation of *I'm Tired of Trying to Be Exceptional*
- The Time of Letting Go of Seeking Approval from Strangers

Ordinary things are the most beautiful things; we just miss them a lot of the time. We're too busy searching for the extraordinary.

Never stop looking for what is beautiful. Borrow my spiritual practice, the one I call *Beauty Hunting*. As often as you can, look around for five beautiful things, then name them. Five is doable, an accessible amount, rather than fifty-seven. The key to what is essentially this mindfulness practice is to identify what is beautiful *right now*. This causes you to pay attention to the *now*. It also very well may cause you to get your head out of your ass. Does for me.

ALLOW

ASK YOURSELF

As I began to contemplate leaving my husband, it felt like there was nothing solid beneath me. Everything looked upside down. It wasn't my life that was upside down though. It was me.

I was the thing that had been tilting, making myself fit in to the tiniest of upside-down spaces. I thought that if I got smaller, that would give me a pass from having feelings—any of them—thereby putting me in control and granting me a feeling of safety. Too bad I was miserable and starving in my self-made prison, with nothing but a false sense of security and an illusion that I was somehow in control of things, which I very much was not. But you know that. Ultimately, I got healthy from that thinking and those harmful behaviors, although I will not say I am *recovered* as if it is past tense. Always *recovering*.

I had practice making myself smaller and cramming myself into things I'd outgrown, and although I was in recovery, it was a reflexive instinct to continue forcing myself into something, even if I didn't fit. Just like with anorexia, I compressed myself so there could be no extra room left for having feelings, let alone investigating them. Nor for questioning my beliefs. And especially no room for growth, because growth meant change.

I put my head in the sand and then wondered *What's in my eyes, and why can't I see?* Everything seemed unfamiliar as I seemed to only recognize my life from a perspective of opening my eyes halfway, and my heart even less. I did this to accommodate my surroundings, rather than myself.

Before I miraculously bought my house in Ojai, my five-hundred-square-foot one-bedroom apartment with zero air circulation felt like it was swallowing the three of us. We'd endlessly bump into each other and yet I couldn't fathom ever leaving this place I'd lived in for twenty years. I was the breadwinner, and there was no way I could see that I could afford to move someplace bigger with just my own income. At least not in Santa Monica or Los Angeles.

I surrendered into *This is just the way it is and the way it always will be*. Into a *That's life* mentality.

I secretly wallowed in a feeling of *saudade*—a Portuguese term that translates to a feeling of melancholy or longing for a person or thing who is absent, or perhaps was never there to begin with, and maybe never will be. I was also mildly obsessed with how people who weren't millionaires afford to live in Los Angeles. I still find it fascinating and mysterious. I was positive there existed no other prospects besides what I thought to be true for me,* and what I thought to be true for me was that I would have a future consisting of cohabitating only in that one-bedroom apartment for the rest of my life. Even as my son grew and needed his own space, and even as my disconnect from my husband grew wider. Apparently, I seemed to possess a crystal ball that told me there was no way I would ever be able to afford anything else on my own. What the crystal ball did *not* tell me was that a) everything was not my fault or my responsibility and b) I actually could ask my husband to contribute more so we'd have a double income.

The thing is, he'd have to give up trying to make films, and that would cost him his dream. Who cares what it cost me? I'd rather have squashed my own dreams and squeezed into the smallest of boxes with no ventilation for the rest of my life before I disappointed anyone. Disappointing myself was standard.

---

* Remember that expression *Don't believe everything you think*? This would be a prime example of when to employ this wise philosophy.

I'd rationalize while in the shower. *Who am I anyway to take up more space than this? Who am I to ask for something different? Who am I to ask for what I need? Who gets to do that?* I figured it must be those same people who could somehow afford to live in Los Angeles without having to rob Peter to pay Paul. I'd thank the gods of hot water and doors that lock who'd blessed me with both of those things and chant *Beggars can't be choosers* in my head as I hid in the only place where I had any privacy: the bathroom.

Answer that for yourself. Who are you to take up more space or to want something different? Notice what arises.

Consider the following to uncover what "the way" means for you:

- When in your life have you been, or are you currently, in your own way?
- Can you look at how you may still be in your own way—without attaching story, judgment, or shame to it?
- Find or make at least one way to create some sense of ease. Just for today. Let it be in the smallest area if needed, so you are not making things harder for yourself. It may require some real slowing down to see where you are hindering yourself.

It's a tough concept if you are a forcer, a non-truster, a pusher. Allowing is the opposite.

I play "Let It Be" by The Beatles when I teach yoga, and I'll invite people to sing along if they feel like it. If you've never tried this, it's freeing to belt out lyrics without caring if you know the correct words or what you sound like. Especially if you are a god-awful singer like I am. It's delicious fun.

I'll often ask *Where in life are you pushing? Where can you let it be?* during those classes, then invite people to place their hands on their hearts if that gesture feels intuitive. Everything I do in my workshop has the caveat of *if you want** or *whatever works*.

Tears often flow, as if every person is finally ready to stop pushing and just let it be, even if for a few breaths.

My yoga classes are yoga-ish, meaning you get to cater the movements to your own needs. You can lie in Savasana (final resting pose) the whole time, you can dance, or you can follow my cues and do downward-facing dog and hip openers. Whatever we're doing in class, or whatever you're doing on your own to connect more deeply to your body, be it warrior two or a vinyasa or simply keeping your hand on your heart, becomes an invitation to observe not just the breath but also tendencies and habits.

Ask yourself:

- Where am I pushing? What does that pushing feel like right now?
- What is one area in my life, or regarding my body, where I can *let it be*?

---

* Not everything. I have a little one, so no, I cannot always answer with *if you want*. If he reads this, he will most certainly try to use this ploy on me, so let me be clear: *Charlie, no. I don't mean you here.*

- What comes up when I consider *letting it be*? A knowing? Shame? Regret? Hope? Grief?
- Where do I feel it in my body? What is the sensation? Am I willing to pause and observe it rather than trying to escape it or label it?
- Do I believe that only *they* get to let it be? That it's something for everyone else except me?

If you believe that last one, we're twinning! I had that same *Bullshit Story*. Sometimes it's not even past tense and I'll fail to see it as bullshit but rather *fact*. Yet, as long as I am breathing, I will continue to commit to putting it down. I will put down that vile *Bullshit Story* and begin again, as often as I need to. We all get to do that with what is no longer ours to carry.

Dear twin of mine, listen to me. You can do this. You may have considered your own *Bullshit Stories* before, and you may have written them down or burned them, but like hungry mosquitoes, they might keep coming back, and sometimes even in disguise.

Which other harebrained *Bullshit Stories* still reside in you? Take note of ones you thought you'd gotten rid of.

We are not our depression, jobs, bank accounts, disabilities, or the lies other people told us. We are also not our *Bullshit Stories*.

It doesn't matter how long you've believed them, or for how long others told you they were true. You get to let it be, and let it go. Even for a few hours at a time to start.

We need to keep checking in to acknowledge what is ours to

carry and what is not, so that we may put down what is not. The good news is that the more we practice refuting them, the easier it gets to put them down.

There's an unarguable fact here, too: As long as we are alive, we get to begin again. Even if it feels like a *Bullshit Story* to you right now, I promise this is an unequivocal truth.

WRITE YOURSELF A LETTER

Once you know your current *Bullshit Stories* and feel ready to make a shift, there's an exercise that can help foster that freedom. I would be remiss, however, if I neglected to mention that this *getting out of your own way* habit can take time to break. It's a sneaky one.

If it has taken you years (face flushes), go easy on yourself. Go back to those vicious *Bullshit Stories*, and you'll understand what you were up against—an army of invisible assailants. Have mercy on that incessant obstructor, ceaseless impeder, and perpetual interferer. Meaning you. Have mercy on you.

Nurture compassion for yourself. It doesn't matter how long you continued to be in your own way, or if you *still* cockblock yourself. There are no caveats on this. It cannot be contingent on you behaving properly or getting it right or being good. Your self-compassion must be unconditional. Be unwavering on that.

Get comfortable in whatever way you like to meditate, visualize, check in, or daydream. Pick any moment in the future, and imagine yourself unapologetically taking up space, allowing room for your wants, needs, desires, and excitement. Notice how it feels in your body and what it does to your breath and the chatter in your mind.

Visualize yourself as someone living life on their own terms and who knows that they get to have whatever they've denied themselves. Staying with that feeling, write a letter to yourself from that space, as if from a future version of yourself. There are no rules, just imagination and play.

I have this letter I wrote that I keep on my bathroom mirror. Constantly seeing it helps me stay in alignment with a future that I say I want. (*The School of Whatever Works* works. I keep telling you.)

Here's the letter on my mirror. I hope it inspires you to write your own.

Dear you,

I need you to read this letter.

I need you to listen to me. I know you want to look away, but stay.

Stay. See that face of yours, the one that, to you, might look like a broken heart?

Are you looking at yourself? Do you see?

That broken heart is offering you a glimpse into everything that matters, even into matter itself, even the things that don't matter . . . yet.

And anyway, it's not broken.

It's coming back together, that heart.

> *Look closer. Do you see how you just needed to tilt your head and squint your eyes a bit?*
>
> *If you drew a self-portrait, you'd see a not-broken-hearted-shaped face.*
>
> *You would see the magic of the whole fucking universe.*
>
> *Love,*
>
> *Future you, who chose herself*

Changing Lanes

We'll believe anything.
How else could we carry on,
unless we believed that we had no choice?
How could we keep driving to a job that sucked our soul,
unless we believed we didn't have one?
So all that sucking was in vain.
How could we have accepted
At least we're not as miserable as most
as reason to stay, unless we believed that it was our bar
and no matter how low it was set, we didn't get to raise it?
We tolerate long lines at places we do not want to be,
with a person we no longer love, by remembering
it's our bar to bear and by bearing it.
How could we have a third date with someone
who asks no questions about us except by believing
Next time they'll ask what I like and what I want.
When years pass with no change at all, we have to say

It used to be different or we'd never forgive ourselves for
what we gave up to feel less lonely.
What we gave up was everything, and there we were,
still so lonely it hurt.
We eat our own hunger, swallow the urge to swerve.
All to remain in the right lane.
Until we notice it's no longer true
that we'll believe anything.
We are not in the right lane after all.
All this time we thought we were
when there were never any lanes to begin with.

CHAPTER TWO

You Are Never Lost

WHO AMONG US can't remember moments when we could not see ourselves clearly—when we couldn't quite remember, without help, how to get back to ourselves?

Raising my hand, without shame. I have forgotten how to get back to myself, or that I was ever there in the first place.

AFTER I TOLD my husband I wasn't happy but before I'd used the word *divorce*, there was this window of time when I somehow absurdly and outrageously fell in love with another man. Over texts and FaceTime. I was no longer sleeping in the same bed or intimate with my husband, but that didn't stop me from waking up to thoughts of *I am a bad person* and *It's my fault*. I'd been perseverating, not just in my waking hours but obviously in my dreams as well. Those same words on repeat. Again and again.

I was in a liminal space, neither here nor there. I knew that if I didn't pay close attention, I'd slip right into the center of the earth. Or worse, down the rabbit hole, *The Bad Place*.*

I could not see myself clearly, so when that old voice came back to remind me I was a monster, I concurred. It was familiar and all-knowing, after all. Anyway, there's just no talking to the devil.

The Devil We Know

There were horns and fangs and scales and terrible coffee breath. My monsterness returned with a vengeance. Those same horns and fangs and scales as when I first saw them in the mirror when I was eight. As scary as it was, I knew this deadly destroyer, like I'd know an old high school so-called best friend who stole my boyfriend and never talked to me again and then friended me on Facebook twenty-five years later with a *Hey U, what's up*. (No, they won't use correct punctuation.)

Those demons of my past I thought I'd loved into submission (yeah, right) rose from the *just kidding, we're not really dead* dead.

I HOPE THAT my retelling of *Monsters, Inc.* reminds[†] you how easy it is to fall back into old patterns. Maybe you'll feel less lost, less inclined to bang your head against the wall, crying *I'm the only one who does this! What is wrong with me?*[‡] *The only one who does this*, as in the only one who can't keep their words to themselves? The only one who can't ask for help, who can't say no, who keeps ending up in relation-

---

* If you've never seen *The Good Place* with the delightful Kristen Bell, it's worth it to find a way to watch. *The Bad Place* is a reference to that. I do read books (sometimes) rather than just watch shows all the time.

† As if you need reminding.

‡ Not a damn thing. Nothing is wrong with you!

ships that aren't reciprocal, who self-medicates and lies to themselves about it, who eviscerates themselves through the comparison of strangers on the internet, and . . . shall I go on? I don't care what *it* is either; you are not the only one. Nice try though.

Believing awful things about ourselves is an easier choice. Until it isn't.

Better the devil you know than the devil you don't. Whoever wrote that quote lived inside my younger self's brain, obviously.

It only stops becoming the easier choice when we practice choosing something besides the path of least resistance.

An almost-instant synapse, if I am not careful, is to ignore what is in point of fact bothering me and instead focus on my body, weight, and an old *Bullshit Story* that says *You're disgusting*. If what is going on feels too far out of my control, like, say, not knowing how to proceed with my divorce, without so much as even batting an eyelash, I can easily start to deprive myself of nourishment and slip back into old anorexic habits. That feels like the one thing I can control. I'll immediately go back to believing I am something that needs to be fixed and begin attempting to fix what is broken, me, instead of what is actually calling for my attention.

It is an immediate response, if I am not vigilant. When I am not being intentional and aligned, I can slip right back into bed with that old hat. This isn't easy to be vulnerable about and share publicly for many reasons, but, as I repeat (a very lot), the reasons aren't that important. I share this with you as a reminder of just how *daily-ish* everything is. Nothing is rarely, if ever, a one and done. Reverting to old behaviors or patterns is human, not a cause for us to hide in shame.

Sharing our stories is collectively healing and powerful, even when sharing what we might perceive to be setbacks, like relapsing into eating disorders or addictions or believing horrible untruths about ourselves. What if, instead of shoving them down in shame, we powerfully and collectively healed?

FROM DOWN THE rabbit hole, I texted my friend, who is a rabbi, that I was in trouble. When we first met, we each instantly recognized the other as an *I Got You Person*. I didn't have a therapist when I reached out to him, and although I hadn't been inside a synagogue in ages, I knew I needed what he had to offer. He replied I got you, and we scheduled a FaceTime for the next morning.

I had nowhere private to talk in my home so I went out to my car. I sat in it and cried to the rabbi. If I turned on the air conditioner it would've made it too loud, and I needed to hear every word he had to say. He spoke to me tenderly and carefully and with great love. After I told him I thought I was in love with someone else, despite only having been with Henry in person for a total of twenty minutes at this point, he said:

End the marriage more carefully even than you entered it.

It reminded me of how, just days before, another friend had said *To exit the marriage, you have to build an ending, and to do that, you'll need to make a map.*

It made me imagine the list of what I am growing. Or shrinking, depending on who's asking. *Cartographer, mother, lip-reader, writer, liar, monster.*

It all felt so daunting as I sat in the brutal August heat and wept in my parked car in my driveway, while inside the house, my husband and son were happily watching *The Boss Baby* for the twenty-ninth time.

The rabbi knew about my inability to cry. When I explained to him that I couldn't stop crying and feeling *everything*, he said it was because I had been suppressing so much for so long.

But now, it's like the basement door has swung open. You'll never be able to pretend again, he added.

He was not wrong. It had swung open, which meant that not only could I no longer pretend I didn't know what was behind the proverbial door, I also couldn't hide behind it any longer.

You Will Never Be Able to Pretend Again

How does that feel in your body when you read *You will never be able to pretend again*? Is there a sense of freedom? A terror, like you've been found out for pretending for so long? Whatever it may be, try to notice it without panic, judgment, or self-criticism. The more attuned we become to our responses, the easier it becomes to discern when Fear or Shame starts running the show.

When I heard the rabbi talk about the basement door, I was shaken up. What would no longer pretending mean? The most significant change that I ever had to adjust to, especially as a little kid, was my father being gone in the blink of an eye. If I could no longer pretend, that would mean I'd have no choice but to make changes, and the greatest lie I ever told myself, an inarguable fact as far as I was concerned, was that change meant imminent demise. My logic used to go like this:

- Worshipped father says that you are bad and making him feel bad. What he actually said was *You are being bad*. But six of one, half a dozen the other. At least to my eight-year-old *not yet deaf* ears anyway.
- You yell *I hate you* to your beloved god of a father.

- In third grade, you decide if nothing ever changes, if you can just keep everything fixed and static, then no one will be able to leave. Or drop dead.
- You're safe if no one leaves or drops dead (summation of my own law of nature).
- The only way to guarantee safety would be to steer clear of the *c* word. *(Change.)*

I sat sweating in my car, spiraling about my imminent death. (See how quickly fear steps in?)

Like he reminded me, I'd been suppressing pain for so long.

Now it is all coming to the surface, he'd said.

I can't remember all of his exact words, but what did stick with me was *Disruption ends in two ways, and only one is beautiful.*

He urged *Do it the right way.*

We agreed I'd have to figure out what the *right way* meant, for myself.

I wanted to choose the right way, the beautiful way. I also wanted to choose myself.

I wondered if one ever got to do both?

THE BASEMENT DOOR had swung wide open and yet I couldn't seem to even open my car door and emerge from my sweltering vehicle. I felt lost in my own driveway, sitting inside a parked car, so how would I ever know the right or beautiful way, whatever those even meant?

THE ONLY WAY I knew how to find direction was through *Heartsight*, which I'd ignored for so long that I'd forgotten it. It had been down in the basement, where I'd shoved it with self-compassion, grief, tenderness, vulnerability, my sex drive, and so many other disregarded parts of me. But now, I had no more hiding place because that door to the basement was apparently just swinging wide open.

I just had to get quiet, listen, and trust. I knew then, with that basement door swung open, that I would make it through the dark part at the top of the stairs and I'd find my way because I was not lost. I had my *I Got You People, Heartsight*, me.

She Did Eat All the Cake

In my twenties, I used to live in this beautiful 1940s prewar apartment in Los Angeles where my neighbor would scream *Get the fuck out of my house* for hours outside my bedroom window. He was a locksmith by trade—although no one ever saw him go to work or do anything with any keys—and I'd lie there listening to him scream, hating myself for sleeping until noon when I had to be at work at the restaurant at three.

Get the fuck out! Get the fuck out! he'd yell in the courtyard, red-faced and hyperventilating. This man and I were, coincidentally, both from the same town in South Jersey. I heard it in his accent when he screamed at his wife, or himself, as he was wont to do. They seemed to never not be fighting. He'd holler *She is a fraud* in the courtyard. *She's left maggots! She ate all the cake! She took an ice pick to my piano! My piano!*

This one morning, his lip cut and bleeding, curly hair flying around his face, there was something different in his eyes. They had stopped roving and were focused, without blinking, on a point ahead of him, as if he'd caught a glimpse of his future. A point of utter loss.

The kind of panic when you realize you really *are* alone and that she *did* eat all the cake.

What Have You Done?

All the *Get the fuck out of my house*s had taken their toll. He had prayed for that woman to be gone, had screamed it into the air. Now she was. I saw the fear in his motionless eyes. It was the terror of *What have I done?*

I have been with that question intimately.

Have you?

I'd listen to them shouting, terrified I'd become one of those life-screamers. People who loved and abused each other. People who wanted their lives to be anything but what they were. I'd visualize myself as a waitress for the rest of my life. Then, I *would* eat all the cake and take an ice pick to a piano and maybe someone would find out I was a fraud, too.

The *What have I done?* an unspoken code between my neighbor and me. The *Oh my God, I've made a mistake.* Like a car we loved that had long ago died, yet we kept it sitting in the driveway as if one day it might be able to go back up the hill. We'd whimper *How can I get it back to the way it was?*

The good news and the bad: You can't ever get it back to the way it was.

I'd sit in that apartment thinking *How did I even get here? Who can I blame this on? Who put me here?*

Blessed Be the Antidepressants and the Night-Light in the Bathroom

Blessed be the antidepressants I went on back in 2008. It was not the meds that pulled me from the labyrinth of despair; they didn't instantly "fix" anything. But they did take away the fog so I could see the light more clearly. The light was not neon or flashing or anything like that. Just a small light, like a night-light in the bathroom. It lit up and spelled *Possibility*. I had never seen it there before. It was the first time I saw any hope of leaving the restaurant. Here I was, fourteen years later, and I needed to find that light of hope again. Except this time, it was my marriage I was leaving, not a restaurant.

It's harder to feel lost when you have light, with the light of possibility, which is *Heartsight*.

What did *Heartsight* lead me to find my way back to? My life.

Not the one I thought I'd lost, but the one I created. Splinter by splinter, I built myself back. I found my way out by finding a way in.

This is something I consistently encourage; it is so often the thing that keeps us immobilized or feeling lost and stuck, the not knowing how or where to even start.

When I was in my thirties and waitressing, I found my *way in* through yoga. Teaching yoga became my way back in to my writing, and my writing became my way in to my career—a career I was "making up" as I went along. I collected all those splinters of myself that I thought had been lost, and I put them together to create something unnameable.

To be human is a constant pulling of our desire to be witnessed with the tug of our fear that no one will want us.

What it looks like to stop abandoning yourself is letting go of fear's hold over you, finding your *Heartsight*, and listening to it.

The extreme relief at allowing this is akin to finding a gas station bathroom after holding it for hours in the car. Come on, you know how good that feels.

May we all remember to look up and out and far beyond and see the humanity in all and remind ourselves that having needs is not a burden. It's human, and may we all remember to be grateful we did not enter the world as a robot in the fake science lab of some weird man in a dirty white robe.

I was never lost. I just believed I was.

It wasn't until I found *Heartsight* that I was able to hear: *You are not lost. You are here.* My entire life was banking on me believing this. Sitting in that driveway, talking to the rabbi, I needed to understand it once again.

Healing Is Not Linear

It's too much to ask of dogs, let alone people, to rely on old tricks. If we don't remain active in our pursuit of alignment with who we say we are, we end up in a rabbit hole, feeling lost. We won't actually *be* lost; it will only feel like it, but our brains won't differentiate.

The way back to ourselves is not about getting from point A to point B and then to point C. Coming back to those parts we've abandoned, as well as staying aligned so we don't abandon ourselves again, is a constant. This is why *daily-ish practices* are vital and necessary. Otherwise, we rely on "work" we did *that one time*, books we kind of read, those three therapy sessions, or classes we attended on Zoom while making dinner. All of these are well and good, but if we are not actively practicing staying in alignment—whatever that means for each of us personally—how are we to stay connected to ourselves, let alone anyone else?

THE SCHOOL OF *Whatever Works* doesn't care how you do it, just that you are intentional.

It can look like eating an entire family-size bag of salt-and-vinegar chips while watching *Succession*, journaling, focused breathing, meditating, dancing in your underwear, painting, or texting memes to your *I Got You People*. You get to choose. But choose you must, so you don't feel lost in the rabbit hole.

That hole is dark, cold, and confusing. If you mistakenly think you deserve dark, cold, and confusing, you'll have a hard time pulling yourself out because you'll convince yourself it's where you belong. I swear on all good shows* that I will climb down there myself and shake your shoulders to say *You are not lost, and this is not where you belong! Let's get out of here. I got you.*

I will pull you out myself, *Indiana Jones Pastiloff* style. Just like my *I Got You People* did for me.

Unclear Directions

My friend Kristen McGuiness and I started something called "We're All Poets," where we co-teach online classes with wonderful guest poets. During our December poetry class a couple years ago, with the amazing poet Ross Gay, I happened to be the guest speaker at Miraval, a resort in Tucson, Arizona, and I brought Henry as my plus-one. I did the class from the bed in our room, because Zoom.

Ross asked the class to give *unclear directions* to something or somewhere.

---

* What are some good ones right now, please?

Before we'd gone to Arizona that December, my neighbor cut down the old oak between our yards. It startled me to see men in the tree, followed by vibrating that made my kitchen floor shake. I hadn't expected or prepared for the tree's demise. It was probably dead, and she probably did warn me they'd be chopping it down, but I am deaf and most days it's just too much to say *What, what, huh?* I just nod and miss the mark. And that is the cost of hearing loss. Thankfully, I have *I Got You People* who interpret for me and put up with my lostness. In this way, I *am* often lost as to what is being spoken, but I am never alone.

After class, I told Henry about Ross's prompt. I was trying to figure out a way in to my own poem. He said *Well, you wouldn't, let's say, give directions to a tree,* as we walked outside to sit by the fire and watch the sun go down.

I thought of that sweet tree in my yard that was now gone.

I began to write the poem right then by the fire.

The sun went down and I read to him what I wrote. He listened intently. There's this type of listening where you are so heard it makes you feel naked. Not the kind of naked where you catch a glimpse of yourself before the shower and wonder when you got old, even though that is your *Inner Asshole* talking again. The kind of listening that makes you feel free and as understood as you've ever felt in your life. The way *Heartsight* makes us feel when we listen to it.

I continued reading: *I want to tell you all about this tree but first I need to tell you the way. Go left then right then left again then straight then backward then left then south. Go any way you want, and you will end up there.*

You are the tree so you do not need directions.

But I'll share these in case you, too, are one who has forgotten.

It got dark and we were in bathrobes, so I stopped my reading and we pulled ourselves away from the cozy heat of the fire and went back to our room.

I'VE FOUND IT possible to navigate my way out of any feeling of lostness when I actively search for beauty. This practice of *Beauty Hunting* saved my life many times (in conjunction with my antidepressants and hearing aids).

Once we find beauty, we must orient ourselves accordingly, as if it is a compass. We must stay close to it, follow it, create it. Also, we have to remember we, too, are what is beautiful. *Beauty Hunting* is a personal navigation system that can lead you away from despair—or at least a little closer to hope—and one that is always at your disposal.

Fault Lines

Henry and I fell in love and dove right into a deeply committed partnership while we were both still trying to disentangle ourselves from our marriages.

Once, I sat on his couch and stared at the gorgeous brick walls around me and the high, white, wood ceiling above, like I was looking for what I could blame for the fight we'd had the night before. And the night before that.

He looked at me and said *I'm sorry for all the last nights.*

Our situation was so intricate and layered, and so entangled with others, that our fights were mostly over how to make it work going forward.

I have long been Queen in the Kingdom of Blame, having ruled over the Land of Blame and its inhabitants since July 15, 1983, a date on which you could, perhaps, find many things of interest should you care to research it. My father's death would not be one, although that is the date.

It's an old instinct to want to find someone to place blame on. Most times it's me. I somehow always place the blame on me. I could be across the world in Tokyo, and I will find a way to blame myself for something in Santa Monica. I so badly wanted to alleviate the pain by blaming our struggle on something, as if that would make the struggle evaporate.

I wanted to blame my dead father, my mom's Alzheimer's, the moon. I wanted to blame my soon-to-be ex-husband and my ex-friend who could not handle that I fell in love with someone before I was divorced, or even legally separated, as it was too triggering for her. I wanted to blame social media, "bad" timing, my own brain, the neighbors, Brian Cox's character on *Succession*. Anyone. Will someone please accept responsibility for this hideous tendency we have to try to destroy?

I was still living with an old *Bullshit Story, I do not get to have this*, which, sadly, Henry clung to as well.

This is good and beautiful, and who are we to have that? Therefore, we unconsciously and repeatedly attempted to destroy it.

We stared at the big map on the wall above the television, like we were studying the countries of South America or how big Greenland was, instead of biting the insides of our cheeks in an effort to not cry or say something that would hurt the other.

Oh, look, I never realized Kazakhstan was that big. And New Zealand? So tiny compared to Australia. It's Australia's fault we fight. There I go again.

Old habits die hard.

The truth is, it is my fault. Also, his fault. Also, no one's fault. Also, both of our fault. Also, everyone's fault. It is faultless.

The fault line doesn't matter; it's simply where it generated from. But the cause of the quake is fear.

I would be damned if I let fear back in bed with me.

You Might as Well Love

We can never know for sure what is possible, or even what is next. It doesn't matter how much we've tried to safeguard ourselves with a false sense of control. It doesn't matter what the circumstances are, what preparations we've made, or what we believe to be certain.

I'm not talking about living in fear of what might happen and having that be your driving force. I mean that not one thing is guaranteed, so we'd best love now. Like Pádraig Ó Tuama says, *You might as well love.*

Because you just never know.

Who Knew That Love Could Keep Expanding

I speak to all of us because despite even the very best of intentions, we all have the capacity to drift from who we are, or from who we thought we were. We also all have the capacity to regenerate and reinvent.

My friend texted as I sat watching my son sleep:

Who knew that love could keep expanding.

She did not pose it as a question, so she must already have known that love could indeed keep expanding.

I am learning. Thanks to you, I replied.

Thank you to anyone who's offered me directions to trees, even when I never found the stinking tree, and even when they did not know they were doing so, which is what I meant in the introduction when I said that although you may not have known it, you made me feel held, and that made all the difference.

It was never about the one particular tree anyway. It was the way I felt at home by some trees but how I would not say that aloud because if I did, it might make that tree die or leave. I learned that at eight.

I tried every day of my life never to forget the ways I could make something disappear.

Except, there is no other shoe to drop. Allowing love in will not make it die or leave. It will only make it grow.

This One Time at Killer Burger

There have been times I've been so desperate for any sense of direction that I would look to anyone else for it, in hopes that at least one person would show me the way and tell me how to be in the world.

In Portland once, I remember feeling this desperation while at a restaurant waiting for french fries. Each table had a giant roll of paper towels on it, and the table to my left had a white cowboy hat turned upside down resting next to the paper towel roll. It had a tiny ketchup stain on its rim. There was something so lonely about that, like stealing something without getting caught, that I had to hide my face. The empty basket of fries, the hat, the guy's one shaking leg, and the other one being used as a napkin. I had to look away.

He was shaking like he was trying to keep something in, but the urge to let it out was too great. I wanted to reach over to him, like I'd do with my mom when she would shake, to place my hand on his leg and gently say *Stop*. Except, I couldn't do that with a stranger. Also, whatever is trying to crawl its way from people's bodies when they shake like that deserves to be freed.

A guy to my right moved his chair just so, about a quarter of an inch, as he carefully dipped each of his fries into a small plastic container of ranch.

Okay, I'll let you live. I prefer mayonnaise, I said, like he asked. He hadn't asked for condiment advice.

He did not wipe his hands on his pants like Cowboy Hat. I was fascinated with him—how he consumed his food and adjusted his body so he wouldn't have to make any eye contact, the way he dabbed the corners of his mouth between bites. He was so intentional that it made me envious.

He must be like that with everything, I decided and considered following him around Portland so I could learn to be that intentional, too.

I didn't follow him around, but I did decide I wanted to begin living a life of intentionality. I still felt lost and wanted to know the right way to be me, but one thing was made clear: my commitment.

I vowed then to be intentional with everything, to the best of my ability.

In this way, maybe that french fry guy was inadvertently showing me the way. Maybe he had shown me how to be in the world after all.

Time-Travel Machine

Kristen and I did another "We're All Poets" class with a phenomenal poet named Brad Aaron Modlin. He offered us the prompt *When did younger you feel discouraged/worried/bad?*

It felt like a trick question to me. In the same vein as the following:

- What is always coming but never arrives? (Tomorrow.)
- What has many keys but can't open a door? (A piano.)
- I am full of holes, but I can hold water. Who am I? (A sponge.)

My answer to Brad's prompt: *Always.*

Younger me always felt discouraged, worried, and bad. When I felt like I lost myself and had no idea where to go, what to do, how to be, I miraculously traveled in time and became that young me again. Breaking up my family turned me back into that lost little kid who felt discouraged, worried, and bad.

If I had a time machine, my lamest and greatest wish since 1983, I would crawl inside and go back to tell younger me things like *tomorrow, piano, sponge.*

Younger me would immediately know that *tomorrow, piano, sponge* was code for:

- *Everything is going to be okay.*
- *Things aren't as they appear.*
- *At least not always.*

I would also tell the me sitting on our stoop on Drexel Avenue:

- *Not everything is your fault.*
- *Tomorrow he will still be dead.*
- *You will never learn the piano—at least not by 2025 you haven't.*

Our body is a sponge, I'd say to young me after I stepped out of the time machine. I'd try to memorize the dirty snow, license plates, and ugly wire fences so I wouldn't forget. Even though I will.

We must wring it out, I whisper.

Deafness has not set in as fully as it will—and it will as I get older. *Can you hear me?* I ask younger me.
Can I hear me? I ask back.

It feels like another trick question because who is the *I*? Who is asking? Who is listening? I would then sit next to younger me in the cold and we would stare into the sky and wonder where things go.

ALLOW

Where do things go?

In honor of the poet Brad Aaron Modlin, now my good friend, I'm sharing his words again: *When did younger you feel discouraged/worried/bad?* Ask yourself. What comes up when you consider this? If it isn't too painful and you're up for the ride, I have a threefold exercise for you. If it feels too hard to think about that time in your past, visualize a younger version of you who felt free and joyful instead. Use your imagination.

Part one: Write a letter to that younger version of yourself. Notice how I asked questions like *Can you hear me?* Ask anything that feels intuitive. Maybe ask *What are you worried or discouraged about? What are you hopeful of? What are you excited about?* You can offer comfort, too, like I did when I said *Not everything is your fault.* You can offer wisdom, advice, love—anything you want to say to that part of you, as they *are* still part of you.

It might heal a piece of you that has been waiting for someone to offer tenderness, even though you swore you didn't need any. That was just you lying to yourself.

> **Part two:** Write a letter back to the you of now from that younger version. You can do these letters in either order. It will often shed light on where things went, as well as other parts of ourselves that might've been abandoned, when we use both of these letters as a sort of call-and-response. Let them be in conversation with each other.
>
> **Part three:** Use the time-machine idea as a way in to something. It can be a poem, another letter, a deeper understanding of yourself, journaling for the sake of itself—anything. There is no agenda except to play with the supposition that this time machine exists and to imagine what you would go back and do or say. Where would you go? What time period? Why then? Write about what happens when you are there. About who and what you see and how you feel. What is there to discover?

Echolocation

When I was in high school, I'd let my friends write on our kitchen wall where the wallpaper was peeling. At some point, someone painted over the peeling wallpaper. I can't remember what my friends wrote so I called my sister to ask if she remembered how *When we lived on Madison Avenue, we let people write on that wall in the kitchen.* She remembered vaguely, but not what was written.

Why did we write on the wall and allow people to write on the wall of our kitchen? We are trash people, I laughed.

I think Mom started renovating the kitchen around then and it just took a while? she replied.

We never remember events the same way, even if we both were there.

I don't know what I was searching for in needing to know precisely what we had written. Back then, I had such little respect for anything, like our house, and especially my own self. I search now to find things that help me recognize that person who cared so little. I study photos for parallels with who I am now. Clues I may have inadvertently dropped regarding who I was to become.

According to the *Merriam-Webster* dictionary, *echolocation* is a physiological process for locating distant or invisible objects by sound waves reflected back to the emitter from the objects. In a poem I wrote twenty years ago, called "The Intimacy of Bats," in which I apparently decided that I was similar to a bat, I'd written: *What I love about bats: their invisible sound. Bouncing off objects, returning as echo. Leaving as one thing, coming back as another.*

Years after writing a poem in which I literally wrote that I was *part bat*, my hearing has become almost nonexistent. Back then, I had no idea I would become deaf. It reminds me just how much we don't know and can never know about how our lives will unfold. How many different ways our stories can go.

When I dream of that house in Cherry Hill where my ex-boyfriend and I once saw a bat flying above us as we made out on my mom's bed, it's like this: my mom, my sister, and I all fight the current owner to buy our house back from him.

My dreams are aware that time won't travel back with me. Although I can get back to the house itself, I am always in my *now* body at my *now* age.

In these dreams, I am relieved to be back. I do not mark walls with permanent markers. I lock the front door. Sometimes there is a bat, but there is never a glassy-eyed ex-boyfriend in a dirty Domino's delivery T-shirt. My first car is always in the driveway, a gray 1988 Volkswagen Fox. My next-door neighbors Kay and Jerry are putzing around their home. Kay hasn't crossed Route 70 yet to go to the Queen of Heaven Church, so she hasn't yet been plowed down by a car and killed. The blue steps are there, the wooden front porch swing, the way the pavement lifted up on the front walk and you'd trip if you weren't careful.

Are we just trying to make sure we aren't lost and that we can trust ourselves? That our memories belong to us and that they really happened? Is it accuracy we are after? Are we trying to ensure that we are not fallible and that everything that ever happened is stored with precision in our minds and our cells? Are we hoping to guarantee that nothing is lost?

I have news:

Some things get lost.

But you can never be lost.

ALLOW

Like Naomi Shihab Nye says in "Gate A-4," one of my favorite poems of hers: *Not everything is lost.*

No matter what you have been told, and no matter what you believe to be fact, you are not stuck, and not everything is lost. Especially not you. You may have *felt* lost or stuck—Lord knows I have, and written copiously about it. Now it's your turn.

When have you felt lost in life? It may be right now. That's okay, too. Remember what I said back in the introduction? You are held.

> **ASK YOURSELF: WHAT DOES IT MEAN TO BE LOST OR STUCK OR BAD OR TO FAIL?**
>
> The following writing prompts will help you dig deeper into this question:
>
> - Write about a time you were lost, in any capacity.
> - Create a glossary of terms for words like *lost*, *stuck*, *bad*, *fail*, or any words you choose. Have fun with it. You can be irreverent or poetic or silly or nonsensical. Just create new meanings for them that you've decided on. You're calling the shots here.

I Belong Here

Once, in London, I told my friend how much I loved being there.

She said *What do you love? I spent most of my time in London at the Tate gallery. I also love the weather.*

Her question caused me to wonder, one of my favorite verbs.

I love how I feel when I am here.

Knowing my tendency to get overwhelmed, or feel like I'm lost, I pay close attention to where, when, and with whom I feel most myself.

Where do you feel the most yourself? With whom? Is it ever with your own self? Where do you feel most at home?

I moved to Ojai because I like the feeling of *I belong here* that it gives me. It's a feeling of being heard by people rather than being looked through, of sitting with my back pressing against a cold window and being happy for no reason because everything feels like its own good reason. It's that feeling of wanting to create, and that is the most important feeling to an artist, who for so long did not allow themselves that want.

> ### MAPMAKING 101
>
> *Make your own map. Draw it, write it, or paint it. Any way that works. It's imperative to not take yourself too seriously with this (because boring). I made one, too, like my friend suggested. I could show you and it might make you feel less alone, but there's no way around it (I tried): You've got to make your own. Or you can go without a sense of direction, like I did for years. Took what I could get and whatever would appear. I've got to tell you though, that's not a great way to live. So why not play with this map idea? For me, the coolest thing was how there were places I didn't know existed, until I made them so. I put* Trust *in orange crayon and then words like* Courage, Exit, *and* Safe *to go.*
>
> *Start with these inquiries, which have been inspired by the workshops I do with Lidia Yuknavitch and what I've learned from her:*
>
> - *Where do you want to go? This can be a physical place, a feeling, a memory, a person, or anything. These suggestions are always portals to find a way in rather than exact directives.*
> - *To where, or to whom, have you forgotten the way?*
> - *Where do you need your own version of a sign that reads* THIS IS NOT AN EXIT *to help you stay in your body when you may want to run away or escape or avoid?*

- *Where do you want to build an exit from? Where have you dreamed of building an exit from? Or maybe never dared to dream of exiting from, despite wanting to?*
- *In what ways have you been hiding?*
- *What are the places that helped you be where, and as you are, in this moment? Places can also be people, moments in time, or made-up places. No rules is the only rule here.*

See where it takes you. Better yet, see where you take you.

No Getting It Back

I've let myself go. I wish I could get it back. I've heard so many people say these words—I've said them myself.

There is no resurrection of an old version of ourselves, no *getting it back*. What is *it* we think we want to get back anyway?

Every time I thought I'd lost something, or myself, and then went searching for it, I realized I had no idea what I was actually looking for. If that isn't the definition of spinning your wheels, I do not know what is.

Like looking at an old photo of yourself. Maybe at the time it was taken you thought you looked *gross*, but looking at it from the vantage point of *now*, you find yourself wishing *If only I could get that back*.

I recite a line from an old poem of mine whenever I need reminding: *Take a picture of your face. Remember that sometime in the future, you will be amazed at how gorgeous you* were. *Be amazed* now.

To get out of the maze you feel you're in, or if you don't know up from down or are drowning in fear, listen for the words: *You are not lost. You are here.* That's your *Heartsight* talking.

Keep listening for it. It is definitely there. *Then,* take a good look at yourself. You, who is not lost, get to be amazed. Not just in hindsight, but now. *Heartsight* helps you do that.

When you find yours and pay attention to it, letting it guide you, you'll know you can never be lost.

ALLOW

BE AMAZED *NOW*

It's urgent that we stop waiting until *later** to recognize our beauty. I am not referring to external beauty, although that may be part of it. It's common to look back at our younger selves with awe and wonder, so why not step into that space now? Why do we wait? It's like waiting for that rickety old bus all over again.

What would it mean to let go of the story of *how hard it is* to be amazed now? You may think it impossible to be amazed now because of all those *flaws* of yours, and all that is *wrong* with you. This is the moment to grab that sticky note from the introduction by the balls. Eat it, if you must. Anything to ingest it. The one that says *We do not have to try to talk ourselves out of feeling good ever again.*

---

* *Later* is like *them* and *I know, I know*. Meaningless words most of the time.

What would it take to allow this now, versus sometime in the future? Try this:

- Touch your cheek.
- Remember how that cheek feels.
- Memorize the feeling and try to carry it with you. Someday when you are very, very old, say, older than your grandmother's grandmother, and your cheek feels rougher than it does at this moment, perhaps it will bring you comfort knowing that this great big life you've led may have weathered your face. *But oh*, the love—the love you've brushed up against with that cheek was worth every windstorm in the world. It was worth every panic attack on the kitchen floor or hotel bed or parked car with your head on the steering wheel while you sat in the driveway in the dead of summer, windows rolled up, engine off. I know that I want to experience *that* more than I want to stay safe. I just didn't know what I meant when I said that word anymore.

Show-Off

The light in the kitchen is such a show-off.
Don't get me started on the cat either, that braggart,
slouching like he knows something we don't because he has
mastered the art of not having to do a thing to prove he matters.
Cat's all *Look how uncomplicated it is to be happy, you idiot.*

Please with the flaunting books, parading their perfect stillness,
how they don't even have to get up to create whole universes.
Pick me up, you know you want to.
Such confidence is disgusting, must they be such know-it-alls?
It's off-putting, like *Enough already, light, cat, book.*
I've had it with the bowl of fruit strutting its stuff,
that arrogant avocado.
Who do they think they are, having such perfect skin?
We don't worry about our skin, says a lemon.
Well, you should, I reply, then stop mid-word.
Because I am speaking to a lemon.
Look, all I'm saying is nobody likes a show-off.
Nobody wants to hear you blow your trumpet about how
you're not a cat person (but you really loooooove dogs),
that you make a mean pavlova,
or about your perimenopause sweat.
Keep everything to yourself.
Even that is too much.
It's like showboating: *Just look at me breathing!*
Look at me daring to exist!

CHAPTER THREE

The Era of *Because I Want to Do It This Way*

I NEVER UTTERED a word aloud about how I felt in my marriage. I didn't dare think or write about it. A couple times, late at night, I'd write a sentence about it. Then, I'd get a black Sharpie, cross it out, and throw away the paper. I have no tangible evidence because I was too petrified to name the thing.

Denial and fear, a soul-killing combo.

I distrusted my feelings when I first left, so I made this game for myself called *Am I Really Unhappy or Am I Just Saying That Now Because I Am Deeply in Love with Someone Else?* A game otherwise known as gaslighting myself.

Years ago, I was perusing files on my computer and found something I had forgotten to destroy from years earlier. It was hidden in a file with a fake name. I shook when I read it. I buried it, closed my computer, and denied every last bit of it.

I'd written: *I feel alone in my marriage. I hate having sex. I am afraid of being alone though. I wish I had someone to communicate with. I feel like I can't write. I have nothing to say. My brain is an empty fucking bowl with nothing in it. I don't know if I love my husband. I am terrified that he would find this.*

That's all I wrote, and then I put it in a file with a fake name and went back to *fine* for years.

Gaslighting ourselves is the dirtiest trick in the book.

You Do Not Have to Earn the Right

Just like my workshops, this book—which is your own personalized *take wherever you go workshop*—is the journey of bringing our light back up to its innate level of brightness, before it was ever tampered with.

When I say your *light*, I mean your magic, your authenticity. The whole of you, had you not abandoned any of yourself. If no one had the dimmer control to turn us down, what would our level of light be? Of course, no one does have the dimmer control, but that hasn't stopped me from believing they do and from acting as if they do.

This is a pursuit of remaining turned up to your innate level of brightness, whatever that may be, despite any of the light controller's efforts. There will be efforts—there always are. Even when our own *Inner Asshole* is the one trying to dial us down. You'll get tools and insights, like you would in an in-person workshop, but the real pilgrimage happens after, when you integrate all you've discovered and begin to embody it.

If the only thing you take away from this book is the ability to stop lying to yourself, I will throw myself a party to celebrate. By *party*, I mean take a nap, and by *celebrate*, I mean dance in my old-lady underwear. Nothing will make me happier than you being honest with yourself about what it is you actually want to do versus what you think you should do. There'd be one more human walking the earth being true to themselves, and with each *one more human* walking the earth being true to themselves, we end up with a whole lot of humans being true to themselves.

The Land of Denial

I shoved my unhappiness so far down inside me that no one else could ever see it.* Everyone did. I saw it, too, but I'd be damned if I left *The Land of Denial* (*TLOD*). I'll just stay over here, where it is *fine*, thank you very much. I'll even remain miserable, as long as it means I do not have to change a thing.

Who gets to leave fine? I'd think, to keep myself in line with fine.

Then, during one very hot July in Europe, something cracked open. *Fine* broke apart into a billion separate particles inside my skin. Words I'd buried to make unreachable erupted. Not only could I not take these words back, I could no longer see anything else besides them. It was as if my superpower of lying to myself was suddenly revoked by the superpower-givers. In actuality, in naming the thing, I stopped being able to be in denial. It became real.

I am not happy. Spoken to my husband.

I did not *consciously* decide to name anything. Something that would no longer remain stifled, ignored, or lied about did the deciding.

What to call that thing?

- Antithesis of the *Inner Asshole*?
- My higher self?
- My integrity?

---

* Lol lol lol, yeah right.

- The expulsion of *fine*?
- My dead father coming through?
- Pain?
- I don't know and it doesn't matter what made it happen because it happened.
- It happened, it happened, it happened.

The truth snuck out. I finally admitted that I wanted out. I did not know how I'd exit, only that I *had* to. Logistics can always be figured out. My light was dependent on me choosing myself, and, friends, I cannot stress this next part enough.

You can't choose yourself when you are lying to yourself.

Let's pause for a moment, in case you wanted to play the futile yet uber-popular guessing game of *But why?* On the off chance you're scratching your head, speculating *Why in the world is she so dramatic when she was the one who said it was a fine arrangement and that he was a lovely man? Why can't she just settle down and be quiet like everyone else?**

Most likely you are *not* thinking these things because, as I like to remind myself, *It's worse than you think. They're not thinking of you at all.*†

Not everything is for everyone or for public consumption. No

---

* I understand I made this voice sound like some far-right open-gun-carrying man who doesn't like women too much and who leaves hateful comments on Instagram accounts he doesn't follow but only knows of them because of his searches for #LegalAbortion or #BanGuns and who can never, ever write *you're* when he means *you are*. He is insistent and will fight you that it's *your* and also that you *loose* things, so no, I will not settle the fuck down, and what does *content* even mean? What about wanting more than complacency? That's what I am talking about, good sir, so please, go back to picking your teeth and *Breitbart*. I will be over here, finding what lights me up, and you have no say in it. (This goes for our *Inner Assholes* and the *Shame Monster* and that asshole *should* and anyone else who mistakenly thinks that they get to have a vote on our lives.)

† One of my favorite quotes that no one seems to know the author of, so if it's you, can we have a meal and be friends?

matter how much you feel you owe it to others to give "explanations," you don't. We get to choose ourselves, even if and when it doesn't make sense to anyone else. Even if others don't see *what the issue is* and try to convince us that we are asking too much or are just never satisfied and that we want too much. Even if there is nothing *wrong* per se, at least from an outsider's point of view, besides our own deep unhappiness, which we thought did not matter.

Forever homework assignment: Stop perpetuating that. It matters. Like I was, you've been lying to yourself that your own happiness didn't matter because we were taught that.

The Presence of Breath

Before you write me off as some navel-gazing memoirist who just got bored with her marriage and decided to upend her life so she could whine about it in a book, I ask that you take a breath. May we all, always, take all the breaths, until we can no longer.

Recently, I took Charlie to Oahu, one of the islands that make up Hawaii, when I was asked to officiate my friend Melissa's wedding to her partner, Scott. Charlie was the official wedding photographer with his Polaroid, as well as the ring bearer. We stood on the edge of the water as I married them under a full moon, and it was just perfect.

I said *Bless Melissa and Scott. They didn't take small, timid steps circling around their love—they took a breath and then waited for the answers their bodies would provide, if they were willing to listen. They were willing. So they ran like hell into it. And here we all are, standing on a beach as we witness the result of taking that breath.*

Can we all do it right now? Bless them? Whatever you call a blessing is a blessing. But a blessing is most definitely in order because look around.

If we allow ourselves to receive, anything can happen. Magic can happen. Let's all pause and take a breath of that magic right now.

We stood for a long time just taking deep, collective breaths.

The next day, their friend Tim, a local who grew up on the island, took us out on a boat ride. Charlie kept yelling *Faster, faster! Make it jump!* Tim laughed and shared how meaningful it was to him when I'd asked everyone to take a breath before the wedding ceremony.

He explained how that was part of the "aloha spirit." That *aloha* can be separated into the words *alo*, meaning "presence," and *hā*, meaning "breath," making it mean the "presence of breath."

He said that often two people press their foreheads and noses together while inhaling at the same time. I was deeply moved by this. By the tenderness of this gesture. My cheeks were already wet from the ocean water, and they became even wetter. I could never have imagined allowing that kind of tenderness until then.

Before anything, may we take a breath. Such a simple thing, yet so much of my life was spent holding my breath or acting and speaking before I paused to take a breath.

Do you bypass the power of breath or avoid pausing to take one?

May we take a breath so we can ask ourselves what is true for us. May we take a breath before we make assumptions about ourselves or anyone else, about what they should or shouldn't do. May we take a breath before we speak or act.

No matter who you are, or the circumstances, a nonnegotiable is that you get to feel how you feel. I say that as someone who, until recently, wore a steel suit of armor over my heart and carried a shield for the denial of all feeling. Not in the sexy, Robert Downey Jr. *Iron Man* way either.

If we lie to ourselves *Pastiloffian* style, if we do not pause and breathe and check in, then we will not know how we really feel. If we do not know how we feel, then we can't be true to ourselves and do it the way we want because *we will not know what we want.* How could we? Oh, the conundrum. (Take a breath. Several.)

Consider if and when you have not allowed yourself to be true to yourself.

Breathe in this question: *Where have I felt unhappy or unfulfilled or hungry or rageful or empty or full of grief and not allowed myself to have it?*

THERE ARE ENDLESS ways in which we've been indoctrinated to judge others when we can't see bruises or any outwardly obvious proofs of *wrongness.* Not to mention the insidious and infinite ways in which we judge ourselves even more harshly, for wanting what we want and for doing it the way we choose.

Breathe. *A lot.*

Recommit as often as possible to asking yourself the truest questions.

The Era of *Because I Want to Do It This Way*

I didn't write a poem for years. As ridiculous as it sounds to me now, I did not think I was allowed to. I wasn't a fancy poet with published books and a Guggenheim fellowship or letters after my name. I was a college dropout turned career waitress turned yoga teacher. I also didn't allow for the truth that I was desperate for intimacy, especially *physical* intimacy, and affection. I did not acknowledge my grief. I ate it instead of food.

I did not allow room in my life to discover what lit me up.

It makes my stomach churn now.

AFTER DECADES OF depriving myself of writing poetry, I stopped that deprivation.

I memorized Derek Walcott's poem "Love after Love" after I heard him read live at New York University. There's this line that gives me chills. It feels like a loving call to action:

Give back your heart to itself, to the stranger who has loved you all your life.

NOT ONLY DID I begin again with writing poems, but I dared greatly, as Brené Brown* calls it. In this way, writing this book was an act of me giving my heart back to *itself*.

Sharing it with you, without shame, is me giving my heart to *you*.

ALLOW

Consider the following questions as openings for you to discover or uncover or create anything:

- What lies did you, or do you *still*, tell yourself?
- What did/do you believe you did not get to have, or that you did not deserve? (Read my lips: Whatever you come up with is *Capital* B *Bullshit* on the grandest scale.)

---

* If I am even using her expression in the right context. Sorry, Brené, if I am not!

- What have you denied yourself? What's been abandoned? Was it yourself?

You allowing yourself to be lit up is the equivalent of giving a love letter to yourself. It's like saying *Here, go on*, after too long going *Oh, I could never. Who am I to get to do that?*

- How would you give yourself a love letter? Could you?

Read my lips one more time. This is *very important*: You can.

Find your own way of giving yourself a love letter. It doesn't *have to be* anything or look a certain way. Just use the letter (or whatever you make it into) as a way to foster tenderness toward yourself.

If you need a little inspiration, find a picture of yourself at a young age. Put it in somewhere you might be tempted to speak unkindly to yourself. Maybe the mirror or your screensaver on your phone.

When you see this photo, take some deep breaths and connect to that part of you. It's still in you.

Having a photo somewhere where you'll see it constantly helps make treating yourself as if you were a small child, or your younger self, a *daily-ish practice*. With that gentleness, that kindness, and that tenderness, we feel safe. We become our own safety.

When you look at the photo (or imagine yourself younger), pay attention to how you would not stifle little you. If they (little you) shared their feelings, or something that was exciting, or if they expressed that they wanted to use their voice, you would not say* *Shut up. You little shit, you don't matter. That is dumb, no one cares. You don't get to be excited. You should be like other little kids. You don't get to do that.*

Instead, you'd say something like *That is beautiful. You get to be yourself. Go on, do it your way. The world needs you.*

Remember that is still you. The world still needs you.

Give yourself permission to go out into the world—or inside yourself by using your breath—to find out what lights you up. Then grant yourself permission to light the fuck up and do it your way.

You are the permission slip, baby.

Kinds of Afraid

Depends what you mean by afraid.
There's a kind where animal fists ball up, an impulse old as dirt
demands you tighten what you let get loose—
got a real *How dare you* attitude, too.
You knew there'd be a cost to freedom, how terrifying it is
to contend with a body no longer locked up,
this nothing left to destroy besides what's closest.
Another: count your ribs in the dark variety.
The tire blowing out in the night sort.

---

* I pray you would not say these things. If you would, my heart breaks for who said those words to you as a child. You are loved. Thank you for being here.

You grip the wheel, pretend not to remember if you ate,
that you don't yet know starvation is a false analogue to power.
You might ask your afraid questions like
Will I have to pay a price for this?
It is ill-advised to wait for answers.
You can talk to your coffee, though, as if a friend.
Tell it *It is safe, you can let go, the earth won't swallow you whole for
    allowing pleasure.*
Befriend the fear that wants you to witness,
rather than submit to it.
Just open your fist and place it on your low belly.
When an urge to clench comes,
place your other hand on top of that soft place.
Once you start to forget it's your own,
you forget to be afraid.

CHAPTER FOUR

Leaving *The Land of Fine*

HAVE YOU EVER denied yourself permission to leave?

Maybe a job? A job you wanted to quit so badly it hurt and yet you denied yourself leaving? How about a room that felt uncomfortable to be in—say, at a dinner party or other social gathering? Have you ever lay in bed, another body beside you, the assumption of sex hanging thick in the air, so you gave in even though you wanted to leave? Have you denied yourself permission to leave a romantic relationship, a friendship? Maybe it was leaving your hometown, toxic family members, or even a catatonic state of grief, fearing that if you seemed happy people might judge you for grieving the wrong way.

Alternatively, is there anything you denied (or are currently denying) yourself permission to let go of simply because nothing seemed outwardly *wrong*?

I'm not here to just talk about leaving spouses or partners. It doesn't matter the exact situation; the question is if you have ever found yourself saying *I'll just stay over here, where it is* good enough. *I'll remain miserable even, as long as I do not have to change a thing.*

If you have ever said anything like this, or have a fear of conflict and try to avoid it at all costs, then you have lived in *The Land of Fine*, second cousin to the aforementioned *Land of Denial*. In *The Land of Fine*, the last thing you ever do is admit that there is anything wrong because, obviously, everything is *fine*.

One could exist for years in these places.* Lifetimes. I did not think I got to have anything besides *fine*. I convinced myself *Whatever. I'm dead inside anyway, or deserve to be.*†

As I wrote this book, each inconceivable thing occurring was followed by *this other unimaginable thing* followed by *this other improbable thing* and so on until I was forced to get clear on something.

I could no longer say *It's impossible*. It *was. Because it was all happening.*

There were so many coetaneous events and metamorphic things, all tending to one point: me. I knew it was time to stop perpetuating the heresy of *If I tell the truth, I will hurt someone else and only I deserve to be hurt*. It was time to let go of *I am bad*. I could no longer pretend it was impossible either. No more pretending, remember? (That goddamned basement door was really throwing a wrench into things.)

Breaking Open

When I finally named the truth that summer, it was as if something inside me broke open. This may sound vague, but if you've ever experienced it, you know what I mean.

It's like something in you was asleep, something you assumed to maybe even be dead. Until one day, when you're just walking down the street, out of nowhere and instigated by nothing noteworthy—

---

* Ask me how I know.
† I was not ever dead inside, nor did I deserve that feeling, but that is how I survived the grief of losing my dad when I was a young child: I shut off and shut down and convinced myself that the only mantra I needed was *Be strong*. Also, after more than a decade of not being able to cry as an adult, I did feel dead inside. Or at the very least, broken.

no one's even around except a couple in front of you laughing and holding hands—everything rises up and starts spilling out of you. Things you thought you'd dealt with and buried into oblivion, feelings you thought you were incapable of having, desires you had no idea belonged to you. They are all suddenly right there, yelling PAY ATTENTION TO ME! So you begin to cry, which startles you. You say to all the things and feelings and desires that have come rushing up and out *I am paying attention. I finally see you.*

I was in Paris on vacation with a writer friend named Michele Filgate when—with no advance notice—lying to myself stopped working.

This was a week before I would impulsively deliver the blow of wanting out of my marriage to my husband, back in London.

There was an unbearable heat wave in Paris. We'd ducked into a café called The Saint Régis for shelter, and with sweat dripping down our faces and our legs sticking to the vinyl seats, I challenged her to a game. If I wrote three poems—*poem* being a loose concept as far as I am concerned—while we sat there waiting for our food, then she would have to buy me a drink. After, it would be her turn.

I used wet napkins to write my poem-ish poems.

> They say the third poem is the hardest, but I think that's a lie.
> Another lie to get you to stop saying things. I'm tired of believing
>   what *they* say.
> I'm tired of not saying things. I don't believe it's true that the
>   third poem is the hardest.
> I don't know who's ever said that, except me, in this café.
> I'm also very tired of lying to myself. I'm tired of believing what I
>   say when I lie to myself.

I sit here in this booth, looking for the poem.
Here's the poem! A girl in a crop top. (What is it with all the crop tops?)
How the light falls on her hair is majestic. She feels my gaze and gets up.
The light is now on a woman with curly hair, slinging her purse on the back of her chair,
inching it closer to the man next to her, who fans himself with a menu.
No, this is it! I've found the poem!
Wait! Here's girl one again. She adjusts her tiny bun, also fans herself with a menu.
Something I already know comes back to me.
It's not either of them that's the poem.
It's the light.
I've been looking for the wrong thing.

After Paris, I met my husband and son back in London. It's antithetical to storytelling and plot to say *nothing in particular happened*, but there was no specific chain of cause and effect other than the following:

- Lost luggage.
- A heat wave in Paris.
- A lot of french fries and mayo.
- A life-changing three-hour play by Jez Butterworth at the Apollo Theatre called *Jerusalem* that moved me to my core, despite not being able to make out most of the dialogue. It didn't matter what the actual words being spoken were because I felt them,

regardless of hearing them accurately due to my deafness. It was an experience of art and connection that transcended sense, literally.

- A French artist named Andriya Filipovic, whom I met on the Left Bank on the anniversary of my father's death, who spoke very little English but who, like the play *Jerusalem*, communicated with my heart in a way that bypassed language. He added my father's face to a painting after I'd shared the significance of July fifteenth with him. The painting hangs proudly in my home and has inspired my own interpretations, using his as a way in, as a muse.
- My friend's party in London, where Angela Bassett and Charlie danced together.
- Having a soulful and life-changing conversation about *Beauty Hunting* and the importance of listening at that party with a man named Henry, who ended up being the love of my life.
- *That's life.* The two words that came out of my husband's mouth, which unwittingly gave me an ultimatum. Stay in denial and unhappiness, or tell the truth and get the hell out of Dodge.

Not *Better*, Not *More*, Just *Different*

I spoke something I had never even admitted silently to myself: I wanted something different. Not *better* or *more*. *Different*.

Different is not wrong or bad, although it may feel that way, or because *they* tell us it is wrong.* It might be the scariest and loneliest thing for a while. I thought I had not earned the right to want *different*, or be *different*, from my creative life to my marriage.

---

* *They* told me it was bad, and my *Inner Asshole* told me every day that I was bad. Fun times!

I didn't think I'd earned the right to want anything other than what I already had.

There was nothing on its own that gave me the glimmer of the fortitude it would take to finally leave *The Land of Fine*, but rather a string of moments like the ones I mentioned, which, when combined, reinforced for me what it meant to be fully alive. And how much I hadn't been.

Something Consistent to Count On

The need to feel that I would never be left has often debilitated me.

I didn't care if it was a lie either.

Just make me feel safe right now, even if you don't mean it.

There was a nagging voice that I never let out since I was a permanent resident in *The Land of Denial*. This voice knew the truth, and if I allowed the truth to be exposed, then my marriage would crumble, and if my marriage crumbled, I was positive my whole world would crumble because I believed I needed it to feel safe.

It was consistent and constant. Robert was steady and loyal. Safety is not love though. Sure, it can be a *part* of love, but it cannot be the entire basis for a marriage or love itself. It couldn't for me anymore.

Some years back, much to my surprise, I woke with the revelation that I no longer felt safe in my marriage. My idea of safety had grown, just as I had. Whether it was *true* or not doesn't matter because I believed it to be categorically true—that I would never be abandoned by my husband. For a long time, that knowing was my sense of security and was enough for me to subsist on, as hard as that is to admit and as bad as it makes me feel for knowing I was not fulfilled and yet unconsciously decided it didn't matter, as long as I would not be left.

I don't think love is ever wasted, and there *was* love, just not an *in loveness* on my end. I have flashes, like we're in a multiverse, where I made different choices, where I stopped wasting anyone's precious time, where I set us both free.

Did I, say, make a different choice when I had this epiphany? No, I most certainly did not. I have this timeworn habit where I will know a thing but pretend not to know the thing just so I do not have to follow through with any *Now what?*s.

I'll do this even as I know I am doing it, which is worse than being ignorant of behaviors or intentions, and it makes you feel like a real fraud, and as someone who has built an indescribable career on authenticity, that is a grave offense. It feels like everyone can see it, too, like you might as well be wearing a big hat that reads FRAUD across the front. Reckoning with that, well, it will make you feel mad as the hatter himself.

Are you also familiar with this behavior? Choosing to willfully ignore something, or lie to yourself and deny its existence entirely by shoving it down into the basement and bolting the door? The one now swung wide open, which doesn't do much to support the claims of a person who says they don't know what's behind it? You can't keep hiding what was behind the door, including your own self, if the door is no longer there. That is what the rabbi meant.

The fear of having to actually do something about whatever it is we find when we are willing to really look with radical honesty can eclipse any desire for momentum. That fear will try to convince us of all sorts of things, such as we did not really see what we saw, we don't really know what we know, we're just making molehills into mountains, we aren't grateful, we don't have the strength or don't know how, and that if we do anything about what we've discovered we will hurt other people who do not deserve to be hurt. And, lest we forget, we aren't deserving of a life we choose and want anyway.

Do you avoid conflict or asking tough questions for fear of what will be realized because you know you will then have to face what comes up if you want to be in alignment and a person connected to their integrity, aka not a fraud? By turning the other cheek and pretending that we did not see what we saw, or feel what we felt, we can trick ourselves into circumventing having to ask and follow through with *Now what?*

This is a ruse. It deludes us into believing we have outwitted uncertainty and/or an unknown future. As if we are *in control* if we only just look the other way, or if we act as if the thing that we are holding in our hands is not really there. *What thing? What hands? What hunger? What unhappiness?*

We convince ourselves that we've succeeded in outwitting life. That we've sidestepped having to change a thing, including ourselves. It might be true that we can evade it, at least for a while, but the cost will be great.

Living in denial in order to avoid change will cost you yourself.

I SPEAK FROM experience when I say the longer you abandon your truth, whatever it is, the easier it becomes to ignore. Then, you can't locate it inside anymore so you're left looking outward, waiting for *them* to tell you.

I did not make a different choice back then, and that's okay. I made peace with that. I hope you do, too, if you recognize yourself in anything or have similar feelings of self-loathing or shame over your choices or complacency.

There are always so many ways our stories can go because *they are not over yet*.

When we don't dim our light to fit in to someone else's narrative, and when we refuse to adhere to *The Bible of Should*, we help each other. So much opens up when we allow ourselves to be uncompromising with our shine. When we just let it rip.*

May we allow our *here I am–ness* and *let it rip–ness*. May we collectively keep refusing to hide in shame.

Don't Listen to Your Randall

Long ago, I had this boyfriend named Randall, who'd get on my case for sleeping as much as I did. *You gotta make moves*, he'd say.

Randall is an iteration of Shame's voice. There are so many disguises it wears.

Randall used to tell me how I had to get out of the restaurant.

Thanks, guy. I didn't realize I was miserable until you alerted me.

Of course I knew. I had no idea *how* to get out though.

He'd snap *You gotta get outta there*.

Shamefully, I'd hang my head. *I know.*

I had to find my own way out because it was my way to find. Your way is yours. If you don't get out, or if you don't leave *The Land of Fine*, that's okay, too. Unless you are miserable. If you are, start investigating what lights you up. Then, pay very, very close attention to that.

During that time, I started to pay attention to what *did* make me feel good, on the rare occasions I did. I realized being of service, or

---

* I wept and wept and laughed and rewatched *The Bear* and wished I had written it. And it made me want to eat as well as be a chef and live in Chicago. So yeah, let it rip!

making a customer laugh, lit me up. I noticed how much making someone else feel good made me feel good.

This was the beginning of *Beauty Hunting*. I began constantly seeking out what lit me up, which, it turned out, was synonymous with what was beautiful. I became relentless in my quest to notice as much beauty as I could, in every moment. That caused me to be less focused on my depression and misery, which allowed me to see cracks in the foundation of things I thought were solid facts. Things like *I am stuck. I will never get out of here. Nothing is possible.* In those cracks I saw light. I followed it.

I began searching for more ways to serve (that did not necessarily involve serving dry chicken pot pies). Being of service—what I now call *Doing Love*—not only got me out of my head and my own sense of self-hatred, it also made me come alive. I also noticed how easy it was and how natural it felt, how it could be the smallest gesture and it wouldn't matter, as long as it was intentional.

It was like this breadcrumb I kept following. If *this* works, if *this* makes me feel good, if *this* inspires me, if *this* excites me, then I will do my best to keep doing whatever *this* is. The breadcrumb led to more breadcrumbs.

When you are feeling inspired and energized and excited, those feelings beget more of themselves and will show up more often, or at least you will then be able to recognize them.

This is an entirely different approach to living than denying how we feel, or going *Yeah, this might excite me or make me feel good, but I don't deserve to have those things so I'll pay no attention.*

Tough Pill to Swallow

Here's a tough pill to swallow: No one really cares if we lie to ourselves.

This means *we* better start caring, or years will pass before we finally wake to the realization that we've become a ghost. That somewhere along the line we conjured a fantasy about how our lives *should* look and were too ashamed to say that they did *not* look like that, so we pretended. In the wake of this realization, we'll find ourselves standing on the sidewalk, ready to knock on every door on the street if necessary, just to get our true self back.

TAKE A SIP of water to swallow that pill. Now what?

No More Just Getting Through

I know I am not the only one who lies to themselves.

If I just *this*, then I can *that*.

Once I do X, then I will Z.

After *blah*, I will *blah blah*. (*But for real this time*.)

During the summer of 2020, I got diagnosed with gastritis and gallstones.

I've sucked my thumb since I was a baby and sometimes still do as an adult, for comfort. When the gastroenterologist said *No more drinking*, it felt like she was telling me I couldn't suck my thumb anymore. I don't realize my thumb is in my mouth most of the time, it's that ancient and instinctual of a reflex to a yearning for comfort. During the pandemic, drinking became like that. Or rather, the truer statement would be that it became *more* like that.

After I left the doctor, I got this vision of my dad a week before he died. His doctor was telling him *Never touch drugs again. Or you will die.*

Did that really happen? Mom says so. I've told the story so many times that I'm convinced I was actually in the room. I was eight and there's no way, even though my parents both treated me like I was forty-six. I may not have been there in body, but as I left Cedars-Sinai hospital, I thought about how my father did not heed that advice. One week later, he asphyxiated on his own vomit while I sulked in my bedroom because he had yelled at me and told me I was *being bad*.

The doctor said that I ruined the lining of my stomach, and it was being made worse by alcohol and Advil. She said that if I wanted to heal (did I?), then I had to cool it. I had to take medication every day before I ate and double up if I was going to take Advil. I liked this doctor. She did not judge me. I told her the truth about everything, which is much easier when a jerk in a white coat isn't looking at you as if you have failed, not only him personally but all of humankind, while simultaneously looking at his watch because you are taking up too much time. She made me feel calm, even though I saw my weight for the first time in twenty years, after actively avoiding knowing the number. It was something I thought would cause me to spontaneously combust were it to occur. (It did not.) She listened and nodded empathetically.

On the way back to my apartment, while I was stuck in typical LA traffic, I decided that I was not ready to die, and yes, I did want to heal.

I was forty-five, having outlived my father by eight years, exactly how old I was when he died. I had a mask around my neck that read NOT RUDE, JUST DEAF that someone had sent me after I mentioned wishing I had a sign that read I AM DEAF to deal with all the masked strangers. I touched it and thought of the many kindnesses so many people had bestowed upon me.

May I remember to be kind to myself, I remember thinking. *Life is so weird, and now I can't even self-medicate to deal with it.* Thing is, I no longer wanted to self-medicate to deal with anything, but my addiction—or habit, or alcoholism, or pattern, or whatever you label it—had little to do with what I wanted, at least on a conscious level. Like I said, a majority of the time I wasn't even aware of what I was doing. *Want* would get overpowered and go out the window.

I had to remember to be kind to myself and just *be* with life? In all its weirdness? Yup.

A lot of my friends in recovery use the term *rawdogging.* It's when you don't use substances to deal with, or handle, life. It sounded gross to me, *rawdogging.* But like I say, whatever works.

SO MANY HABITS are born from a desire for comfort.

I believed that anything that provided comfort, or helped me get through the day, was fair game. Until I decided I no longer wanted to just *get through.* What kind of life is that anyway? *Getting through.* Like life is one big dentist appointment.

I DID STOP drinking during that period of time. It wasn't easy at first. Breaking habits generally isn't. Like my thumb-sucking, it was almost reflexive, which was dangerous. I had to become very intentional and mindful. The way I understand it, being mindful is about just noticing, so I spent most of my time making sure I was noticing what was around me, as well as inside me.

I long recognized that I often drank *to deal*—as well as to *not* deal—or for no reason at all. I drank every day, mostly without even putting any thought into it. I was well aware it was a habit that served to help me avoid, which I needed no help with at all. I was a master avoider, with or without booze. I hadn't been able to access my feelings since I was eight. The last thing I needed was to push them down farther and yet I did that on the regular. To assuage my own shame and guilt about my drinking, I justified it (again, to myself) by claiming that drinking helped me feel. That wasn't true either; I just confused the feeling of being tipsy or buzzed with feeling alive.

I made it easier to stop by making it harder. I made it more arduous to access alcohol by not keeping any in the house and by not going out to dinner. At that time, I could count on one hand the times that I'd gone out to dinner as an adult and did *not* drink, so it was challenging not to associate the idea of going out to dinner with drinking. For me, they went together like Bert and Ernie, peanut butter and jelly, pea and pod, french fries and mayo. (That's how I like my fries, so don't come for me with your ketchup tears.)

I was cranky, and I wanted to numb out more than anything. Until I didn't.

I took long walks through the streets of Santa Monica. I'd stand in front of the multimillion-dollar homes just north of my building and make up stories about the people who owned them and what they were sitting around having for dinner in their dining rooms just two blocks from the ocean and how expansive their lives must feel having so much space. I'd go *Beauty Hunting* like I was being paid to. Like I was on a mission to notice every goddamned beautiful thing on the planet, which had somehow been put on the path of my walks.

All the beauty in the world, and it was right there.

Something that comes up a lot for me, and that I have to share because it never stops blowing my mind, is that the *idea* of a thing is often harder than the thing itself. The lead-up to giving up caffeine, booze, sugar, or whatever it may be, and how we often obsess over *how hard it's going to be* and create entire scenarios in our minds of the sheer torture. Then, we actually *do* the thing and realize the *thought* of doing the thing was so much harder.

After habituating and exploring different things rather than numbing myself, I was able to trust that I could go out and be present without feeling like I needed a drink to *get through*.

What exactly was I trying to get through? What was I so terrified of by having to stay rather than check out? What was I resisting? I'd spent almost my whole life up until that point willing the resistance to be gone, which is its own kind of tenacious resistance.

Full disclosure: I did stop drinking during that time during the pandemic, for a few months. I *rawdogged*, until I went right back to the same exact old behavior. I tried again two years later. Lasted a month. It wasn't until my son turned eight and I was able to finally see myself for the first time. I finally saw me as an eight-year-old, too. I wept—being able to cry is still such a new thing that it sometimes startles me with its unfamiliarity and its wildness—when I truly saw for the first time that I'd just been an innocent little kid, too, just like Charlie. A kid who'd done nothing wrong or bad, like my sweet boy. It was the first time I had ever seen myself with anything resembling softness. Ever.

But, we are never too late.

I was then able to name it. The first time I dared utter it aloud was not just to a couple friends in confidence, but during my TEDx talk called *Nothing You Do Is Wrong*. It was a title inspired by my son, who said that to me a week before the talk, apropos of nothing.

It's what I'd been waiting my whole life to hear, at least since 1983. If I had said it, I'd be a liar, but I'd never feel that about Charlie.

I decided to believe him.

What a gift he gave me, and like all the best things about us, this one, too, was invisible.

I doubled down on refusing to hide in shame, so on that stage I said *Like my beloved father—whose heart gave out, not from my badness but from his own self-abuse—I am an addict. To leaving my body, to self-medicating. To alcohol. This isn't a new revelation. I just never, ever said it aloud. Then I'd have to do something about it and I didn't want to. I wanted someone to make me.*

No one was ever going to make me.

Thankfully, I was done believing everything I think just because I thought it. I did not *think* I could, but I stopped drinking because I got crystal clear that I was not done with living.

Only with waiting to.

I catch experiencing that longing to escape sometimes, but I get curious about it now instead of giving in to the numbing. Answers to the questions we ask ourselves don't matter as much as procuring a habit of getting curious and inquiring, rather than immediately giving in to an old reflex without cognizance. *This is not an exit,* I say to myself. Like those signs hanging in buildings that let you know that *No, this is not the way home.* I'm standing here with you in solidarity, and curiosity, in the refusal to escape life.

The Bravest Thing

One of the bravest things we can ever do is to stop lying to ourselves.

It is only then that we can allow our desire to be named and honor what is true for us, at least for that day. I let myself name not only what I no longer desired (to be in my marriage) but also what I did want. And that, by far, I find to be the more terrifying thing because then I had to allow it in. I named that scariest of scary things. I'll call it *Big Love*.

It meant intimacy, partnership, trust, friendship, connection, sex, tenderness—essentially all the things I had locked down in the basement before barring the door.

- In what ways have you, or are you currently, lying to yourself?
- Are you willing to do your own internal investigation into what makes your heart skip a beat? How your breath gets shallow at certain times?
- Are you willing to look into the eyes of whatever it is that feels like a lie inside of you?*

Be Willing

I was legally separated—not divorced yet—and still sharing a home with my soon-to-be ex. Meanwhile, I was deep into my relationship with Henry. It was that *in-between place* we sometimes find ourselves in during transition.

Maybe you have been there, too, in some way? Ending one thing, beginning another, and how sometimes there is a spilling over and the lines all get blurry?

I went to Montreal, where Henry was filming a television show. I sat in a tent with the actors and drank coffee and talked with them about divorce and yoga and second chances until they got called to set, and without so much as batting an eyelash, they'd embody their

---

* Look, if you aren't ready to do the whole dead-in-the-eye thing, can you maybe look near the eyes? Maybe the forehead? The left ear? Just get near the damn lie and see what the burn feels like. How hot is it? How much more of it can you take?

character sand start the scene. Their ability to transition with such ease was incredulous to me. It felt like I was watching a magic disappearing act.

I used to say I wanted to be an actor. It wasn't really what I wanted though. I did love it but I knew I did not want it as a career. I would have acknowledged this, had I been willing to be honest back then. I did enjoy slipping into other people, becoming different characters, the adrenaline rush and sense of community in the theater or acting class, and the way it felt like escaping into someone else's life. I knew I didn't really want to put in the work it would take to make it my career, and the world of trying to *make it* in Hollywood frightened me. Every shift, I'd wait on industry folk, who were always *this close* to something happening. And who, for the most part, stayed that close, never getting any closer. But who I also imagined wouldn't recognize if they got closer. They'd spend their lives reaching for what's next or better or more. I witnessed the tolls that leading a life like that took, how unable so many seemed to give away their attention, as if they'd miss something more important were they to do so. How desperate for a sense of worth (and often income) struggling actors seemed, how (understandably) insecure, how much they seemed to be yearning for validation. I recognized this as if I were looking in a mirror every time I approached a table. The last thing I needed was another reason to feel bad about myself. Still, for a long time I claimed I wanted to *make it*.

I never actually specified, even to myself, what making it *meant* though. Only upon reflection is it clear that I just desperately wanted to *make it* into the light in some capacity. I wanted to not hate myself to death. I wanted to *make it* out of what I saw as only darkness around me, ahead of me, inside of me.

I didn't have the language for any of that at the time, so I said *I'm trying to be an actor*. Want to know what that meant? It meant I waited at the host stand to be discovered.

No one discovered me.

I didn't want to be discovered though, but I was too scared to see any of this back then. So I didn't.

Invisible to me was how badly I wanted someone to save me, to tell me it was going to be okay, to give me permission to stop hating myself. I wanted someone to give me a medal, because even though I said *I don't care* and never let myself cry, it still felt like I was going to die when my dad died, and I didn't die. If I'd had the courage to let my grief out, I would've wailed for my dad and never stopped wailing. When he still wouldn't come back, because he never would, I'd beg for a medal for still being there.

We have to give ourselves the permission *and* the medal, which so often go hand in hand. We can spend our lives waiting if we don't. We can only save ourselves, choose ourselves, give ourselves the permission. I didn't have that knowledge during those years. The truer truth is that I did. I just pretended not to.

I stood by and held my breath until someone said *I pick you* even though I had no idea what I was waiting to be picked for, besides simply being *chosen*.

That didn't even happen until I left my husband. I finally said *I pick me*. There really are so many ways to say that. Most don't even need words.

While I was still waitressing, I heard Wayne Dyer say something that shook me awake regarding what we said we wanted in life. He asked *Does it feel natural to you?* I took it like he was asking if when we imagined our so-called dream, if it was like *Yes! That is my life!* I *can see it now,* our arm hairs on end with excitement at feeling like it was all going to work out because it already felt so natural.

I saw nothing. I certainly didn't see me on a set somewhere fanning my face with a script to try and keep my makeup from running. I saw blank space. I heard only ringing in my ears, except more like a warning signal than my tinnitus had ever sounded before. My arm hairs did not stand on end either. They wilted.

It felt so obvious that I checked to see if a light bulb had gone off above my head, like I was suddenly living in some cartoon world where words like *Duh* and *So Obvious* would appear in floating bubbles across my face. *In no way does being an actor feel natural to me* was what came through. I did not have a name for it then, but that was my *Heartsight*. I loved performing, but I did not want to make it my livelihood.

I was looking to feel something like love. Something that might help me to stop being the rotten person I believed myself to be. I did not understand that then, but I knew I would not be going on any more commercial auditions or try to impress self-declared *big* producers whom I already knew from waiting on them three days a week but who would not remember me if their life depended on it. I knew after I heard Wayne Dyer's question that I had to find what *did* feel natural. Problem was, that meant I'd have to stop lying to myself, and I wasn't ready for that yet.

I did take baby steps. I admitted I did not want to pursue acting, but I didn't dare try and get honest about what I really wanted. That would take years.

That day on set with Henry, I watched, awestruck, at how it appeared like the most natural thing in the world for the actors. I forgot I wasn't just sitting there oddly observing people, for whatever reason

I might do that. People being normal, old, everyday people, albeit in hair and makeup and very good lighting. It inspired me to see them doing this thing they were brilliant at and made money doing. (Anyone going into acting, or writing books for that matter, who is entering into it *for the money* needs to rethink that.)

For folks who believe it's a fairy tale to be able to get to do what you love in life: It's not. We all get to have a life that lights us up. Watching them act and get to do this thing they obviously loved to do inspired me to double down on my commitment to lead a life where I don't feel any guilt for being lit up. Where I consistently remember that I'm not getting away with something by experiencing satisfaction or excitement.

We are not getting away with anything by feeling joy. Not a single one of us.

Gay Hendricks calls it your *zone of genius* when you do what you love doing, and that was the zone I wanted to live in. Unapologetically.

You're Allowed to Live

Many of us live like we are getting away with something by existing. Like by daring to even exist, we are showing off. We live as if we aren't allowed to have, think, do, be, say, wear, or go.

We wait for the *Permission-Givers* to tell us *It's okay. You can do it now.*

Or *Sorry, my friend. You don't get to have that.*

These *Permission-Givers* can be spouses, parents, society's norms, social media, our beliefs around age, the *Imaginary Time Gods*, religion, our fears, or our own *Inner Assholes*. It doesn't matter who it's coming from, as long as we believe that they are the boss.

When we *allow* ourselves to call in whatever we have been denying—be it love, joy, sex, food, pleasure, rest, creativity, saying *no*, writing poetry, or whatever it is—a new world opens up. That's the world I now live in: *The World of Possibility*.

The World of Possibility

The first thing to know about *The World of Possibility* is that anyone can live here. You enter by making space for allowing in your life. Which is to say space for yourself.

The Allowing Of

If you feel stuck as to what you want to allow in your life, try writing this sentence and playing with what comes up: *I am ready for the allowing of* _____.

What a sublime blank statement. What would you put in that blank space, at least right now? Remember, you get to put whatever you damn well please.* Before I left *The Land of Fine*, I forgot that part.

I went back to sleepwalking. I was on the *autopilot of fine*, where I had no anchors and no daily or *daily-ish practices*. It was like I unconsciously believed I did not need any because I had *gotten it already*, from years of leading my retreats and workshops and coaching and listening to the likes of Wayne Dyer and such; as if I had things figured out and could sustain myself on all that *work* I'd once put in.

---

* Isn't there something about *damn well please* that just sounds authoritative? That's right, baby. You are the authority on your life.

What Kind of Life Is One Where We Have Nothing Left to Learn?*

Both ruminating and beating ourselves up are easier choices. I did both. I slipped into old, familiar ways of being, then became mortified with myself for slipping into those old, familiar ways of being.

On another Montreal visit, early on, when I was still in the stage of castigating myself over how awful I was and what I had done to my family, I took myself to lunch. I felt as if I were in mourning, even though I was clear on my love for Henry and that I wanted to spend my life with him. I just couldn't reckon that with how selfish I felt.

The pub I went to was crowded so I sat at the bar. As I waited for my food to arrive, I pondered what was inside my sadness. Were I to crack it open, would it be yolky? If I sucked on it, would my lips pucker? Would my teeth chatter and then fall out, an effect caused by daring to look straight into the center of sadness? (No, they would not, but I clench and grind so badly that I incorporate my teeth falling out into my dreams almost nightly.) When it cracked open, would sadness have a face and a name? Would it be as ordinary as, say, sitting at the bar inside the Pub Saint Pierre in Old Montreal at three p.m. because that's what you do when you feel like you might die from overwhelm and guilt? Overwhelm and guilt have huge mouths. They could swallow you, leaving only a carcass to go through the motions that you very much have to keep going through.

I sat next to a man using his finger to draw a map on the bar top to describe something to another man who was nodding and drink-

---

* I implore any one of you to *lovingly* shake my shoulders to snap me out of it if I ever again resign to growth in this way. Not too hard. Just a gentle rattle to wake me the *f* up, okay? I am happy to repay the favor. Reciprocity, right?

ing a pint of pee-colored beer. I tried to figure out where in the world the finger map could take someone.

I wondered, if I opened up my sadness, would it be as plain as the nose on my face or as exciting as watching paint dry? What did I expect? A marching band? (Probably.)

I imagined a bunch of miniature ponies all somehow holding up little signs to remind me how rotten I was, all the reasons *why* in a bulleted, organized list. Maybe when I looked inside, I'd find a tiny fortune, like my sadness was a fortune cookie. It would read *You're not really sad. Stop it.*

Maybe the fortune would read *You don't find what you're looking for. You* are *what you're looking for.*

Most likely, it would read *This isn't a fortune, and your sadness isn't a cookie, for fuck's sake. Now go eat a cookie.*

Did it matter why I was sad? I wondered if I could just be with it. With the not knowing. With the longing for what I could not name as well as what I had and, therefore, no longer needed to long for but couldn't stop. Either out of habit or because I couldn't see what was I holding.

It's right in front of you. Why are you still begging for the thing that you already have? the fortune cookie would also have read.

At the bar, I studied people's faces, looked up weather patterns on my phone of places I'd never been, and picked my cuticles.

I was so afraid.

I was afraid to go back to California, to leave Canada without Henry, that I didn't know what to do or how to do anything anymore. Afraid of how I let everything slide and hadn't earned any income in far too long, of what would become of my home, of custody of Charlie, that I would not be able to move from the barstool because I was so afraid of every possible thing that I could be afraid of.

But man, I just kept staring at that guy's map. I knew I'd have to make my own for my life and that I could not get stuck inside the fear or else I'd stay there.

I didn't have to stay stuck because everything, everything is changeable.

You hear me? Everything is changeable.

I watched an ant crawl onto finger map man's shirt, and it no longer seemed dumb because suddenly I remembered: *I get to crawl out, too.*

We all do.

THE UNEARTHING

- What have you accepted, without questioning, for whatever reasons? Don't get caught up in the reasons right now.
- Are you now willing to question it?
- What are you afraid you may discover? Does that fear cause you to avoid asking questions?
- What have you believed to be *just the way it is* because someone else said so?
- What is one way you can begin to challenge any of these beliefs? Start with one, and go from there.

As they arise, name the things, but listen up, ladybug: This is not an *everything all at once* thing.

That's how I get myself into trouble. I forget it doesn't have to be *everything all at once* and end up in defeat and overwhelm. We can begin, at any moment, to chisel away at the truths we've held to be true that were, in fact, not. Daily deciding.

Turn *fine* on its head and see what you find under there.* Get your hammer ready.

Now, tear that shit down.

Trust

Do you lament choices you've made? Like there's this other life where you made alternate choices?

Maybe there is some sort of parallel universe where I didn't drop out of NYU and I have three kids and a dog. For now, let's say that *what is so* is *what is* and we do not have the option to click over to our other life where we chose differently.

How can things be any other way than how they are? Pause with that.

This isn't *Sliding Doors*. It's not that we can't change. It's that we can't change the past and what has occurred. We can only change the stories we've attached to what's occurred. We always get to change our minds about what we are going to do and who we want to be moving forward.

May we trust in the divine timing of our lives. When we choose trust, we stop seeing our face on the cover of *The Doing It All Wrong Book*. Even if we *were* doing something wrong, when we have trust, we understand that we get to start over and begin again and that it is not too late.

---

* My son is obsessed with *Captain Underpants* these days. For good reason. Dav Pilkey is incredible, and his imagination is enviable. Charlie keeps telling me this joke that goes: *Mommy, what's under there?* I go: *Under where?* He howls with laughter. *You said underwear, Mommy!* I purposely fall for it every time now because it tickles him so. I try it on him when I think he is least expecting it, and he never falls for it. He won't say *underwear*. Nope, he says, *I will not fall for it*. But still he laughs and laughs that I even tried. Anyway, let's see what's under our notion of *fine*, shall we?

> **STICKY NOTE ALERT**
>
> *Get a pen and write* TRUST *on a sticky note. Or on your hand, your foot, or the wall. Get red lipstick and write it on the bathroom mirror. Trace it and stain your finger. Let that red remind you to trust. Take some rocks and use them to write it in sand. Write it in the air or with your toe. Spell it out with Cheerios. Live it, breathe it, eat it. Wake to trust, after sweating all night in tangled wet sheets.*

Our Life Is Ours

I lost one of my best friends because I had an affair.

I did not have an affair.

Her mind was made up though, from the get-go. I tried explaining myself, despite my body contracting at the self-betrayal of having to defend my actions, especially to a best friend. I did this because I loved her and was willing to do whatever it took not to lose our friendship. But no matter how much I tried to get her to see things from a different perspective, she could not see it in any other way besides what she believed.

ROBERT AND I had met Henry together at my friend's party in London, where they spent a lot of time talking. It was only on our way out that I even met him at all. A near miss. Alas.

We had this beautiful conversation about listening and *Beauty*

Hunting, and after asking if he minded if we moved away from the noise where the magician was performing so I could hear him better (yes, there was a magician), he looked at me and said *I think you are just about the best listener I have ever met.*

I have a reputation of being *the best listener*. This is *only* from people who have experienced my workshops or know me well; never has a stranger said anything of the sort. Usually, I get *airhead, checked out, not paying attention, snob*. I don't present the way most people think deaf people present, so it's understandable that it isn't on their radar to consider deafness. They just think I'm rude. It's one of the reasons I have such fierce allegiance to not assuming or making up stories about others (and ourselves). We just never know.

I was thrilled to discover that he also lived in Los Angeles. I called Robert over, excited at the prospect of getting together with our new friend when we were all home. Henry said he didn't do social media, which I jokingly commended him on. We took a selfie, exchanged information, and said *We'll be in touch*. And that was that.

There was nothing romantic about our interaction that night in the slightest. Just joy at feeling alive, connected, and very seen.

CHEATING WAS AN inexcusable offense to my friend, one she could not forgive.

Years back, her now ex-spouse had cheated on her, causing their marriage to end in a brutal divorce. I was aware of how excruciating that period of her life was and had deep compassion for what she'd experienced, as well as what that wound gave rise to within her. My situation with Henry brought that old pain back to the surface, she informed me.

I WAS FULL of adrenaline after we left the party where we met Henry. We got back to our Airbnb—the same Airbnb where, two nights later, I would unexpectedly and unrelated to meeting a stranger at a party ultimately end my marriage when I confessed my unhappiness as I sat on the floor by my husband's feet.

ABOUT TEN DAYS after our return from London, Henry texted both Robert and me to say hello and how nice it was to meet us. He reached out using my phone number because we'd exchanged numbers at the party. I told Robert as he was on his way out the door to his weekly soccer game in Santa Monica, and we were both chuffed our new friend had made contact.

The next thing I knew, eight hours had passed. Henry and I had been texting all day. Nothing untoward or sexual or even flirty, but I told him I felt guilty for some reason.

He said *Because it's intimate.*

I was desperate for intimacy and hadn't acknowledged that until that moment. I can admit now, that was when I knew I was in love with him. I felt it in every part of me, and the feeling was undeniable, even though my brain said *Not possible.*

AFTER TEXTING EIGHT hours on that first day, we took it to the phone to continue. During that call, he asked me if I was happy.

I replied *I am. Mostly.*

Then, I told him it was funny he should ask. I shared how two nights after meeting him, I'd accidentally blurted out to Robert that I was not happy. Retelling it made that basement door swing open again because, let me tell you, I had closed it immediately after that night and had planned on pretending I'd never opened it at all.

I can't say, because there is not a parallel universe, whether I would have had the grit to go through with leaving had I not had a catalyst: Henry. I'd like to think yes, but I know it helped me.

MY FRIEND SAID it was insensitive that I didn't understand how triggering cheating was for her, knowing her history with it and everything. That it was the worst thing I could do, and also that divorce was the most traumatic thing for kids and that I'd hurt Charlie by breaking up my family.

AFTER THAT FIRST texting marathon, we did it again the next day, except we added FaceTime. From that point, we couldn't stay away from each other. Albeit, only through texting and FaceTime because he was still abroad. From the moment I told Henry the truth about being unhappy—the second time I'd ever uttered it to anyone—I became crystal clear that I would leave, and despite how implausible it is that I could know I loved this man, I did. From that very first day of texting, I never touched my husband again.

WHEN I FIRST told my friend about my text exchanges with Henry, I said *I think I might be falling in love with this guy. I know it's absurd because we only met once in person for twenty minutes.*

She wanted to hear none of it.

We can never avoid everything in life that can potentially trigger us.

Body comments have the potential to send me into a spiral. I know this about myself. To avoid that, as best as one can ever avoid any spiral or trigger, I've set a boundary of *No comments about the physical body's appearance*, thereby dodging the trigger. Of course, this does not always work.

Sometimes we can be caught off guard by what triggers us. I imagine my friend was surprised by her own visceral reaction to something in my life, but the truth is, I do not know.

It was hard to have this rug pulled out from under me all of a sudden, taking my support system with it. I tried to put myself in my friend's shoes, but I did not consider what was going on to be an affair. Even if it was, she'd often remarked how miserable I seemed in my home life.

My brain knew that what felt like coldness or lack of support wasn't about me, but logic doesn't get much say in matters of the heart. She thought that it was wrong, and I'd be lying if I didn't admit that a lot of my self-talk in those early days was prompted by her words and our friendship ending. I was vulnerable and very susceptible to someone confirming that I was a bad person. She said as much, just like my father had the night he died, so it made it easier to become a terrible monster once again.

It's wild how easy it is to find confirmation that we suck when we are looking for it.

I COULDN'T ADMIT to anyone else that I was in love with someone I had only been in person with for a few minutes. I assumed I was making up the whole thing because I was unhappy and I was probably projecting. I did not yet have the guts to use the word *divorce* with Robert, and although it was never going to be because of Henry, I wanted to be sure of my feelings for him. As my friend Lidia put it, *You need more data*, and getting that data would require being with him in person again, for more than twenty minutes.

HENRY AND I continued on for a few weeks while he was still away, texting and FaceTiming all day and night and falling in love.

I WAS TAKEN aback that my newfound happiness did not trump any outrage my friend might have felt. The few other friends who knew about it were over the moon for me, even if they felt bad that my family was going to split up because, as we know, we can hold more than one thing. They knew I'd been unhappy, because everyone apparently had seen it, so seeing me lit up like that made them ecstatic.

I want the people I love to be happy, even if I am not, and even if I wouldn't necessarily do what they were doing. I want to champion their happiness and always be an *I Got You Person* for them.

I still have a hard time comprehending that our long friendship dissolved because of what she *perceived* to be my infidelity in a relationship that was mine, not hers. Or how it had anything to do with *our* friendship.

With time, I've doubled down on my commitment to accepting what is so, instead of spending my energy wishing it was not, or shoving it down to the basement.

YOU KNOW HOW I said I had wanted to get free but without causing any collateral damage? Well, I've got news for you: There can never be *no collateral damage*.

It's why I never did anything about my unhappiness before that moment. I was not willing to cause damage.

While it was true that I was not willing to cause damage, I realized I was very much willing to cause damage to myself.

I reckoned with this newfound insight as my friend rebuked my behavior. I decided I was no longer willing to avoid facing the truth so that I would not cause anyone else harm, nor was I willing to harm myself in order to spare someone harm.

That was true for our friendship as well. As it turns out, I would not have done anything to save it because I didn't. I ended up choosing love and what I knew to be true.

Our friendship dissolving is one of those heart-wrenching situations in relationships where no one gets to be right, only hurt.

I learned we can definitely appreciate someone else's pain without fully understanding it. It's a kind of empathy, and not without heartbreak. I miss us, but I now can see that my friend simply could not be an *I Got You Person* for me, so *always* is not always possible. Sometimes we can't show up the way someone needs us to. Sometimes we have to choose ourselves.

She chose herself, and although it hurt, and it still hurts, I do not fault her. I also chose myself and ended up hurting others.

Broken Open, Part II

Change meant death. I'd believed that since I was eight, so after I did *the thing*, I'd incessantly check to see if I was still there. That I was still a person in the world, like with skin and a heartbeat and everything. I'd feel myself in order to gauge if I was disappearing, little by little, like Marty McFly's siblings in his photograph in *Back to the Future* after he traveled back in time, which then altered the course of events in the future and subsequently erased their existences.

I'd touch my legs, my arms, my head, repeating *I am here. I am not dead.* I did not trust that I was deluding myself. I'd continually feel myself. (I can only imagine what that must've looked like to passersby.)

I WAS AFRAID of so many things—how to make it all work, what would happen with my son, what would happen with my home. I was terrified that Shame might be right when it said *Finding this kind of love for the first time at forty-seven is embarrassing and weird, and you are too old and should be ashamed because the life you had was fine. You're a bad person.*

Shame told me to keep quiet and stay put.

ALLOW

WRITE YOURSELF A LOVE LETTER

In my workshops, I do an exercise in which I ask people to write a letter to themselves in the voice of someone who loves them. I have them begin with *If you could see what I see* and end with *PS I wrote this myself so it's what I already know but may have forgotten.*

It's also a beautiful thing to do for someone else. You can share with them what you see that perhaps they cannot.

Notice any sensations in your body when you think of this someone who loves you, whether they are dead or alive or non-human. Stay with those sensations as you write yourself a letter in their voice.

BRIDGE THE GAP

Ask someone you trust to write a letter for you. Read what they see and appreciate about you that you maybe haven't been willing to see yourself. Consider ways you might begin to bridge the gap between what is in their letter, or the one you wrote in the voice of someone who loves you, and how you are walking through the world. Consider any *Now what?*s on how to close the gap (at least a bit) between how you appear to someone who loves you and how you see yourself. Between who you really are and how you have been hiding that person.

With these letters, a portrait is formed. Most likely, it's closer to a truer you than who you believe or allow yourself to be. If you're willing to believe these words, you might find yourself discovering ways you've been lying to yourself about what you really want. It's not about what *they* want. We just forgot or were taught otherwise.

Pause and ask yourself *Who do I want to be? What would feel fulfilling?* Observe how often *they* (that includes Fear and Shame) show up. Keep inquiring, as if you are the one who gets to answer, because you are. If you feel ungrounded, go back to those letters that remind you who you really are. Tattoo them on your heart.

Start asking again *What do I really want? Is* fine *enough?*

Start digging into cultural narratives and standards you've been taught about what it means to be *good*, *right*, *beautiful*, and *successful*. Play with different ways to dismantle the stories you've bought into or made up about how your life *should* look. Then, turn them on their heads by doing it your way.

It's unnerving in the best way possible to look at something with an altered perspective. Like going into a handstand at the wall in a yoga class and observing how everything looks upside down. Everything is still there, and nothing is actually different except your point of view, which, after a while, you get used to. Then, everything *is* different, all because you chose to see it in a new way.

Shame

For years, every morning, I licked my fingers
to see if I'd eaten in my sleep.
Crumbs on the tongue meant muffins.
For years, every morning, I licked my fingers
to see if I'd dug through the trash to shove them
in my mouth like a prisoner withheld food.

I was desperate for sustenance, then counted the ways
I hated myself for feeding.
Who gets to stop being hungry?
For years, every morning, I licked my fingers
to see if I deserved to be a person.
All that chocolate under nails, blackberry seeds in teeth,
while my customers took careless bites of turkey meatloaf
in bodies that stayed, that knew how to behave.
Forks in fingers free from old peanut butter,
knives when they needed to make an important point.
What a thing that must be: to know
who you were without being told!
How I wished for this fork-waving assurance.
For years, every morning, I licked my fingers
to see something, anything.
Old habits die hard and I'd lick,
expecting to taste disappointment
from what I'd done in the dark.

Oh, what I've done in the dark.
For years, every morning, the things we did.
How Shame told us to be good.
How the dark allowed us to be bad.

CHAPTER FIVE

Shame Loss

TERRIBLE MONSTER. That became my self-appointed moniker (again) when I left my marriage. I'd already spent decades believing I was a monster who made her father die, so I had the role down pat. I didn't self-appoint the nickname as much as I woke up one morning and it was in bed with me, like it had never left.

I did my best—often failing—to lose the shame I was holding on to about so many things, including my new relationship and its "inopportune timing." Every day, I tried to put down that rat bastard.

I forced myself to ignore the rat bastard, as well as (try to) not take it personally when other people didn't approve. Even when I received emails telling me how disgraceful I was, or rude comments on social media, and horrifyingly, an anonymous letter in my home mailbox, which was so invasive that I still get chills when I think about it. Even when I lost a treasured friend. I had to remind myself, and frequently ask my *I Got You People* to remind me, that my life was mine to live, that I owed no one any explanations for my choices, and mostly that I was not a bad person.

I am grateful for those people who gave me support as well as confirmation that choosing myself was not the evil act of betrayal

Shame would have me believe it was. I would have used anything as evidence that I should turn back to the place that was familiar. Had I gone back to the familiar, to *The Land of Fine*, I'd be abandoning myself, again. My *I Got You People*, thankfully, would not let me do that on their watch.

No matter how many times I asked *Tell me it's okay? Remind me I am not bad? Am I going to be okay? Did I ruin everything?* they lovingly stressed that I was supported, that they were there, and that it was going to be okay. They did it as often as I needed (a lot) and not once judged me or acted like I should know the answers already. They were just there, and that kept me going.

In this, I discovered *Shame Loss*.

Do you ever cling to something, someone, or a belief, only to realize that you don't know what it is you are actually holding on to? What about shame?

If you answered *yes*, open your hands and look closely at whatever it is you are gripping.

See? Nothing there. Just hot air.

I CAPITALIZE *SHAME* here because it's a character with a voice, personality, habits, and sometimes a body, often our *own* body. Even though it's got things that make it seem real, it's not, but most of us don't realize this because the rat bastard looks, sounds, and feels so real.

IT ASTONISHES ME how many people weep when I read aloud Mary Oliver's poem "Wild Geese" in my classes. I barely get started before noses are running with emotion after the line about not having to be good. Hands cup mouths, followed by revelatory intakes of breath. I am also the snot-faced weeper, no matter how many times I've read it.

It's like Queen Mary O. is giving us a hall pass that makes us collectively remember, at least for a couple minutes, that we don't have to always get it right, be perfect, or be *good*. Whatever those words even mean. I imagine, that in her Mary Oliverness, she is saying that we get to be our own permission slips.*

How many years have you spent trying to be *good*? How long have you let shame live rent-free in your mind and body? Do not attempt to calculate because it doesn't matter and can send you into a shame spiral over how long it's been, which defeats the purpose of *Shame Loss*. Take an honest look inward.

It is not necessarily *simple* to simply *be* with what you find and try not to attach a story or meaning to it. If you are willing to give this a go, I'd wager you have the chutzpah to ask *Now what?* and follow through with whatever shows up as best as you are able.

When at long last I admitted how profound my hearing loss was and that I needed hearing aids, the earth did not shatter from shame. This did happen though:

- I was able to discern the difference between being broken and not being able to hear. That I could not hear did not mean I was broken.
- Someone who took my yoga class in West Hollywood, who'd never said more than two words to me and about whom I made up a story that she hated me, read the blog I wrote containing this confession of deafness, where I'd stated I did indeed need

---

* I keep having these images come into my mind of a grown-ass person dressed as a giant permission slip for Halloween. Or just because. Someone's got to do this. Send me a picture if you do.

hearing aids but that I didn't have the money for them. She promptly acquired my phone number, called me, and donated a pair of hearing aids to me from her audiologist friend.

- I began to feel less stupid, alone, and left out because I could hear better. (I know I am not stupid, but spend your life not understanding what's being said or what's going on, and you begin to feel as dumb as a talking rock who can only say phrases like *Huh?* or *What?* or *Sorry?* or *What did you say?*)

Word to the wise: If you *don't* follow through, you get to let yourself off the hook and begin again. We really do make it harder than it has to be.

What's Not Mine Anymore

Shame Loss is choosing to put down what is no longer ours, and perhaps never was. It unlocks the door to our freedom and—in one of the great (worst) practical jokes—gets us to see that the door wasn't even locked in the first place. It's a mean joke.

Letting go of shame awakens parts of us that were buried under it.

Each time we are able to release it, we free our trapped components and rescue abandoned ones.

I did want to rescue my abandoned parts, but I needed help. I also needed community and whatever else might help me get the courage to kick my roommate (Shame) out of my house. So I created *Shame Loss* because that fucker had to go, for all of us who'd been boarding it.

Shame Loss is a communal and collective approach of eliminating shame through naming it, sharing it, and transforming it. There's strength in numbers, so when we meet it together, its power over us diminishes.

We can also do it without community as an everyday (everyday-ish) solo thing by remaining conscious of what the shame is; by naming it and consciously choosing something else instead of shame; by paying attention to where we hold it in our body and softening those spots; and by speaking to it and letting it know that we no longer need it. The more ways we find to help us kick it out of the house and the more we practice doing so, the easier it becomes to alchemize shame into something else. Like art or any type of creativity. Like being of service to someone else. Like gratitude. Like love.

Shame mutates. It can become tenderness or compassion. I've felt it happen.

The crux of *Shame Loss* is leading with the thing that causes you shame. I am not suggesting that you walk into a room and announce to strangers that you're carrying shame from being sexually assaulted. I am suggesting that you no longer hide.

This does not necessarily mean that you speak it aloud, but that you don't actively try to hide yourself, or the parts of yourself you think are faulty or rotten. *Shame Loss* is an adamant refusal to hide any longer.

Make it a constant awareness, and know that the ingredients of this practice are your own, created by you and catered to your own personal history.

Friend, it is not your birthright to feel bad or to carry shame. (I hope you'll remind me of this when I forget, too.)

OG in Your Alchemy

In the past, you may have felt awakened when you've been able to let go of shame. You also may have felt awakened from the power of words, art, death, sickness, or love. They *all* have that life-giving power to wake us from our walking slumbers.

As reawakened or inspired as you are though, you might still fall into the common trap of *Who cares anyway? I don't matter. I'm not special.* It isn't something only writers or artists fall prey to. Any of us can succumb to this. That's Shame talking.

Shame tells things as a way to try to keep us small, quiet, and well-behaved. Like Fear and our *Inner Asshole*, it thinks it's doing it for our own protection because if we stay small, quiet, and well-behaved, then we won't get hurt or embarrassed or disappointed. Like that has ever worked. Shame is conniving but not very smart.

If you only knew how often I've said *It's all been said before. It's all irrelevant. It's all pointless* when thinking about creative pursuits. Of course, I did start this book and I did keep going, with all of it. It can never have *all* been said before anyway. No one else has the ability to "get there first" because no one has our particular story or the precise shame we harbor. No one has our particular *here I am–ness*, our individual *let it rip–ness*.

THE NEED FOR ownership and *This is all mine* gets us into trouble. Write or speak this aloud, like I do: *Get over yourself.*[*]

We are not original in our crappy self-talk or our fears. We can be original in how we alchemize them.

---

[*] You can use first or second person, depending on your mood.

Put Down Your Boxing Gloves

Are you ready to stop fighting yourself? If you are not, skip ahead. If you are, ask yourself this: *What is a* Now what? *for today that will allow for softness instead of pushing against myself?*

If you're not ready to stop fighting, that's totally cool. Old habits die hard, and I'll be here tomorrow and the next day and the next.

I no longer harm my body or starve it or force myself to exercise for hours on end because of old beliefs that I don't get to relax or that I must be punished, or to distract myself from feeling, or to batter myself into being *good*. I don't obsess or drown in guilt for not torturing myself anymore. I let myself rest, and if and when I do exercise, it is because it makes me feel good or because I want to. It is no longer because I think I deserve to be punished. I am proof that old habits actually can be broken with practice and support. I haven't succeeded in breaking my salt-and-vinegar-chip or detective-show-binge-watching habits, but slow your roll, because I've broken many other old habits.

Mean Girls

No one has been meaner to me than me. That hurts to write. Does it hurt to read because it feels familiar?

I used to write little notes everywhere that said things like *I am disgusting. I am gross. I don't even deserve to be a person. Why did I eat? Why can't I control myself? I am a monster. Why do I keep letting myself go? Why did I make my father die? What is wrong with me? I am a bad person.*

Then I'd crumple them, like that would make me not have written them in the first place. I'd just write more and then leave them everywhere so that there were these crumpled little terrible missives all around me, as well as inside me. There was an urgency to how I couldn't stop writing awful things to myself. I couldn't stop thinking them, and I thought that writing them down would get them out of my mind, therefore making them stop. That never worked. I couldn't bring myself to throw the papers in the trash, as if I knew that I did not really get to let these thoughts go because they were mine, and they were true.

Have you also been the meanest to yourself? If yes, I see you hiding your face in your hands. You deserve softness. You don't need to hide anymore.

Prayer for Softness

This is a prayer that comes from you, derived from your own body. It can be felt only by you.

Like they are hand tambourines, shake your fists and pray for softness. You may have tried before, but now is the moment you are ready to remove the sheathing you've encased yourself in, hoping that it could shield you from pain and grief and loss by not permitting vulnerability. It did shield you from these things at times. When you are numb, you certainly don't feel, or you feel less. But it also protected you from the most beautiful things in life—deep connection, intimacy, accessing your emotions, your sexuality, desire, and tenderness.

Softness isn't discriminatory.

It comes and goes where it's needed. If, like me, you didn't just harden your heart but your whole body, the gods of softening know. They know how you clench your jaw to the point of breaking through your own mouthguard, three different times, and how your teeth are now ground down to nubs. They know how you used to wake every morning with curled fists, like you were fighting yourself in your dreams. They know how you used to believe you didn't deserve anything, especially when you were soft in the gut. If you are willing to listen, you'll hear them telling you, with such softness, how untrue that all is.

Pray for softness when the only sound you can hear is the vibration through your feet. Pray you meet that old broken record in your head of *Do not let me feel, let me be strong, may I be hard* with compassion, and then pray to abandon those battle cries for good. You don't need them anymore.

One day you will remember your immutable self, but like it was someone else. You will only want to hug her and tell her not to worry so much because one day, not too far in the distant future, she will recognize her own capacity to re-create herself into something soft and beautiful.

Come. Sit Down. Talk to Me.

Things I want to remind us of as we soften:

- Don't be an asshole to yourself. It can be hard. We live in a world with a lot of assholes. We also live in a world with a lot of kind mensches. (Hello, you mensch, you.)
- Stop being mean to yourself. It's boring.
- You're not perfect. Thank the god of spell-check. Perfect people are a myth. So is *productivity* or *busyness equals worthiness*. I will happily and effortlessly demonstrate what not being perfect looks like for you anytime.
- You're doing a great job. You're a delight, even if you're grumpy in the mornings.

- Try to do some good in the world. Pick up your trash. Look people in the eyes. Say thank you. Try not to judge so much. Breathe. Drink water.
- Why are you comparing yourself? What is that getting you? Check in to see if you can identify what the payoff is from that idiocy. Then let it go. What it's costing you isn't worth it.
- There's no race. There's no *set way* to be a person.
- I wear a bracelet that reads DON'T BE AN ASSHOLE. I forget a lot. Let yourself off the hook if you do, too.
- I stand over the sink at midnight while eating a loaf of bread and a chunk of stinky cheese, which then makes me say *Look at me. I'm a dumpster fire.* Google *dumpster fire* and see whose face pops up. Not mine. Not yours. We are not dumpster fires.
- Don't google yourself. Do what you want, but if you've put anything out in the world you feel tender about, I advise against googling your name. You'll find one of the aforementioned assholes, and it might hurt. I'm not going to say *Don't let it hurt*. Let it hurt for five minutes, then keep going. Or an hour, or however long it hurts, but no, you may not take it on as truth.
- Be unwavering in who you know you are.
- If you don't feel like you know who you are, start asking questions. Investigate. Listen. I think you do know though. You are a worthy human being, deserving of love.
- Go *Beauty Hunting*, especially but not solely within yourself. Look up and out.
- Do not forget to look within, too.

The Voice

You might find yourself talking to the bathroom mirror. *Here we go again*, you might even say to the toilet, which does not care in the least. Because it is a toilet.

    The Voice has returned. The one who constantly lists your flaws. *Eyes too small. Can't ever find your keys or matching socks. Bad at math. Can't hear for shit. Talks too loudly. Eats before bed. Has stubby toes. Is unlovable.* The one you mistakenly thought was gone because *you did all that work on yourself with people who knew things. Or so they said.* The one you presumed was beaten into submission by your repeated posting of *I am enough* memes, by friends saying *Just because you can never find anything doesn't make you a bad person.*

    Naively, you thought you vanquished it. You imagine an exorcism in your bathroom and laugh. *The Voice* says *You don't exercise enough.* You say *I said* exorcise *not exercise!* but you silently concur that it's correct, you do not exercise enough. *The Voice* is calling you out for this laziness. It always seems to know.

    It says nothing in response, which you take as it listening. You get in the shower and the water feels good. You remember you get to feel good, despite what *The Voice* repeatedly tells you. You write *I get to feel good* on the mirror with your finger. You are not lazy. You know that you do not need to do the elliptical for eighty hours a day, or every day, or any day. You know you are being lied to. *The Voice* has gone quiet. For now.

What Matters Is That I Felt It

Last summer, I was swimming in my friend's pool and we were goofing off, pretending to be Linda Barrett (played by Phoebe Cates) from *Fast Times at Ridgemont High*. My friend filmed me in slow motion on her phone, and I was shocked at how not self-critical I was when I watched it. I loved it. The playfulness, the sexiness, the way I was laughing. I posted it on social media.

We Are Forever *Works in Progress*

Days after that moment by the pool, Shame taunted: *You are a fraud. Look at you writing about losing shame when you fell right back into old patterns. All those self-destructive habits that reared their heads around the dissolution of your marriage, while you pretended they didn't. You should be ashamed of yourself. And look at you letting your weight fluctuate like that. Why can't you actually get anything done that you commit to getting done? Why do you always let yourself go? Why are you so lazy?*

Shame is a liar, but I am not. I never pretended to be okay when I wasn't. After I plummeted to the depths of *self-flagellation*, I asked for help. Then, allowed myself to receive it.

How dare I talk about *Shame Loss* and still have these things come up?

I dare because I am human.

We are forever *works in progress*—one of the most frustrating parts of being human yet also one of the greatest, if not *the* greatest.

Put It Down

How is shame keeping you from expressing your most authentic self?

Get nosy about this. Try writing what comes up when you ask yourself that question. Don't lift your pen from the page or fingers from the keyboard until something feels true. Or just stop when you feel like stopping. Maybe getting in bed helps you uncover where shame is keeping you from expressing yourself. If it is, go take a shame-free nap.

Sit with that question, even if no tangible answers arise. The question is the thing.

We are dynamic beings, so the answers will be forever morphing and shape-shifting. This curiosity and diving into wonder are how we live life with more *full-body yeses*, as Katie Hendricks calls it.

It comes down to our receptiveness to listen and *just be* with whatever we find, including new questions that arise.

We have two options in life, albeit nuanced: Shut down or keep going.

I am only interested in the keeping of the going.

Be relentless in your asking and your determination to keep going.

Here's what these two opposing forces can look like:

KEEPING GOING: You get out of bed when you feel like you want to die, even if it is for a minute. Or to get a drink of water. You let the person standing in the doorway ask you what you need. You let them stand there for a long time, without you apologizing when you can't answer what it is that you need. You have no idea, but you let them stay because you understand this means *I Got You*.

SHUTTING DOWN: Closing yourself off. Hiding so no one can see you, not even you. Especially you. Closing the door on the person standing in the doorway. You're so shut down that you don't even see them. Or you don't believe they mean what they say anyway. You close the door on yourself.

Who cares if you crawl back into bed or if you only get up to move a few feet to the couch? You got up! Doesn't matter what it looked like or how long you remained up. It's the staying open and letting in life and love, even if it has hurt us in the past. Even when we are afraid it might hurt us again. It very well might, but we are here to love and be fully alive.

Shame is the broken thing that takes up too much space, not us. Forget all the things that tell us our bodies are broken or too big. That they don't look like they should or are too old or not enough in any way.

May you continuously wonder, *Am I willing to lose shame? To put it down, for now?*

It's okay if your answer is *No, I'm not willing to lose shame*.

Why is it such a hard habit to kick sometimes? I don't have a PhD in Shameology, but I can tell you that when I was nearly dying from anorexia, I wasn't unaware of that fact. People would act like maybe I didn't realize. I knew damn well. I was also clear that I had no intention to heal. That would require letting it go, and I believed it was my identity. I did not know who I would be without it. It was mine, and I wanted no one to take it from me.

Shame can be like that. It can feel like our whole identity, and if we were to lose that, who would we be without it?

There's often a belief, one I had at least, that I don't get to lose shame. That it's my burden to bear, and one I deserve to carry forever. How dare I have the privilege of letting go of the shame surrounding the monstrosity of killing my father? (I killed no one, in case you've only been skimming so far.)

One *this* in *You get to have this* is *You get to let go of shame*.

It's okay if you are not ready to let it go yet. Maybe you will be tomorrow.

There is no timeline or wrong time to stop carrying what is not yours to carry.

Shame Holds No Power over Us Once We Name It

Naming shame can be formidable, but it's also liberating. There is such power in giving ourselves permission to name a thing, such grace in allowing ourselves to not be *defined* by that naming.

It renders it powerless when we look it square in its beady eyes and say *Not today, Satan.*

It may hold power over us again, but so what? We're talking *now*.

I took a thousand steps backward, and instead of recoiling, I'm going to lead with the thing that caused me shame and share about it.

After I left my marriage, I fell back into the arms of my *Inner Asshole*, who repeatedly reminded me I was bad and deserved to be sentenced for that, just like when I was little and it first showed up.

I couldn't fathom how I'd be able to go through with extracting myself from my marriage logistically, as well as emotionally and financially. I ended up in *The Land of Overwhelm*, where I reverted to what got me through that place before: self-punishment.

I stopped eating. I lost weight, and people began commenting on how *amazing* I looked. Bless them, for this was the worst thing they could have said—and this is where Shame really kicks in—because I started feeding off their comments and obsessing on how I could maintain and stay *amazing*.

I have a strict personal policy of not commenting on people's bodies, regardless of whether it is meant as a compliment or not. I've also asked others to respect that boundary, but it's not like I can walk around with a sign that reads DO NOT MENTION MY BODY IN ANY WAY. Besides, it's convoluted. I did not want comments, but oh, how I did. I very much did. I was dying for them, literally. It gave me something to focus on besides what I was actively avoiding. I was ignited by their feedback in the very same breath that I hated it for sending me farther into the depths of my eating disorder. The thing was though, it was myself I hated.

It wasn't the folks who said things, even though many of the things were obvious testimonies to the insidious patriarchal culture we've been raised in. Before I lapsed, I was not overweight in the least, yet after I began shrinking, people—including my very intelligent friend who intimately knew my history—said things like *Wow, how did you lose all the weight? Good for you! You look so good. Was it a diet? Tell me how you did it.*

I did not say *By leaving my husband and feeling like a monster who doesn't deserve to eat. By being terrified. By going back to what I know. By starving.* I did not say *How did I do it? By slowly killing myself.*

I did, however, point out the thoughtlessness of her words, especially considering she was a good friend who knew I had almost died from anorexia. It had been so unconsciously programmed in her.

Socrates said it best. *The more you learn, the more you realize how little you know.* My friend knew and yet, when we've been conditioned, sometimes that conditioning takes over and dominates our perspective. It's like we have this primal need to be accepted as beautiful so we feel worthy and like we belong. Of course, this *beautiful* is according to how *they* define beauty.

We've normalized starving women. In every sense.

I was thriving on—and dying from—the attention. At the same time. Paradoxical as any of the other weird things about being human.

It doesn't matter what the content of the comment is either; comments about my body still trigger, despite being in recovery. They serve in bringing all of my focus to my physical appearance, which I do my best *not* to solely focus on because I tend to use it as an avoidance tactic and a deterrent to feeling.

I've found the healthiest thing is to abstain from remarking on bodies, period.

I was aware of what was going on, which, like I said, is the hardest aspect when it comes to Shame. Yet I continued with my destructive behavior, feigning ignorance.

I'm trying to eat, I swear. It's just that I am so stressed and sad and it's causing me not to have an appetite. That was partly true, but I was consciously depriving myself. As I'd done innumerable times in the past, I had convinced myself that the only way I could deal with anything was to be empty.

I did my best to stay empty.

While I sit here naming the shame as I write, I have an epiphany. I actually did not take any steps backward. All steps I took, even the *no steps at all* steps, brought me to this exact moment.

Healing is not linear.

What can feel like a regression can be a path toward moving forward. That is, if we don't recoil in shame over our perceived regression. Looking at it as objectively as I can, I see that my willingness to share how I slipped back into anorexia as a way to cope feels brave. The sharing feels brave, not the starving. It does not look like someone who took a thousand steps backward and is trapped there in the land of regression.

When we look closer, we often see that what seemed like backpedaling was actually growth.

In my "Shame" poem, a line asks *Who gets to stop being hungry?* I'd like to clobber myself with a soft balloon until I comprehend the entirety of that heartbreaking lie. So many of us have placed stock in it, consciously or not.

You Get to Commandments

- Nourish yourself.
- Feed yourself.
- Be the size you are.
- Take pleasure in your body, in food, in whatever you want.
- Eat, without guilt or punishment for doing so.
- Name and then satiate your hunger.
- Exist! That's right. You get to exist as yourself, wholly, in whatever way you damn well choose.*

Do you recognize yourself in any of the things in the poem, even if your life details are different?

I was desperate for sustenance, then counted the ways I hated myself for feeding.

If you do, please know that it's not you you're seeing. It's Shame.

Shame wants us to count the ways we hate ourselves. Not just for feeding but for existing. Remember, however, that one of the tenets in the *You Get to* Commandments is that you get to exist.

The best thing we can do to squash shame is to stop counting the ways. Hopefully, eventually, there won't be any more ways that we hate ourselves left to count.

---

* If you don't believe this then go get a balloon and do your own head-clobbering and start to remind yourself of these things, every single day. We can be weirdo balloon head-hitters together. Actually, probably not because balloons are bad for the environment, so let's use imaginary ones.

If They Really Knew Me, They Wouldn't Like Me

Aren't most of us afraid that *if they really knew me, they wouldn't like me*? Isn't this why we hold so much inside ourselves? That, my friends, is the work of Shame.

What are your things you did in the dark?

You don't have to shout these from rooftops or post them on social media. Just breathe and turn inward. Tour your own dark rooms, those cubicles where things that are labeled *Bad* and *Shameful* have been stored, and then let them out of the dark.

They can't hurt you anymore. They certainly do not define you. Turn on the light and go look at your gorgeous self in the mirror. Do not roll your eyes at me when I say you are gorgeous.

Do you see yourself?

- You are still here.
- You are not a monster.
- You have nothing to be ashamed of.

How to Be a Successful Model

Gather your young people. Gather the old. Gather as many as you can. Show them your "mistakes," your "brokenness," your "failures," your "faults," your "bad things." Let them witness each one. Then, make sure they know that there is no such thing as too late or getting it wrong or ruining it.

Show them paintings you did and explain that when you weren't thrilled with how one was coming along, you'd begin again by painting over it until something emerged that took on a life of its own. Then, show them how you dance with that.

Show them an empty trash can and make sure they understand how there very well could be tons of discarded canvases in there, if you'd kept believing the *lie of ruin* or the *lie of not good enough* or the *lie of bad*.

Show them how far you've come, not with achievements or dollars or followers, but with your commitment to choosing for yourself what *good* means, as well as choosing yourself, period. Show them the gift in not taking yourself too seriously, or not *as* seriously. Show them how much more attractive you are now, not because of any physical attribute or diet or plastic surgery or outfit, but because you no longer loathe yourself and how that is about as sexy as it gets. It's up to us to model that.

I always wanted to be a model. Not really, but I wanted to be beautiful because I believed that if I was, it would make me finally become *good*.

I could never be a model because of my height—at least that is what I was always told. There was no end to the litany of crimes I committed by daring to exist in my body, unaltered. Anyway, I can finally be a model. So can you.

I'm not saying we don't need money. We do; we live in the world. The payoff that comes from modeling your life as if no proof is needed is priceless. It is everything.

You'll be free of the poison, or mostly free. Have you ever had food poisoning? I'm not trying to stay with the toilet metaphor on purpose, but when it's finally all out of your system, you just feel so good. If that feeling isn't worth a million bucks, I don't know what is.

Not Everything Has to Be So Damn Hard

> **STICKY NOTE ALERT**
>
> Not everything has to be so hard.
>
> Write down those words, or some variation of them, and stick them everywhere. I wrote this so much it's now a permanent, stuck-in-the-brain sticky note. I don't notice it's there anymore, although when I got an MRI for the terrible headaches* I was having, I did worry they'd ask what a sticky note was doing in my brain. (They did not.)

I am reporting from the other side—that is, my very first office in my very first home, in Ojai, which I bought against all the odds. Remember, so much is always against the odds that it's like the most glorious explosion of *I got no fucks left to give*. It's like sleeping for the perfect number of hours, your body waking without an alarm, someone you love standing there with a cup of coffee in hand, and let's throw in some gorgeous yellow roses from Trader Joe's.

---

* The headaches come from my neck and jaw, and guess why? Yup. My clenching and my shoving everything back inside me and tightening and locking. It's caught up with me. Take it from me: You cannot outrun anything, especially feelings, even if you think you are.

ALLOW

DEAR SHAME

I have imprints from where I carried shame in my body—my shoulders, jaw, temples, belly, hips. The etchings are deep. Some days, I still actively carry it. Those are the days I use whatever works to put down shame.

Writing a letter to your shame is a tool for *Shame Loss*. Here's how to do it:

- Name the shame.
- Talk directly to your shame so you can get it out.
- Is this shame from a particular experience? There is power in naming it, especially once you realize that doing so does not hurt or kill you.
- Play with detaching from the story and meaning you've given it. Try making it mean other things. For example, let's say you are carrying shame around money and the fact that you are in debt because you left an abusive marriage and it cost a fortune on credit cards to get out. Say you've made being in debt mean that you are irresponsible and that you'll always be broke or that you are a failure. (I want to hug you so badly, by the way.) Flip the script. Play other meanings, or no meaning. Make it mean that you are brave because you did what you had to do to escape and rebuild your life,

and you did not let fear stop you. Make it mean you are one courageous badass, who now has an opportunity to discover what lights them up and begin climbing out of debt rather than out of a grave. Sometimes the act of writing the event that occurred and meditating on it as *just a thing that happened* that has no meaning, in and of itself, is the most powerful tool.
- Can you identify where you are carrying shame in your body?
- Place your hands on whatever body part(s) it might be residing in. Repeat *I love you; I'm listening*, as if your hands are speaking to those parts. If you feel inspired, use that mantra. See what comes through. You can whisper it, speak it aloud or in your head, or move your lips soundlessly. Use it anytime throughout the day to ground yourself or feel more connected in and to your body.
- Freewrite for five minutes (or any length). Without stopping or editing, write from this body part, as if it had the ability to speak. What would it say?

The body will tell us what we need most.

Altering Time

Not to nitpick, but I said there were doughnuts when my father died.

Didn't mean to lie but you know what they say,
the road to Hell, what it's paved with,
maybe I'm belaboring a point, but it matters I said
when instead of *after*, as if the moment he last gasped for breath
a platter appeared, glazed and jelly—cruller too on the nose,
a sacrament from well-meaning neighbors.
As if doughnuts descended down as he transformed into air.
I don't know if he transformed into anything, or into nothing.
But facts matter, they live on, same as a lie.
They came after it was too late to change
what was said in anger,
when all we could do was ask *Chocolate or plain?*
and pretend posthumous doughnuts could undo the wrecking.
I can maneuver time if I move a *here, there, when, after, during.*
Tell a story enough times and it becomes THE story, with a slant.
You get a message from your dead friend's ex-husband
with a photo of thirteen pairs of shoes lined up by a bathtub
Finally going through her stuff, figured I'd ask before I donated
You realize you've altered time to again make death impossible.
The story of how your friend took her life lives in you,
but is eclipsed by the story
of eating gnocchi in Rome as she held your baby,
your breast squirting milk on the bread, you eating it anyway.
Until that picture of her worn shoes,
you'd made only the pasta possible,
only Rome possible, only the silly photo where you kissed
on a bridge next to the baby's stroller
as your mother pointed out birds possible.

It's hard to put things where they really go sometimes,
and we can't help but put words like
when during after before
where we wish they went instead.

CHAPTER SIX

You Are Right on Time

ALL OF MY life I have been called a late bloomer.

But late according to whom? Compared to what?

Who gets to decide our timelines or how efficient we must be in order to maintain *their* schedule? I don't know about you, but I am tired of *them* telling me what is what. In fact, I am right on time. Because I say so.

The *Imaginary Time Gods* (*ITG*) let me know, by my meeting the love of my life just days after I admitted to myself I was not happy in my marriage, that I'd committed an (imaginary and) unacceptable crime. According to the *ITG*, after you leave one relationship, you must let an adequate amount of time pass, determined by *them*, of course, before entering into *another* one. Otherwise, other people may *think things*.

The *ITG* were mortified with me. Especially my decision to invite Henry to attend my Italy retreat in September 2022.

By that point, Henry and I already knew that this was *it* for us. The retreat was a beautiful, as well as complicated and painful, experience. I was in hog heaven and, at the same time, tearing myself apart with behemoth claws. Our falling in love was in no way an acceptable timeline to the *ITG*, or to the friend I lost who did not approve.

I had already left Robert, although we were still cohabiting, just in separate beds. I had planned for him and Charlie to join me in Italy during my second retreat week because I was doing two in a row that year to make up for all the lost income during COVID. Henry came for the first week, and they would be there the second.

I wanted to throw up at the thought of Robert arriving just as Henry was leaving.

They arrived the day Henry left. There was a torrential downpour, and at three in the morning, already missing Henry more than I could bear even though we hadn't yet parted ways, we stood hugging in the rain in front of his hotel in Florence. Sopping wet and clinging to each other, afraid of what would happen if we let go.

My nervous system felt as if it were malfunctioning, and my right hearing aid had broken earlier that day. You know when it rains, it really does pour. My right ear is my *good* ear, so I was fully deaf without my aid. I held on to Henry in that downpour until eventually I had no choice but to say goodbye. In just a few hours, I would squeeze my sweet boy, kiss him one thousand times, have breakfast with his father, then pick up a load of retreat attendees in a van I'd rented, which Robert had agreed to drive.

With Robert driving me, Charlie, and six other people, we headed right back to the villa I'd left not twenty hours before, where I'd spent the week with a man who was not my husband driving this van. A man I was deeply in love with.

The van got stuck in the mud on a Tuscan hillside. Like I said, it really pours. We all got out and tried to push, but to no avail. As we waited, I squatted to pee and fell into a puddle of mud in the ditch where our van was stuck in the pouring rain.

And so it began. Retreat number two.

I had one barely working ear and another part of me missing as well. It felt like that without Henry.

The people who showed up to spend a week in Radicondoli were goddamned unicorns though. Both retreat weeks. I was a nervous wreck heading into that second week, and all the uncertainty and covertness made me unable to catch my breath. The anxiety over not knowing how I would disentangle myself from my marriage and what that would look like, especially financially. How we'd manage custody, how to tell Robert I'd fallen in love with someone else, and would I, as it was not the reason for my not being fulfilled or for not being in love with my husband?

I felt flattened by my belief that I was a monster, so *how in the name of all the pasta in the world was I going to lead a retreat?*

I will tell you how I did it.

The amazing unicorns who came to my retreat demanded I show up exactly as I was. They said that I always held up everyone else, and now it was my turn. Another instance of being able to persist due to a corroboration that I was held and could let go of the reins for a bit. I allowed myself to be exactly where, how, and who I was. Also to be vulnerable and held. I told the truth, doggedly.

I did what I was teaching and writing about: I allowed me to be me.

The first night, when I was down an ear, bone-tired, delirious with guilt over Henry having just left and my family now being in attendance, riddled with fear over how I would make any of it work, and afraid I possibly had just made the biggest mistake of my life, my friend Kari tenderly stepped in and led our opening circle with Ceri.

There was no hierarchy of student or teacher. We all sat in a circle in the yoga studio on the top floor of the villa, candles flickering around us as the waning light from the sunset slipped in through the sunroof, casting shadows across everyone's faces.

A couple friends in attendance gave offerings, like writing and culinary classes and grief and rage workshops. It was a collaborative, beautiful expression of what happens when we allow ourselves to be who we are, as we are. Everyone insisted I rest, and those who had clocked that I had relapsed into anorexia kept making sure I was nourished. They took care of me and I let them, even when spikes of guilt arose that said *But they paid to be here*.

We all received the gift of witnessing firsthand what happens when we embody being an *I Got You Person* for each other. What happens is that we are able to do what we thought we never could do. What happens is that although they *did* pay to be there, they received confirmation that it was also safe for them to let go and receive support if needed, no matter the scenario, just as I had modeled. That is priceless.

With that kind of support, there is no room for shame, so we are able to be who we had not been letting ourselves be. The power of shame's influence cannot be underestimated, but do not underestimate the power *you* have by being an *I Got You Person* either, nor the power it has to free you when you let yourself receive.

That week, I wasn't so much "running the show" as letting it be. I heard the song "Let It Be" playing in my head on repeat, and my hand kept ending up on my heart, just like when I played it in my yoga classes and asked people to place their hands on their hearts. It was an unconscious habit, and I was not mad at it at all. No downside to it.

That week we were all just people choosing love and choosing to eat a shitload of pizza. And it was everything.

The Time Gods Do Not Exist

At first, I raged that it had taken Henry and me this long to find each other and that our time together would be less as a result. I tried to remember that I was right on time. This was not easy.

The fact is, timing is an invented thing. No one ever knows how long we've got. Ask my dad. Oh, right, you can't. He dropped dead in 1983 when he was thirty-eight.

I had to keep finding ways to come back to the *now* and *now* and *now* and *now*. This also was not easy, but I declared myself a sworn enemy of the *Imaginary Time Gods*.

Plot twist: It is never the perfect time. It is never too late to begin again. It is never too late to ask yourself who you want to be or what you want. It is never too late to explore what you want to create or let go of. It is never too late to find love with another.

It Is Never Too Late to Find Love for Yourself

Sometimes it's like, *Son of a monkey, gods of timing! Why do things always come when I don't have time or when I am smack in the middle of buckling my kid into his car seat?*

It's never a good time. The *ITG* can shove it.

FROM THE SPACE you are in right at this moment, rather than yesterday or next week, ask yourself:

- Who do I want to be?
- What do I want?
- What do I want to create?
- What do I want to let go of?

What a phenomenal gift it is to give ourselves to look inward with unflinching honesty, even when we're terrified, and ask *Now what?*

Here's something you can say to yourself each time you dare to inquire within: *Now what am I going to do about what I just discovered, starting today?*

Look, I don't always follow through with *Now what?* Sometimes, nothing comes up except *Now I will watch Netflix, is now what.* You get to say one *thing* and do something that is *not that thing.* This does not make you a monster. Let yourself off the hook, and go again.

We've only got to do our best with being intentional.

The *Body Prayer*

You get to begin again. Until you die. This is not an allegory. Can you imagine the level of ideological carnage if we all believed this though? The patriarchy, capitalism, and all the rest of it would be thoroughly screwed.

To which I say: *Screw them!*

We get to decide who we want to be, what we want, and how we want to feel. Every single day.

If we want to embody whatever we say we want, we must begin to *feel* that in our tissues. For someone who struggles to stay in her body, who struggles not to disassociate and float away, this *feeling it in the body* business is not so simple.

The *Body Prayer* is the cornerstone to helping me stay in my body. It supports being in alignment with who we *say* we are or want to be. I have to have fun with mine though or I'll check out. Not taking myself too seriously is a nonnegotiable.

As a ritual and tool to create intentionality, I start my day with my *Body Prayer*. It can be repeated whenever it feels intuitive, not just in the mornings. Like during a traffic jam when you're yelling expletives at the *idiot who didn't put his damn turn signal on*.

When I start with it, before the world starts in on me with work and emails and social media, I feel more grounded and confident in myself—the self I want to be, rather than who *they* said I was.

I experience less struggle loosening shame's hold when I begin my day with it. As I go through my day, you know what happens? It logs in my brain that I'm in congruence with myself, which makes me feel confident. When I'm not, that's also okay because, you know, off the hook, beginning again, being human, et cetera.

The more my brain logs that I am in alignment and that I'm congruent with who I say I am and the future I want, the more it starts to feel as if it's real and possible. The more it starts to feel that it *is* me rather than just me *trying* to be something.

The more my brain can log that I am living in alignment, the more I *am*. It becomes a natural state to be in, and that, dear *I Got You* friends of mine, feels fucking amazing.

Sometimes I lie in bed and repeat my prayer silently until I need coffee so desperately that I am willing to make out with a coffeepot just for a sip. At other times, I sit somewhere the light is streaming in and let it bathe my whole face as I recite my prayer because that feels luxurious. (Try it!) I often add to it in the moment or notice I've stopped saying certain parts that no longer seem relevant or necessary. Sometimes I write it down. Writing something down has a way of solidifying it for me.

Do yours in whatever way you'll respond to it best, but do try and make a habit out of it. It doesn't have to be in the same spot or using the same words every day, but the more consistent you are with your invocation, the more you *become* it.

WRITE YOURSELF A *Body Prayer* to recite when you need grounding or help staying in your own gorgeous body rather than detaching from it.

Here's one of mine:

May I remember to breathe. Oh, Lord of forgetting, may I remember that a leopard can change his spots and whoever said otherwise has never met me.

May I remember that I am right on time, except for when I am actually late, like the times I get my son to school an hour after it starts.

May I remember that there is no universal timeline, despite what they tell us at birth.

May I remember that you can lead a horse to water, and even when you forget the rest of the sentence, you can still lead him to water.

Lord of nuance, may I remember that my weirdness is not a character flaw; that everyone is weird, and if they aren't weird, they're boring, so . . . I choose weird.

You can lead the horse to water, but you can't make him drink! May I remember that!

May I remember that finding your purpose is a daily quest and the idea that we only have one is a trap to make us feel bad, and we don't have to wait until the cows come home to begin again.

May I remember to not get trapped by old ideas. I don't have to beat a dead horse, and I never want to.

May I remember the things I do not have language for, to hunt for beauty in the least likely of places, and to allow everything to breathe, including me because I forget to way too often.

Today may I floss my teeth, read a poem, allow for pleasure, nourish myself, and detach my phone from my hand.

Today may I count my chickens before they hatch if I feel like it.

May I remember to tell Charlie more about my father, his grandfather, and to not get angry every time Robert gets him a Happy Meal, which he admittedly only wants for the toy.

May I remember that I am enough without having to get more, be more, or do more, and without having to prove it to anyone. May I repeat this seventeen more times.

In my darkest hours, may I find the compassion to go easy on myself, to put on kid gloves because the world is hard enough.

Today may I not forget myself.

Creating and Solidifying Your *Body Prayer*

I begin with the words *May I remember*. I think we put into our *prayer** what we already know and perhaps have forgotten. We know it somewhere, even if not on a conscious level. The *Body Prayer* is like a recipe for our favorite comfort food that we might have known by heart at one point, or actually had written down, like Aunt Sally's

---

* If you don't want to call it a prayer, call it whatever you want. You get to have that. Discernment. Autonomy.

recipe for potato latkes. But who knows where that could be? We maybe sort of kind of think we might remember at least some (fine, one) of the ingredients. When at last we do locate the recipe and peruse it, it all comes back to us and we go *I did know it after all.*

Come up with a *Body Prayer* as often as you feel inspired. There are no rules at this school, so forget *should* and the *right* way. Add to your prayer, modify it, whisper it, speak it loudly, or say it in your head. Sing it, if that's your jam. I do sometimes, even though I can't carry a tune. The idea of it (or you) having to be *good* can go take a hike.

It's important that we do anything we find that brings us even a sliver of joy. Singing makes me happy, so I do it. Anything that makes me smile—as a person who owns exactly zero photos of myself smiling as a child—is a good thing in my book, in *our* book, rather. This book, once you hold it in your hands, becomes *ours.*

There is no *one-size-fits-all* when it comes to this prayer. It is an invitation for expansion. Yours.

I think about how anxiety-ridden I get at the dentist and how I'll be all mouth wide-open, literally the most nonerotic way a mouth can open. It can be my millionth time in that exact position, and still, how is it that I can't stop wanting to fight? How suddenly I don't trust my hands? I worry they will grab the dentist to try to protect myself.

How when I rub my eyes, he whispers *Germs. Be careful.*

How when he says *Rinse,* I whisper to myself *Careful now, careful,* like we're writing a poem together.

Then, my hands come together at last, as if praying. But maybe they are just lonely. Who can blame them really, right?

All I am saying is that if it looks like a prayer, let it be a prayer. Name it one.

WHEN IS THE right time to say your *Body Prayer*? Any time.

It can be a pause before you start your day, during the middle of it, or at the end. *They* tell us that we do not get to pause, and that is some more *Capital B Bullshit*. We absolutely get to have that. *That* meaning pause and rest. Both are necessary, yet we've been misled to think of them as luxurious. It is a lie that rest must be earned.

What in your life do you do deliberately? Let this ritual be one of those deliberate and intentional things. I cherish anything I say or do that I am deliberate about. I want to feel that whatever I am doing is by design, rather than default.

How many things do you choose simply by default? Consider this without making it mean you suck if you realize you are indeed operating from default. My forever goal is to be able to look at something without immediately attaching a narrative about what that something means.

The *Body Prayer* is your personal language, a declaration of *how* you want to feel, what you are committed to, and what you need. To do this, you must be willing to not lie to yourself.

Let it become a constitutive part of you that you don't even have to think about doing, or maybe you have to think of a little bit, like brushing your teeth.

Stop Cholula-ing Yourself

When I worked at the Newsroom Café, I'd wake up sweating in the middle of the night and shout out to no one *Oh my God! I forgot that table twenty-seven wanted Cholula sauce!*

I coined something I call *Cholula-ing ourselves*. It's that thing we wish we had remembered, the things we wish we'd said, the person we wish we'd been. It's the thing that has us wake up yelling in the middle of the night, sweating regret.

I don't wish that feeling of regret on any of us.

In my workshops, I talk about that panic over the forgotten Cholula. (I don't know why it was always Cholula, except that I love it, because I forgot anything and everything the customers asked for, from more water to a napkin to putting in their order.) I ask people to speak up if they sense they might wake in the middle of the night with remorse over a missed opportunity. If there is even the slightest nudge that they might feel *Oh, I wish I had said what I wanted to say but was too afraid to*, I remind them that *now* is the time to say or do the thing.

Don't Cholula yourself.

And Then Stop Abandoning Yourself

How do you stop abandoning yourself?

I know it seems like a daunting task, but it's an everyday learning and unlearning. A daily softening, a never-ending remembering and beginning again.

What does it mean to be *soft*? Anything.

Soft is whatever you say *soft* is. There's no one, single, foolproof *how* for this. It is a constant practice to stop abandoning ourselves.

For me, one way is allowing myself to cry instead of pushing back my tears with such force that I throw up from migraines. It's letting Henry hold my hand, even when I feel like running away and hiding. It's not calling myself a monster. It's choosing to stay in bed instead of exercising or writing (or doing anything) and not beating myself up for it.

Trap ahead. Beware! Catch yourself, with anything, if you find yourself saying: *I will tomorrow. I don't have time today.*

I fell into that trap for years. Tomorrow never comes.

It doesn't matter if *softening* looks like taking a nap, putting down the phone so you stop scrolling and comparing, taking a walk, eating or making comfort food, saying something true and kind to yourself, masturbating, or writing yourself a love note. Anything that encourages tenderness, especially toward yourself, is an act of softening. Softening is anything you do because it lights you up and because you *want* to do it.

TMI

As in, *too much information*. I have received comments on social media from "private" accounts (the kind with no photo of themselves and zero followers) accusing me of being an oversharer. Those who can't fathom why anyone would talk about their feelings to strangers on the internet have said *TMI, girlfriend*. FYI, that is one of *should*'s many unpaid interns spouting the party line when she tells us not to share so much. But I'm not talking about that TMI. Today—right here in this book—we're going to allow it to stand for *Today may I*. Today may you do, say, and feel whatever the fuck you want to do, say, and feel.

You are right on time, and I, for one, am here for it.

Let Yourself Off the Hook

A big part of getting to the place of believing that you are right on time is letting yourself off the hook for not being *perfect* or *getting it right*. Neither of these concepts exist, so let yourself off the hook for what was never possible anyway.

Life is forever beginning again, and ain't that some shit?* Letting ourselves off the hook is a deeply compassionate act. It is the missing link in so many of our lives. It was in mine.

We can have every intention to do _____ or be _____, but despite that, we may not do _____ or be _____.

We then have options.

Option A

1. Hate ourselves.
2. Scroll Instagram to compare ourselves to everyone else *who does not suck*.
3. Put our head in the sand, proverbial or not.
4. Decide there is no point to ever committing to anything because we suck. (See point 2.)
5. Eat seven bags of salt-and-vinegar chips because what else is there in life? (This is a hard one because S&V chips kind of give me life, but no, there is a whole world out there besides those salty, heavenly bodies.)

Option B

1. Let ourselves off the hook.
2. Begin again.

---

* My friend Stephanie Monds always says this, and I love it and her, so I borrow it often.

Do not pass go: Option B is the answer. It's Option B! There is no other option.

Off the Hook Book

Here's an idea to help turn this *letting ourselves off the hook* business into something actionable: Get a journal or notebook and write *Off the Hook Book* on it. Or write *Cookbook* if you want. Whatever works. It's entirely for you. Consider it a private dumping ground where you can list, in any fashion, everything you want to (or wish you could) let yourself off the hook for. For that particular day. I like to do this at night, before bed, after I've checked in to see if I've been in alignment with myself, my values, and who I say I am.

Generally, what we think about before bed marinates in our subconscious as we sleep. This is why ruminating before bed is asking for trouble and why I sleep with my phone in another room. That way, it's not the last thing I look at before going to sleep. The ritual of getting these things out of your body and onto the page is a physical representation of *letting it go*. We then, hopefully, wake fresh, with an intentionality as to how we want to live that day. At the end of that day, we get to review how that went and repeat the process. And on and on. It's a ritualization of letting go and releasing anything we didn't feel to be in sync or that we labeled a *fail*. Getting it out on paper and then closing the book before bed is a powerful act of grace.

Often the things we list are questionable, and many will eventually, hopefully, cause us to go *Huh? I don't need to let myself off the hook for that.* For example, letting yourself off the hook for speaking your mind, for resting, for not exercising when you were sick, for experiencing pleasure, and on and on. By naming these things and seeing them in writing, we can see how hard we are on ourselves and how a lot of the standards we set for ourselves are impossible to maintain and will always lead to a feeling of failing. It's like a setup. It *is* a setup.

Some of the things you end up listing in your *Off the Hook Book*, like the ones I listed—speaking your mind, resting, not exercising when you were sick, and experiencing pleasure—will begin to transform into what you need to actually give yourself a medal for, rather than let yourself off the hook for.

Make it a habit of writing in your *Off the Hook Book*. This practice helps you not be so hard on yourself and is the other half of the *Body Prayer* exercise. We can start our day with words like *May I remember to be kind to myself today, may I remember to not deprive myself, may I not compare myself to other authors and end up feeling like shit all day long until the cows come home*, and then go through the day and do the opposite of each of those things. It is essential that we have the other half, the letting ourselves off the hook, so that we can begin again. Otherwise, we throw up our hands and say *I can't do anything right, so why even bother?* Then, we don't bother.

If, or *when*, it is time, you can always put yourself *on* the hook to hold yourself accountable, but this must be done with compassion. If you need help with that, you have it. Your *I Got You People* are there so you do not have to do it alone. If you believe you have no people, I implore you to stay open, as if your life depends on staying open. (It does.)

With this openness, you'll find yourself in *The World of Possibility*, where others are waiting for you, including me. This means that you'll have to say those three hardest words: *I need help*. Then, be open to receiving it.

> **STICKY NOTE ALERT**
>
> *You are right on time.*
>
> *Go write it down, before you forget it again. Do not buy into the* ITG.

I OFTEN SEE the most amazing, beautiful, confident humans say they want to step into who they are. They step to the edge of the diving board and then just stop. Or they turn around and climb down the ladder. Some just stay on the edge. Usually, it's paralysis caused by fear of what *they* will think creeping in. It could be anything though, because the *Inner Asshole* and Shame and all of their kissing cousins are insidiously clever.

I was one of those who stood on the edge, moaning *I don't know how to dive*. Until one day I said *Oh, well! I don't know how to dive* and jumped instead.

I learned how to ask for what I need and what I want, as well as how to allow myself to feel my feelings. I learned to stop constantly apologizing, especially for being deaf. I asked my body questions, then listened hard for the most honest answers.

- What about you? How did you learn? What did you?
- What are you willing to learn? To lean in to?
- What has been your education? (I'm not asking for your résumé.)
- What do you want to, or are you willing to, unlearn?
- What are some things you've been taught, consciously or not?

- What would you like to teach? Say, to the next generation? Or to the person going through something similar to you?

Because We Forget

I had a dream once in which I had a conversation with my father. I was an adult in this dream.

I asked him *Were you afraid?*

I was. At first.

Why?

Because I knew I was dying, and I wasn't finished. A sigh issued from his dream body.

Did it hurt? I asked.

Not in a way you will understand.

What did it feel like then? In the dream, I had a desperate ache to understand what it felt like.

It felt like forgetting. It was that fast, the undoing. And just like that, gone. I saw you at thirty-eight, he continued, *my age. I understood your own forgetting and how difficult it is to keep a life going when there's no body anymore.*

What did you understand? I asked as I reached to touch him.

That you might forget small details, but that you'd carry my legacy. And that you and Mommy and Rachel would know I loved you and did the best I could, he explained.

Did you? Do the best you could? I couldn't touch him, no matter how hard I tried. And I tried.

I don't know. Yes. Maybe. No.

Why is it so hard to do our best?

Because we forget, the dream said.

Because we forget.

ALLOW

Write, meditate, or draw something in response to the following questions and prompts:

- Answer these questions: What would happen if I started doing what I felt like doing *now*? What would the cost be? What would the cost be if I don't?
- Play with the vision of what comes up for you when you ask yourself the above questions. Sit with it in meditation or write or draw it. The *how* doesn't matter, in terms of accessing your vision or truths, as long as you contemplate the things that arise. Let this vision live in you, as if it has come to fruition already. Give yourself goosebumps from how that feels for you.
- Jot down any moments throughout the day today when you felt you Cholula'd yourself, no matter how minuscule or how big. Note any time you stopped yourself from doing, being, or saying the thing you felt called to do, be, or say. Examine why you stopped yourself, but do not get stuck inside the *why*. Notice if you shut down because of the fear of what others might think.
- If it was that, or whatever the reason was for your shutdown, let yourself off the hook for it. Do not skip this part. It's not about just a listing of things. That's part of it, and this is the taking-action part, the *Now what?* aspect. Take a deep breath and . . . let yourself off the

hook, whatever that means for you personally in this moment.
- Reflect on things others have said that you can recall (including your *Inner Asshole*) about your timing being off. Consider which of those things you've unquestioningly accepted.
- If you're into rituals, then go get the sticky note or wherever you wrote those things that you've been taught, sold, lied to about, bought into, and shamed into believing. Any education you no longer want to claim, go and cautiously burn that paper somewhere. After you burn it, get some blank paper or another sticky note and begin again. Repeat this ritual as often as it feels empowering or clarifying. You don't have to burn it, but find some kind of action that allows you to feel the destruction of this old belief. That's the reclaiming part. You get to reclaim yourself and your own education and burn down what you've been told or what you've believed that is not true. Whatever way you find that works in helping you unlearn harmful beliefs is the most perfect way. Whatever works never fails.

You might've already forgotten—that's how quickly it happens—so let me remind you: You are right on time. May you remember.

How to Get Connected

Once, on a plane, I sat next to a woman named Fern.
Like the plant, she said.

Fern, *like the plant,* was trying to make it to the hospital,
before her seventy-eight-year-old sister passed.
She couldn't figure out how to get online and wanted
to keep tabs to see if her sister was still alive.
It's very important I get on the internet, Fern, *like the plant,* said.
Here, let me help you, I offered and got her connected.
Don't worry, it can be complicated,
I said and passed the phone back.
My son said I'd better get a drink on the flight,
Fern, *like the plant,* said.
So I ordered her a gin and tonic and she told me stories
about her kids and grandkids and her sister
and when she started to cry *I have to make it in time,*
I don't think I said anything at all because
what can you say that wouldn't feel like a promise
and who was I to promise her anything
so I took her hand and held it for the duration of the flight
but I guess that was a sort of promise, too—
the kind that says *I'm right here.*

CHAPTER SEVEN

Love Is a Verb

WHAT DOES *DOING* Love look like for you? Let it be the smallest thing, the simplest, the thing that costs no money. Let it be mundane, the most ordinary thing. Let it be anything, as long as it is intentional.

We know how many ways there are to say *I love you*. There are as many ways to *be* love, and to *do* love, as there are stars.

I TOLD YOU in chapter one about my friend Stephanie. A nurse in Georgia, she has nine children, one of whom is no longer living. I'd given her a scholarship to come on my Italy retreat in 2023.

The scholarship is in honor of a beautiful, ten-pound, otherwise healthy baby who passed away twelve hours before his mother was to be induced. Julia, a Russian woman living in Norway, reached out to me from the hospital room right after she delivered her lifeless son. She'd been following my social media and writings and was aware that I'd accidentally cultivated this huge group of women who had lost children. I'd then started publishing essays by women who had lost children on the website I had back then called *The Manifest*

Station, and the community just started to naturally build. That's always the way it happens.

I created the scholarship to help grieving mothers after Julia came to my Italy retreat in September 2016. She attended through the generosity of donations from people who read about her after I shared her story (with her permission). It was only a few months after Aleksander had died, and I brought my own son, who at the time was four months old. She kissed his forehead and held him and laughed and cried and slept and ate. She said it was the most healing experience she could have ever imagined and that she wanted other grieving mothers to have it. She gave me five hundred dollars to pay it forward, and thus it began: the Aleksander Fund.

By the way, Julia and her husband now have a healthy, perfect little boy named Steffen. He was born in May 2020. I'd been descending farther and deeper into depression and despair when she reached out to tell me he'd been born, and I wept like a goddamned baby. She had been through so much, and it is not mine to share, but the losses she endured were unbearable and this felt like the greatest miracle in the universe. She hadn't told anyone she was pregnant. After so many losses, she couldn't. She was afraid speaking it would make him go away. But he's here. Steffen, Aleksander's little brother.

STEPHANIE HAD BEEN a recipient of the Aleksander Fund, and we have stayed close during the years. Nowadays, we'll sit in the same room without having to say a word to confirm anything. Spoken language is helpful, sure, but it's not necessary. It is a relief to not have to open your mouth to make noise so the other person knows that you love them. Our *I Got You People* just know, and vice versa.

This leads me to share a scientifically proven thing* called the *I Got You Effect* (*IGYE*), which has three distinct parts. It's the butterfly effect, without the butterflies. Edward Lorenz declared that a butterfly had the potential to create tiny changes that could alter the trajectory of the world.

Here are the *IGYE*'s the three parts:†

- Being an *I Got You Person* for other people, whoever they are, including people you love and people you don't know.
- Mastering the art of receiving. When an *I Got You Person* shows up for you, do your darnedest not to deflect it or doubt that you are worthy to receive. Allow it, with as much ease as you can handle. The *ease* part may take time, but eventually you'll get good at it. Or good-ish.
- Being an *I Got You Person* for yourself. You've already forgotten. Sit with this one. As often as you are willing, recommit to finding a *Now what?* that helps you discover how to be an *I Got You Person* for yourself. All those *Now what?*s, all those *day by day by days*, they make up our lives—our big, beautiful, expansive lives that we get to live fully and without apology.

I HAVE STUMBLED upon my *I Got You People* in the unlikeliest of places—although what is a *likely* place? When we find them, we must hold on. Not grip or attempt to possess, but like you are holding something sacred. Nurture and tend to them; pay attention to the gaps, the quiet, the laughter, the small bowl of mixed nuts they love so you may remember to have them ready for when they arrive.

---

* Or it should be, says the least science-y person on Earth who is me.
† But note that the last two are harder than the first, and the third proves most difficult for people.

We can also re-find people. This isn't about reconnecting with an old friend on Facebook, but rather finding someone we did not know prior, on a conscious level at least. Yet when you meet, it's like you have known them forever.

Love in Action

A couple years ago, Henry came back for another guest appearance at one of my retreats. We had chosen our love, despite the circumstances and timing and practicality and all the reasons we might have talked ourselves out of it. We became each other's *I Got You Person*. On the second-to-last night, he woke me while it was still dark, which made me nervous once I realized it wasn't morning. I sleep without hearing aids, which means I hear nothing. I immediately assumed something had happened. He kept gesturing to my hearing aids as if to say *Put them in*. He had a serious, *I mean business* look on his face, too. Naturally, I panicked.

The other shoe is going to drop voice can run my life.

There was no catastrophe. He woke me so we could go lie in the hammock, under the stars. Rain was predicted for the final night of the retreat, and he wanted to have this experience with me.

No one back home had died. Exhale.

I'd never tell you like that, he said. *If it was something bad, I'd be holding you.*

I took note. *This is love. This is what it looks like.*

NAKED, WE TIPTOED out into dark and headed toward the pool, carrying towels to use for blankets.

I wanted to memorize everything. That way, I wouldn't be able to forget what *Doing Love* can look like, feel like, show up as.

What was above me, who was next to me, what was inside me. The way the rope from the hammock pressed into my naked body, leaving indentations on my skin.

I committed each and every star to memory—more than I had ever seen, too—so when my hearing aids were not in my ears and when my eyes were closed, they'd be there still. Stars resting behind eyelids to keep me company when I felt afraid. When I was terrified that I had missed the call by not hearing it, they'd be there.

We saw two shooting stars and delighted like little kids. We wished on them.

Mine was *I wish to always feel as gotten as this.*

Desperately Seeking Susan Grace

Imagine in your mind's eye, if you would, a silver chain with a circle on it. Then, look closer and you will see that the circle is actually a tiny heart.

Crystal, a woman whose two sons were killed while they drove back to college together after Thanksgiving one year, had given it to me.

After they passed, she began a company called The Graceseeker. It's a fitting epithet because when she enters a room, you go *Ah, here comes grace.* Everyone does, not just me. That's just who she is.

She sent the silver chain with the tiny heart as an offering during a time when I was consumed with shame for all the destruction I believed I'd caused.

One morning, I sat down in my office, in the home I'd bought, and saw that chain sitting on my desk, so I put it around my neck.

The note accompanying the necklace read, *The circle necklace symbolizes connection and friendship, the kind that doesn't waver. The kind that sits with us in the beginning and in the middle. The kind that has no end.*

She was talking about *I Got You People* and the *I Got You Effect*.

Everything felt pointless to me during that period, but then I touched the necklace around my neck and wondered if maybe pointless isn't a bad thing? A circle has no points, after all.

I traced the outline of that little heart on the chain and began to feel a deep and pointless love holding me up. The kind that doesn't waver. The kind that sits with us in the beginning and in the middle. The kind that has no end.

The Call Is Coming from Inside the House
(Are You Going to Let It Keep Ringing and Ringing?*)

I had a wake-up call last year.

Hello? Is anybody at home in there? You're out in the world, offering help to whoever asks, accommodating anyone who needs accommodating, except yourself. What's that about, and more important, what in the name of your favorite show are you going to do about it? And what is your favorite show right now?†

I locked the doors, but it was too late. The call was coming from inside the house.

I squeezed shut my eyes in anticipatory fear. It hurt to face the

---

* Disclosure: I often let it ring and ring and ring *because I am deaf and do not hear the damn ringing*, and many of you won't answer because apparently it is passé to actually call on the phone rather than sending a text. Sigh. I feel old sometimes.
† The caller did not ask me my favorite show, but you know I'll use any opportunity I can to talk about my shows. And also there was no caller. It was me! Me! Me!

truth, but I'd like to report that it did not, in fact, kill me. The caller* was referring to the fact that I was a constant *I Got You Person* for everyone. Everyone, that is, except myself.

I exhaled, opened my eyes, and began again.

This is my best stab† at chronicling what happened after.

Relief from the Soup

I answered the call and then it was my turn to call out. I shared how sad and desperate and alone I felt.

My darling Ceri, who is now my partner at my international retreats and who might not be human but some kind of earth angel, brought me back to center. She wrote me the following note:

> *There are no words for the soup of loneliness, but there can be the looking around for art you can make and finding someone in need of someone to walk them home, which I hesitate to say because you are always GIVING AND GIVING AND GIVING, but on some days and the very dark ones, find a dollar and find a person and give it away and do it again until you cry, realizing that your mind had a little relief from the soup for a little while. Also drink water. I love you so much.*

Without saying it verbatim, she was suggesting I *Do Love*.

It is always the thing that will bring us back.

She was also *Doing Love* herself, her care with choosing her

---

* That is, in fact, a Scream movie metaphor about the *caller*. Look it up if you've never seen the films, although my hunch is that you get the reference because I had never seen any of them and I still knew about the phone calls.

† OMG, I swear *stab* wasn't on purpose, but after rereading, I see I can't let go of Scream, even in my subconscious. Help?

words, knowing I might again abandon myself. Truly seeing another is a radical act of love and helps us better see our own selves.

It's worth a mention that since Charlie was two, our way to say *I love you* has been *A hundred dollars!*

I used to go *Do you know how much Mommy loves you?* I said it all the time.

One day he replied, *A hundred dollars?*

That was that. It now meant *I love you*.

Ceri telling me to find a dollar and a person—well, if that isn't love showing its hand.

Sticking with Soft

These days, when that voice in my head tells me it's time to *take a good hard look at myself*, I turn the other cheek and tell myself I'll take a good *soft* look at myself. I try to see where I may be out of alignment with who I say I am. *Doing Love* doesn't have to be a parade. It's choosing softness.

Shit's hard enough. I'm not adding to it anymore. Sticking with *soft*.

DURING ONE OF Stephanie's visits, we were gearing up for one of our creativity sessions where we commit to doing something creative for an hour. To stay intentional, and to take the pressure off the results, I came up with a proposal. We'd have designated pockets of time, which didn't have to be long, when we simply create. It didn't matter what we created or how it turned out, only that we did it.

We sat on velvet couches opposite each other—hers green, mine blue—and committed to the task at hand as if it were dinner and the kids were starving. *We've got all the ingredients,* I said. *Now let's make the thing.*

I couldn't get started. I have gastritis and my stomach was hurting. When I told Steph about it, she offered to rub my stomach. She gestured for me to lie on the carpet, so I did what she said. One must listen to nurses.

Only recently have I allowed anyone to hold my hand or maintain eye contact during any moments of intimacy or vulnerability. Previously, I'd intuitively go *on guard* as a reflex. As far as touching my stomach, if anyone got near, I'd become rigid as a corpse.

I was talking to my pops, my stepdad Jack, about this recently. I will never not appreciate how lucky I am to have gotten a second shot at having a dad through him. How even a couple years ago I could never imagine myself allowing tenderness.

I would have eaten glass before I had my stomach touched, held hands, or faced someone sleeping (as I do with Henry). I could neither receive tenderness nor show it, unless there were no stakes or it was my son. Especially anyone I was close to or anyone who loved me. Hardness was how I survived. At least, I'd always thought that. It became a part of me. I became *it*, period. No separation. It seemed impossible to undo what felt like my DNA structure. No way to remove the nothingness, the shell of armor. It would be like peeling my skin from me.

My hardness was as intrinsic as breath.

And yet, as I lie on the floor while Steph massaged my belly, I softened. When I am able to soften, as I did with her, it feels like a magic trick.

Years of depriving ourselves anything, including touch, and that part of us—or the whole of us—becomes wild with hunger.

When we let love in, the transformations that happen are remarkable. That is, when we stay soft and don't kick out love before we think it'll kick us out.

The Ripple Effect

Recently I received a letter from a woman who wrote about an instance from five years ago. I'll share a bit of it, with her permission, so you can be reminded how often you may have no idea what gifts you have given, just by being you. How letting yourself be authentically you is what *Doing Love* means. Sometimes it takes years. Maybe you never get a letter like this—for which I am so grateful—that shares how your love has transformed someone else, but please know this: It has and does and will continue to.

> *Dear Jen,*
>
> *I wanted to say thank you for giving me courage. I stood up in front of seventy-five people at your workshop and announced that I was gay. Something I've known my whole life but was too scared to say. (I literally could not even whisper the words to myself until I was thirty.)*
>
> *After I did it, you looked at me and you said, "We love you!" Twice!*
>
> *Maybe I didn't seem it, because I was still scared and hesitant and trying not to close, but I am so grateful because in that moment of vulnerability, you covered me in love.*
>
> *I may still have a long road ahead with needing to come out to my close friends, family, and dad . . . but when I do, I will take your words with me. "We love you!"*
>
> *Love,*
> *Justine*

Becoming Love

Sometimes you've got to become your own Charlotte. As in, everyone's favorite spider. Even if you hate spiders, you've got to love her. I'm talking about the most famous spider of all time, the titular character from *Charlotte's Web*, obviously. Why do you think I positioned my I GOT YOU tattoo so that it can be read by me, or someone else, without seeming upside down to either? To remind me I am also gotten and supported and can stop constantly bracing for the next terrible thing to happen. It doesn't always work, but I'll be damned if I ever give in again to *I might as well always just expect disappointment*.

For whatever reasons, there are days I still struggle to let go of expecting to be disappointed. I'm less concerned with the reasons though, than I am with asking *Now what?* I'm interested in the doing, as in *doing* love. Reasons are stagnant. They can turn into webs when we over-scrutinize the reasons, which creates inertia. While that might feel like movement, asking *But why?* can get us stuck spiraling in that web, spending all our energy trying to find a way out. We can find ourselves once again wondering *How did I get stuck in this mess? Again?*

If I ever saw a spider demonstrating what *Doing Love* meant—I haven't, but still—it's her.

Wilbur the Pig was due to get slaughtered, and Charlotte, that little lovebug (spiders are not bugs but the endearment still suits) saved his life by getting him to believe in himself. I don't speak Spider, but there's no doubt in my mind that she was absolutely saying *I got you* when she created four webs and wrote the following words on each one to remind the little guy how amazing he was: SOME PIG, TERRIFIC, RADIANT, HUMBLE.

That is peak *Doing Love* right there, my spider sister.

I'll look at my I GOT YOU tattoo and think how our girl would absolutely be an *I Got You* for herself, too, not just for other farm animals. I simply have a feeling she was a highly evolved spider like that. I try and channel my Inner Charlotte when I find myself hiding in shame, or living like I'm dodging dropping shoes.

To let go of constantly preparing for a shoe to drop (or the other one, if the first one has already dropped) requires you to actually *be* in your body. This is simple, and like most things touted as *simple*, not necessarily easy.

Pause and focus on your breathing. The length of your exhales, and if they are shallow or deep. Notice *how* you are breathing. Is it through your nose, mouth, or the back of your throat? Are you holding it in? Is it steady?

I find it helpful to repeat *I am here. Now. I am in my body now* to anchor me as I scan my body in an attempt to simply notice its sensations. Without judgment or attaching story to it, I attempt to witness only. *Attempt* meaning that sometimes I am just a judgy storyteller who attaches meaning to everything and who doesn't *simply notice* even one stinking thing. Honesty with self is key, folks. Keeps us humble, too.

As you scan your body and breathe, contemplate: *What is happening now? What sensations am I feeling now?* No matter how minuscule or mundane the sensations may seem, you are fine-tuning in the most powerful way possible by really listening to your body's responses to everything, as well as to nothing in particular.

With this kind of bodily awareness, which gets deeper and more in tune the more we pause and drop into being connected to our bodies, it becomes easier to notice any urge, no matter how slight, to revert to old habits and ways of thinking and we become capable of catching ourselves *before* we revert. We sense a contraction, a quickening of the heart, a shortage of breath, or tingling palms. Whatever it may be, we have paid attention to what our body feels and does and when. We are able to register a sudden jaw clenching as an *I'm afraid* and how, without even realizing, we'd trained ourselves to instinctively put our old armor back on to protect ourselves from hurt. We are able to notice that reflective instinct and have compassion for it. We can then pause, come back to our breathing or the mantras helpful in those moments. *I am safe. I am here now. I am in my body. Come back.*

The more dialed in to our own bodies we are, the quicker we can recognize our unconscious patterns of shutting down, protecting, staying small, and denying love and shift it into a conscious pattern. How a tightening in our trap muscles clocks as panic, and normally we'd impulsively run to the bathroom, hyperventilating, to pick our face in the mirror until it bleeds (me) in an effort to either make the feeling go away, deny it, or confirm we were right to panic because just look at our bloody face in the mirror; we can't even trust our own selves to not destroy us. When we catch ourselves *before* we respond unconsciously, which we absolutely can do by recommitting to actively paying attention to our body and its signals, it offers an opportunity to then make a more conscious and loving choice.

The Catch

When we catch ourselves pre-slippage, before we fall back into unconscious old patterns, we are able to compassionately choose something different, with intention. That is the *Doing Love* part, no matter what we choose.

It's that we paused, we listened to our body, we took care, and we refused the path of least resistance. By doing this, we have sent ourselves a signal without even having to say a thing. This level of intention sends a message saying *I matter*.

It is in this way that we walk through the world inherently embodying love. It is a beautiful way to live. It's much better than, say, being a person who's simply getting through the day, surviving by running on autopilot, ancient reflexes, old beliefs.

It is possible to be here, now in your body, and when you are, you'll find you are no longer in that terrible land you'd been spending too much time in: a future that had not occurred yet where things are *loud and very bad, shoes always fall on heads, and the only thing on the menu is old disappointment.*

Do not go back there. That place you keep finding yourself? It doesn't exist anyway. The way we stay here and now is by choosing to *Do Love.*

Ask Yourself: How May I Serve?

The thing about *Doing Love* is that it can be absolutely anything, and that *it can be anything* creates infinite opportunities. *If* we are willing to stay open and intentional.

In February 2020, I was in Portland, having dinner with some friends before a book event at Powell's. After having had a baby four years earlier at age forty-one, I was starting to fantasize about moving out of my apartment to a place with more space and better ventilation, to upgrade my 2005 Hyundai, and also maybe get some new hearing aids. We toasted the still new-ish year.

It's 2020, and finally I am making money, I said over spicy tuna rolls in what felt like mere seconds before a global pandemic hit and the universe laughed and laughed at what I had dared speak aloud.

I did not laugh. I said *See? There it is! The other shoe.*

The pandemic came.

My income went.

At the time, I earned the bulk of my money through live events and travel. As a deaf person in a masked world, what also went was my ability to understand what was being said. Ever.

Despite my antidepressants and the arsenal of tools I had (or thought I had), from teaching my workshops and classes and books and friends and every blessed thing that used to work, depression kicked in hard.

Back then, I had one sole tattoo. Typewriter font. Inner left wrist. I GOT YOU.

I kept looking at my tattoo. Unlikely, or perhaps as likely as it seems, that I GOT YOU tattoo was the thing that made me remember how I saved my life before, when I was still waitressing, by asking *How may I serve?* Then, by living from that like it was my North Star.

We had no way of knowing back then that it was only the beginning of the pandemic, but that's what it was. It wasn't completely altruistic. I'm not that saintly. I partly used *How may I serve?* and my own tattoo message as a way to get my ass out of the bed, as a distraction from my depression and anxiety, and to avoid figuring out my own income and career.

I posted on Instagram *Do you have food to eat?* not because I personally could feed everyone, but because I knew the community I'd fostered would lift each other up, that the *I Got You Effect* would happen.

Someone left a comment saying they didn't have food, and another follower sent them groceries; someone lost their job, and another sent cash. One said she was letting her son sleep in late in the mornings because he woke up starving and she didn't have money to feed him, and someone sent me money to forward to her. It was beautiful to behold this embodiment of *I Got You.*

Dayna, a woman I'd never even met in person, reached out and asked if I wanted her to start a GoFundMe to help me streamline this system of people helping each other that I'd inadvertently created, and I most certainly did. I then offered a donation-based virtual workshop and put the earnings into the GoFundMe. I did something I called "Chat and Feed," which was an interview series with all sorts of folks to inspire people to donate if they could. I created a dance challenge called *The Dork It Out Dance Challenge*.

All of this was an effort to keep finding ways to generate money so that when people asked for support, we could provide help. I did not have a name for it yet, but looking back, I see I was employing *The School of Whatever Works*. Whatever worked to raise money to feed those hungry people is what we'd do.

We were not ending the pandemic or creating long-term solutions. It was a small gesture to offer hope. A reminder that they weren't alone and that they were held, even if it didn't feel like it at the moment. And that they had *I Got You People*, even if they lived thousands of miles away and might never meet in person. Perhaps they'd get a chicken, too, and maybe some toilet paper if they could find it. It wasn't saving their lives, but when you feel hopeless or alone, or like no one has your back or cares, feeling a sense of *I Got You* does save your life.

I know. I have been on the floor, hopeless and alone. Until I felt *I Got You* and remembered I wasn't.

Every person I asked to join in the conversations said yes, and with such humility and love. There was no hierarchy of careers, no judgment, no camera crew. We just sat in our bedrooms, sometimes in pajamas. I joked that it was my *fancy talk show* because of its utter lack of fanciness. A desk lamp lit my face, which apparently looked so bad that it prompted three separate people to send me a ring light.

Each interview was simply two humans who wanted to do the most primal of things: feed people.

Something else happened. The whole community fed each other. We remembered that in order to be of service, we just need to find a way to *Do Love*.

Love as a verb. Whether that means donating time or money, sharing a link, listening, showing up, waking someone in the middle of the night to stare at stars, or reminding someone they are *Some Pig* and quite *Radiant*, or whether it means doing nothing at all except simply being there, exactly as you are.

When we are brave enough to ask for help, *love* becomes a verb. Our willingness will remind others how brave it is. The same goes for receiving help and then perhaps giving it again. The ecosystem of love is an endless and forever loop. It gives and takes and gives back more and takes and gives more, and it never runs out.

Reciprocity

If you are not currently living a life filled with reciprocal relationships, I urge you to do everything you can, using whatever works,* to remind yourself that you get to have reciprocity. That your people are out there, the ones you won't have to beg to love you or show up.

Your *I Got You People*, if that phrase resonates.† Whatever you want to call these people, it doesn't matter. What matters is staying open so you recognize them when they appear.

---

* You are now a student in *The School of Whatever Works* (*TSOWW*). Feel free to add your own curriculum and get rid of any that is not working for you. This is your school. You design it. You can use my lesson plans, of course, although you may find that they don't work for you. Trial and error. This school asks that you employ whatever works, as long as it doesn't intentionally hurt yourself or anyone else. Welcome. You are now enrolled.

† As for what doesn't resonate? Chuck it. Take what works.

> **STICKY NOTE ALERT**
>
> *Jot down these two unarguable facts:*
>
> We all need help some of the time. *It's an integral part of being human. I spent years being the person who gave help while denying I ever needed any. I lied to myself, then believed the lie. I relied on* I am strong, *per my childhood mantra.*
>
> Receiving is the hardest part of the help equation. *I had to give myself the grace I gave to others and grant myself permission to receive help.*
>
> Here are the five parts of the help equation:
>
> 1. *Realizing that we need help.*
> 2. *Accepting that realization.*
> 3. *Finding the courage to ask for help.*
> 4. *Believing we are worthy to receive help.*
> 5. *Allowing ourselves to actually receive help.*
>
> Close your eyes. If you don't want to close them, don't. Don't make a thing that's not a thing.

IT'S RIDICULOUS HOW we'll say *Finally* when we let out our breath, as if someone was making us hold it all this time.

For your consideration:

- Who's been making you hold your breath?
- Who's been making you stay?

- Who's been making you show up for the friend who doesn't show up for you?
- Who's been making you despise yourself?
- Who's been making you fight your tears so no one sees you as weak, so hard that you get migraines?

It had been me. All along.

When we stay open, we find our people. Then, if we listen close enough and are willing to believe, we hear it. The *I Got You.*

The Secret to Everything: Staying Open

The secret to every good thing in my life is being open. Actually, it is choosing to *remain* open. Also, totally not a secret.

The *staying* part is harder. Especially if you've been hurt or feel like you've already been so open for so long and nothing has come of it, *so what's even the point?* It requires a lot of trust, but I promise staying open will transform your life. People, things, opportunities—they all become more visible when you are open.

HOW TO FIND YOUR PEOPLE:

- Remain open. Even when it is *hard*. Especially then.
- Allow for what's possible. (Everything.) You might have forgotten that though. Look for evidence of this. Find people who model the truth of this in their lives, whether in person, in books, or online. Let them show you what *The World of Possibility* is like.

- Remind yourself that you don't know it all. That you have not met all your people. You have not yet experienced all the love you'll experience.
- Remember that our story can go so many ways. It's not over.

It's Time to Stop Thinking That Everything Is Always for *Them* and Never for You

Who gets to have that?

If that question stirs in you something painful, pay attention. What is that stirring trying to tell you? Is it that you don't get to find your *I Got You People* or *Person*? Is it telling you how badly you want it? Or that you shouldn't?

Try to identify, with softness and compassion, what any response you're having may be trying to get you to hear. Then, you get decide if it feels true.

If, during this check-in or at any other time, you find your *Heartsight*, listen to it like you've never listened to anything before. If you think you found it but are not sure, you have.

You believing you have *Heartsight* equals your having it.

Remember that love can look like ease or like pain or like watching someone sleep. It can look like an argument or like sitting silently on velvet sofas or like belly rubs or like waking someone up who can't hear alarm clocks or like uncertainty.

Doing Love can look like anything, too.

You can do love, be love, and even give love away; it will always come back to itself. Love will keep expanding if you trust there is enough, and if you trust that it will also keep coming back to you.

ALLOW

LOVE IN ACTION

Set a timer for yourself, and for twenty minutes, note things others have done for you or you have done for others (or yourself), no matter how seemingly irrelevant, that are actually love in action. Notice if you are now able to recognize these acts for what they are and how easily you allowed yourself to give or receive with grace.* Keep going, even if you think you are finished or got it all out, and even if you find yourself writing *This is dumb. I dunno. I have no people. This author is such a dork*, keep writing. If the timer buzzes and you have more, keep going.

Do not let the idea of it making sense or being good writing enter your tricky little brain either.

What even is *good*? Who gets to say?

As you sift through all these acts of love, allow yourself to decide, on your terms, what *good* means, until you begin to use *meaningful* instead, or better yet, *love*.

Love instead of *good*.

Is this love?

Now, that is a much better gauge for living our lives. Don't you think?

---

* *Warning:* Just do not forget to reciprocate it to yourself, or you, too, will get that creepy call that will be coming from inside your own house.

The Coal Town Bus Route from Lewisburg to Philadelphia

Roofs so used to night any light makes them cringe,
turn tar faces from sky to pavement.
I'd think of Shetland ponies, trained to trudge
in coal mines, through damp spaces, weight on
their small backs, taking fast, uneven paces.
And how they got used to that.

I imagine hooves hitting hard ground
sound like tongues of sewing machines
clucking at my mother all night
as she works in the basement,
television on mute, just for company.
My mother, forever in my mind.
My mother, with pins in her mouth,
fingers pinching fabric in place.

I'd dream of the lift and descent of a hammer
breaking open the earth,
breaking open parts of ourselves,
splitting what's solid, cracking patterns,
like days falling into one another.
How all things without change will do.

Our eyes would adjust, as theirs had.
They'd bump bodies, bang heads,

crawl through soot and rock,
darkness becoming a source of comfort.

They finally emerged from swamps,
eventually changing forms.

We also could adapt to living differently.
Like them, we could get used to anything.

From basements, buses, tunnels, have I risen.
I, too, have changed forms.
From old beliefs, have I emerged.

We, too, are capable of all kinds of change.

CHAPTER EIGHT

The Will to Grow Must Outweigh the Need to Stay Safe

I DID THE thing I knew would kill me: I allowed for change.

THERE ARE CERTAIN sounds, no matter how garbled from my deafness, that make me feel safe in a way I crave. Most words that land in my ears are altered or have had parts amputated. I imagine myself in a room where I hang out with these words that bring me comfort, their arms wide open, ready to take me in. *We got you. It's going to be okay. Everything is going to be alright.* Despite and against every odd, every hindrance, every broken hearing aid, I am able to hear these words.

I *have to* hear them, feel them, believe them. My survival feels dependent on them.

It's going to be okay smells like my Bubby, my dad's mom, who was a walking *Bubbeleh, it's gonna be alright.* They smell like her brisket, her floral dresses, and her wet mouth, especially at the end, in the nursing home, after she'd lost all her teeth. These words effortlessly reassure me with the sounds they make, no matter who is speaking them.

Sometimes, however, the words take a little bit longer to sink in.

You are worthless, I'll say to them, especially when I feel immobilized by my fear of change. *It's not going to be okay. You lie!*

Look at Yourself (I Mean Really Look)

Even as I lie naked on a bed, next to the man I'd fallen deeper in love with than I thought was possible, I wished to be brave. I was unable to see that I already was. I was unable to see how much it took for me to do what I thought would kill me.

Our *Inner Asshole* or Shame causes dysmorphia, in every sense, not just body dysmorphia (although that looms large from those jerks, too). This is a perfect example of an instance when we need our *I Got You People* to help us see what we cannot, because—as I've asked you more than once—how many of you have had moments when you could not see yourself clearly?

If I could go back in time to that bed, I would cover my naked chest with the sheet that had fallen onto the floor and I'd speak to my sleeping body. *You have gumption in spades. Look at you, doing the scariest thing you can imagine. Look at you, finding your body again after all this time. Look at you, softening.*

In the wake of a change that you were terrified to make, what would you go back and say to your pre-change self? Reflect on that.

Let me say to you what I said to myself when I was able to stop resisting. When I was able to accept what was actually occurring, rather than my stories.

I said: *Look at you, softening.* I was!

Look at you, doing what you never thought you could. I did!

Look at you, doing what scares you. Still!

And for the rest of my life, I hope. It continues to scare me, and I will allow for it anyway.

Take that in, and then, as softly as you can, really, really look at yourself.

Accidental Coffee Shop Owner

I have a specific stance around fear in that I think the only truly fearless people are sociopaths. Total theory, mind you, but it is my theory. The rest of us have fear, albeit in varying degrees, because like everything in life, fear is a spectrum. Most of us have fear and do it anyway. Or we don't. If we wait until we are fearless, however, we will never do it because no one is fearless. No one I know, at least.

I believe in being fearless-ish.

I used to say this thing all the time: *Go buy your fear a cup of coffee and show it how it's done.* I'd repeat in workshops, coaching sessions, keynote speeches, and retreats. But then I stopped teaching during the pandemic and seemed to forget that expression of mine, along with almost everything else that kept me in alignment and feeling like I was who I said I was and that fear didn't get to be the boss of me. I noticed that I was not only *not* buying my fear a cup of coffee and telling it what was what, I was running the whole damn coffee shop on my own, mopping the floors and being the barista and doing whatever else it told me to do. I realized I had become fear's bitch.

I had to get tired enough of cleaning pee off the toilet seats of that coffee shop and burning my hand while steaming the milk and dealing with unruly customers to stop letting it control me.

Change Does Not Equal Death

What happens when that which once made us feel safe as a house no longer does?

Nothing. We don't die. We keep breathing is what happens. We unload the dishwasher is what happens. We file for divorce and return emails and refill the water pitcher. We brush our teeth and lock all the doors and spend a few seconds searching for what we've been used to until we realize it's gone and yet, here we are, as functional as we ever were. Unloading the dishes as ever.

My will to grow had, after all those years, outweighed my need to feel safe. After a lifetime, my need to have things remain static had been trumped by my will to grow.

The greatest lie I ever told myself was that change equaled death. It was an unarguable, mathematical fact.

Leaving my marriage was the biggest one I could imagine. It did not result in the death I believed would follow suit. I won't ever lie to you, so I will admit what I have already alluded to: I was so petrified of change that I needed assistance. Henry is not *why* I left, but he was the catalyst. Look, anything can be a catalyst.

Or Am I Just Scared?

Where in your own life have you also been avoidant of change in ways that possibly hindered your growth, joy, creativity, desires, or needs? Or prevented you from leaving whatever the thing, situation, or person might've been? Is there anything in your life, or within yourself, that needs to remain static in order for you to feel a sense of safety? Pause to ask yourself as gently and honestly as you can *Is this true safety, or am I just scared?*

BEFORE I DECIDED to tear down the garden, so to speak, and leave my husband, Robert came into my office one day to tell me that the roots of my angel's trumpets plant were growing under the house. *They might uproot the house, something something.*

I was devastated and stopped listening. He was moving his mouth, but it might as well have been a metallic mouthpiece, a brass instrument.

I don't care, I love it, I cried to this cornet man threatening to take away my happiness.

He'd already started pulling the roots from the soil, and there was nothing I could say because nobody was listening anymore, not even me.

The Uprooting

I was inconsolable. I went in the bathroom to vent and anxiety-pick my face. I talked to the mirror, aka myself, as I am wont to do. *I can't go on without my plant. I will die without it.*

The mirror, aka me, looked at me like I was lying because I was lying. I just didn't realize it yet.

I did go on.

I went on without my plant, as it once was. I went on without my marriage and without the sameness I had counted on for security. Despite the uprooting, I survived.

The mirror, aka me, knew I was not telling the truth when I said I couldn't go on. Yes, I was terrified, but I would not die without the sameness of it.

The amazing part of him digging up my cherished angel's trumpets wasn't my utter despair, but the fact that he replanted it somewhere else, despite my protests that it wouldn't work and that it would never rebloom. It did work. It is now in a new spot in my front yard, as well as on the side of the house and in the backyard, where he'd propagated it, which I also claimed would be ineffective. I find it incredulous how sure I was. How much I knew what I knew and no one could convince me otherwise, and how ready I was to die on that hill of impossibility.

The blooms are as gorgeous and fragrant as ever, only in different spots. If that isn't a will to grow, what is?

Payoffs

For a long time, my marriage *was* a safety net. I did not have to give of myself or be intimate. I did not have to have sex. It was a way for me to embody *You get to have this* except the *this* was a relationship that required no intimacy from me, body, mind, or soul, just like I thought I wanted. Win win.

Intimacy terrified me to the point of absolute aversion. I was clear on the things that could happen when you allowed yourself to be intimate. *The other person can see how rotten you really are, or you can let yourself be vulnerable and then they'll just up and leave or drop dead, so no thank you* was my firm stance on that.

So many things can happen when you allow yourself to be intimate. I was correct in that assessment. I just had the things that can happen wrong.

We always get something out of our way of being, habits, and patterns. Even if what we get out of it is not something perceived as *good*, there is some kind of payoff.

MY PAYOFFS FOR STAYING:

- I got to not be bothered. In every way imaginable, including *sex*.

- I got to not have to change, which was my lifetime goal.
- I got to not have to be intimate. (See the previous page for the pseudo *dangers of intimacy*.)
- I got to not have to be vulnerable, which, despite apparently helping loads of folks feel safe to be vulnerable, I could not allow myself to be.
- I got to come and go as I pleased and find connection and joy with everyone else except my husband, as well as not be questioned about that.

In fact, this *unbotheredness* led me to think he didn't care all that much, which in turn suited me because then I didn't have to feel as guilty. I still found things to feel guilty about, but I didn't have to feel *as* guilty.*

The payoffs are often invisible to us, even though we are benefiting from them in some way. They only stop being invisible when we have the audacity to really look at ourselves, until the will to grow gets strong enough to overcome the fear.

Don't Miss the Point

In your life, is there anything that does not feel intentional or aligned with who you say you are? If not, please come over and have dinner with me. You are amazing, and I want to eat food with you, you mensch.

---

* I'm a terrible Jew. I keep scheduling my Italy retreats during the High Holidays because I *forget*, but sometimes I am such a Jew. (See above: guilt.) I will always refer to myself as Jew-ish, and Rabbi Steve Leder has assured me I am not a terrible Jew and that I can indeed still have a bat mitzvah if I wanted one.

Gay Hendricks, my teacher turned friend and neighbor (but still teacher), writes a lot about *unconscious commitments*. He says that it's one of the most important and controversial things in all of his work. It was from him that I learned that these unconscious commitments are one of the main ways we hold ourselves back, and I started identifying my own.

One day last summer, I asked him why he'd used the word *controversial*. He said he thought people resisted the idea because it is so powerful.

I asked *So powerful, as in it would mean that we have agency, as opposed to things just happening or life happening to us? Or the dreaded "That's just the way I am"?*

Exactly, he said.

We might claim that we want to stop living in chaos or hustle mode, but our thoughts, and subsequent behavior, give us away. They did for me at least. We'll say one thing but do another, like hamsters on wheels, because somewhere, once upon a time, we made an unspoken commitment to *This is just what I get in life. This is it. This is what I deserve. And so it is.*

As if there were a contract called *That's Life* that listed in great detail what we deserved and what we were permitted to get and who we could be in our lives, and we signed on the dotted line at some point, many years ago. Or before we were even born perhaps, like *Bullshit Story* inheritances.

Chaos and always having to hustle is not a contract we signed when we came into the world, and if you did sign such a contract: IT WAS A MISTAKE! YOU WERE A BABY! NO ONE SHOULD HAVE GIVEN YOU ANYTHING TO SIGN!

One way to recognize unconscious commitments is to consider

what it is that you may frequently complain about or that seems to give you grief, and then really examine the patterns surrounding it, without judgment.

I experience endless frustration at my disorganization. It makes extra work for me and keeps me in a constant mode of low-key (and, at times, high-key) panic. It causes me to endlessly be searching for things. There's a constant sense of misplacement, and I mean that in every sense. I'll bemoan it *all the time*, and swear up and down that I want to stop being this way and that I want to create a system to have more ease and less disarray.

The key here is to acknowledge the frequency of it, as well as the lack of changing any behaviors, like I claimed I wanted to. *This* is the portal into understanding and then letting go of an unconscious commitment. That is, if we don't fall into a trap of beating ourselves up over the frequency of it. If you can avoid that trap, you can look at it almost like a scientist to try to really figure out what you might be getting from these patterns or behaviors. When you unearth an unconscious commitment and replace it with a conscious one, in Gay's own words at his home in Ojai near my own, *You get an awesome amount of power very quickly.*

Gay used the example of someone who has continuous drama in their relationships. He said that if they were to say it—that is, name the thing—that they could create a shift just from that simple (but not necessarily easy) thing. He said *It's a bold move, but one that works very quickly, if they are willing to say, "For some reason, I have an unconscious commitment to creating drama."*

I was unconsciously committed to chaos. I grew up with it, and somewhere along the way I decided chaos was my lot in life.

After claiming and owning your unconscious commitments, Gay says the next step is to ask yourself *Where might I have developed a commitment like that? Like the need to hustle, create drama, live in chaos, or whatever it may be?* The next step after that is to replace it with a conscious commitment; what you actually want and how you want to be.

He said *My old teacher Jiddu Krishnamurti said that once you understood this idea, you didn't need any more therapy.*

I kept myself in overwhelm and disorder, and I happened to be very familiar with it so it was easy to stay there. Same with my financial woes. I had an unconsciousness commitment to the belief that I did not get to have financial freedom. That my life would never not be one of hustle, because who got to have that?

How do these words land in your body? Do you recognize yourself in any way?

Keep in mind that *Shame Loss* is not one specific action but rather the willingness to say *I will not take you on*. If you do recognize yourself, I implore you to call in your own expression of *Shame Loss* and not to get in bed with Shame.

Consider contracts you unknowingly may have signed—or maybe even knowingly, when you thought you had no agency over the matter—and are now ready to tear up.

What might the payoffs be for your continuance of these things?

The most important part of all these questions, prompts, and self-inquiries is that you do not use them as an opportunity to feel bad about yourself. You'd be missing the point by repeatedly using these things to go *See? I suck.*

It's okay to miss the point on occasion, but don't make it a habit.

Try not to say to yourself *See? I suck.* Or try not to say it as much. Because you don't suck, weirdo.

We Have the Capacity for So Much

We all have the capacity for so much.

I taught myself to hold in my grief and not express it through my capacity to withstand. This made my threshold for pain very high. My tolerance, off the charts.

Just because we have great capacity for things does not mean we *should* have the capacity to do it all alone. We must be relentlessly discerning with our capacity. Katie Hendricks, Gay's wife, lovingly asks me this question that I find useful and that I urge you to also consider:

What do you want to expand your capacity for?

Freeing ourselves from our unspoken contracts, unconscious commitments, and *Bullshit Stories* expands our capacity for everything else. We then have the capacity not just to be tender and gentle with others but also to ourselves. We forget ourselves most of the time.

As a child, young adult, and until I was in my forties, I didn't think I knew how to be soft. I wasn't affectionate, as a child or as I became an adult. As I got older and began leading my workshops on authenticity, a side effect of tenderness began to emerge. Then, with the birth of my son, I no longer had to work at being gentle.

For years though, I kept this capacity for tenderness like a secret department so no one would not expect it from me.

I trained myself so well not to allow my feelings to register that I eventually lost the ability to register them. This *no feelings permitted* was as an act of survival when I was a kid. Because I thought it was *my* fault my father died, I believed that I did not deserve to grieve or feel anything besides guilt. Hardness was how I saved myself from dying of grief for a long time.

Turned out, I was dying in other ways.

Granting Permission to Go

Why fix it if it ain't broke? I used this justification with exactly no one (no one was asking) except myself. As if I needed validation for my own experience.

I *did* need validation. Listen, there's no shame in wanting or needing that at times. It's when we can't function without it, or become dependent on it, that it becomes an issue. Validation helped when I had little trust in myself. Thankfully, I have the tools to know how to ask for support. My *I Got You People* were there to offer it.

I was searching for validation that I wasn't making up my unhappiness in my marriage. I asked people I trusted what they'd experienced when they were around my husband and me. They said that they'd seen two people who had a working system going, that we occurred as roommates or co-parents, or like two people leading separate lives. Two people who didn't seem like they liked each other all that much. Over a decade ago, a good friend had said to me *It's like you're starving in your marriage.*

No one was surprised by my leaving, except those who knew how profoundly skittish I was when it came to change. Those people were there, cheering me on for doing my scariest thing. Except the friend I lost, who, maybe in her own way, was cheering me on, too. Maybe she just couldn't stick around for it.

No one could recall seeing us laugh together or be affectionate or silly or playful with each other. It was as if I had sudden amnesia and couldn't recall anything so I needed their point of view as confirmation. I was lost inside the bad neighborhood of *I am a monster who destroys everything.*

Or rather than their confirmation, I think I needed their permission.

I was looking for someone to tell me it was okay to go.

I had to know in my *own* body that it was okay to go. While it is true that nobody could do that for me, their confirmations did help me doubt myself less, which in turn helped me be courageous enough to give myself permission.

It *is* okay to go.

I'm talking about it being *okay to go* in any capacity. Wherever it is you want to go but didn't think you got to. You get to have support with that, too.

No one can do it for you. You have to choose it for yourself.

There's no way around it. (I looked.) You must become your own permission slip.

You Can't See Me, Right?

Resisting change allowed me to believe I was safe, but my lack of fulfillment in my marriage was right there, in plain sight.

I was never any good at puzzles, and I was particularly not good at solving the following:

If I am in control by refusing change, therefore *safe*—the thing I want more than anything—then why am I still unhappy?

No one bothered to tell me the answer, as if it was anyone else's job to. I pretended not to notice this riddle wasn't adding up.* I covered my eyes and hoped that made me invisible—another way of living in *The Land of Denial*. I prayed this would fool *them*, whoever *they* are/were.

---

* Do you notice me trying *really hard* to resist the urge to blame someone else for their inability to give me a solution to what was only mine to ever know the answer to and to which there was no *right* answer? If you don't notice, then let me tell you flat out: I really, really wanted to blame someone else.

They all saw. It wasn't that it was not there. It was just squeezing its eyes tight, saying *You can't see me, right?*

A TRICK AS OLD AS TIME: If I pretend the thing is not there, then it will make it *not* be there. Then, nothing will have changed, and safety is still mine.

This is dupery! Although you may believe, as I did, that this *is* the thing that helps you survive. It very well may be, but for only a while.

TRICK'S INEFFECTIVENESS: I'm still deaf, even though for years I pretended I wasn't. I thought that if I didn't name my deafness, then it wouldn't be so. This did not work.

Yet I tried the same thing in my marriage.

I WASN'T GOING to share a specific impetus that made it clear to me that leaving was a nonnegotiable because it felt like I should keep it close to my chest, but omitting it would be a disservice. It's an example of what it looks like to no longer be able to pretend that we can't see what's right there.

It was that night in London when *I'm not happy* slipped from my mouth. It was an unplanned yet seemingly very deliberate slippage, like it had been waiting in the wings of my throat to make its grand entrance.

After we got back from the theater and a strained evening, after Charlie had fallen asleep, I said to Robert *It makes me sad that Charlie never sees us affectionate with each other. Or laughing together, or romantic, or connected.*

That's life came his reply.

And that was the crucible.

No, it isn't! I wanted to cry out. *That is not life! Life is what we make it!* I said nothing though at first.

I had to get my bearings and make sure not to reflexively shut down so I would not have to deal with it.

I'd always known on some level that he ascribed to this perspective, but I chose to look the other way and avoided that knowing. And because he never said as much aloud, I could pretend I didn't know.

I stood in the kitchen of our Airbnb staring at him for a long while after he said that. Then, my fist slammed down onto the countertop, seemingly of its own accord.

I reject that, I said, the *thump* of the slam startling us both.

I do not want to live my life like that is true.

That's life is like saying *That's just the way it is.*

That's life is like *Oh, well. What do you want from it? More? What did you expect, and how dare you expect that? Who gets to expect that?*

Once he named it out loud, I could no longer pretend to not know what I knew. (That damn basement-door analogy showing up again.) I had to either walk through it at that moment or go back to sleep and keep lying to myself.

See what happens when you name the thing? It becomes real. Like Gay said, when you name the thing, *You get an awesome amount of power.*

I knew that if I wanted to be who I said I was—someone who was about *Doing Love* and who thrived on authenticity and connection—then I could no longer keep the facade going that we were connected. I could no longer lie to myself that I didn't need connection in that way either. I could no longer be part of a union that wasn't one in the way I wanted to have a union and pretend that didn't matter. As if I bought into the narrative of *Oh, well, that's life.* I do not!

I do not buy into that narrative. But I had been living as if I did.

I do this thing where I'll make a soundtrack in my head to accompany whatever is going on. It took determination to stay connected to my integrity in that instant, so I thought of Eminem.

It was in one of my workshops in Philadelphia in 2011 that I started to talk about the *Just-a-Box*. I told them how I wished for everyone to bust out of their *Just-a-Box*. I asked *Who would you be if nobody told you who you were?*

I explained how no one is just a mom, just a waitress, just a girl, just a yoga teacher, just an anything. It's so minimizing to think that way, like we only get to be the one thing. Not only that, but life decides what that one thing is we get to be.

I came up with something called the *hi-ya flow*, where I'd play "Lose Yourself" by Eminem while they kicked and flowed and yelled *Hi-ya!* and I'd say my ridiculously simple (yet effective and very fun) instruction of *Dork it out! Dork it out* means to be really, really fucking free. Like that whole *dance like no one's watching* free.

It felt like a now-or-never moment that night in London, so I conjured the famous musician as my wingman. He looked me dead in the eyes (in my mind) and said *I got you*. Naturally, he used the famous lyrics from "Lose Yourself," which I knew like the back of my hand from playing it in my workshops on repeat.

Then it was as if *I am not happy* couldn't help but follow suit and come out, like it was attached to *I reject that*.

Although I did not officially leave in body that night, I left. I could not turn back. I knew—thanks, my dude Eminem, for your encouragement—that I *was* going to seize everything I ever wanted. I refuse to let my fear keep me feeling stuck or lost anymore, and I will not apologize for it, even though it may hurt someone. I am no longer willing to hurt myself though.

Day-by-Day–ness of It All

Some days the fear of it takes me by the throat and I want to freeze time to avoid any further disruption. That is when I recommit to my *daily-ish practices* to help bring me back to center. I'll breathe and remind myself what I have done already and how I did not die from that because *Look, breathing. Not dead.*

I will keep reminding myself and anyone who will listen, *ad nauseam, forever, every day, until the end of days*, that this life is a *day-by-day* thing. May we have the *day-by-day–ness* of it all ingrained in us.

A Weirdly Comfortable, Yet Very Overpriced Place

You know it. That place you choose to stay because you are afraid to go somewhere different. The place where growth is simply not possible.

When you do subsequently see clearly and yet choose to do nothing, or pretend not to see it, it feels like you are the biggest fraud on the planet. It did for me. After I finally left, I'd sit at my dining room table and take in everything around me.

All the beautiful detritus my allowing change had caused.

Beautiful Wreckage

The consequences of going through with a terrifying change, despite what I'd decided beforehand, do not always have to be dire ones. They will not necessarily be ruinous, leaving your life in upheaval.

In fact, the space created was monumental, literally and figuratively. My life was turned upside down in a way, and I'd done the turning, but what I found in that topsy-turvy world was that it was beautiful. A beauty I had not previously experienced emanated from everything.

I experienced an expanse that was not there before, as if someone had built an addition onto to my house while my back was turned. There was a leeway, a highway of creativity, and a stretch of life in front of me where anything seemed possible. By letting go of what I'd been clinging to, I created an opening to find me again.

I entered this new arena and began to bloom. I wrote until the sentences ate each other. I made art. I made a mess. I hung photographs and art everywhere and anywhere I wanted. I walked around in my underwear freely, with the windows open. I did painting after painting, like I was about to have an important exhibit and was on a tight deadline. I was not on any deadline (except for this book), but the urgency to create overtook me.

It was a glorious urgency, rather than an anxious one. It's like seventeen espressos but without the jitters and buggy eyes.

I was inspired and awake. My son and I danced in our pajamas before breakfast and made up loud, silly songs. We stayed in bed to cuddle knowing that it was the most justifiable excuse for tardiness.

My dining room table had always felt too small, the surface of it not even big enough for both dinner plates and elbows. It became enormous, like I could invite the world over and there'd be room for all, plus plates, and even elbows. The table became piled high with poetry books stacked to the ceiling, unopened mail, fresh flowers, paintbrushes and paints, old photographs, sticky notes filled with things I wanted to remember and love notes to my son, toys, crayons, candles, and art he'd brought home that said *Charlie's Thankful Turkey*.

I opened my red Dutch front door, just the top part (my favorite part of my house), and sat back down to visualize myself as a thankful turkey, which made me laugh. I knew the effects of shoving emotions back inside, so I allowed myself to grieve. I mourned what was gone.

There is an acceptance that must occur with new environments or we risk bypassing the beauty by being too focused on what is no longer there. In spite of it being me who'd initiated it, there is still loss. I breathed and focused on welcoming this new landscape.

Amid that grieving process, I experienced the deepest gratitude I'd ever known. There was loss to be sure, but there was also love that was still there, and for that love, I am endlessly grateful. I became aware of what was right in front of me that I simply could not see before. My hand, on what felt like its own, picked up a pen and a sticky note. I listed what I was grateful for at my now seemingly gargantuan dining room table, with what felt like a new pair of eyes.

Our idea of safety shape-shifts, if we allow it to.

You might one day let go of that which you'd been clinging to for dear life because you believed that without it, you'd die. But on this day, you realize—much to your own shock, a shock you feel at *still* being alive—that you will not die from letting go. And so, you let go.

In *The School of Whatever Works*, we encourage students and teachers—one and the same—to find anything that makes them do things like laugh or make lists of what they are grateful for. If it is a drawing made by a second-grader, so be it. Use it. Find any way in.

Daily Dining Room Table Assignment

Do this wherever you want; even in traffic or on the toilet works:

- Can you find the funny? The miraculous? The absurd? The delight? The beauty? Look around. Don't forget that you get to decide what those terms mean. You get to renegotiate what delights you, what you find beautiful, what a miracle is.

- See if you can identify them, whether you are still too scared to make a move, or whether you already blew the whole thing up and told your fear to get lost. Whatever your position may be, play with finding these things. Look under everything, leaving nothing unturned.
- Even in hard times, can you find a way to laugh? What about now? If you can't find a way in to levity, I challenge you to find some way to take the piss out of yourself. Laugh at yourself. I do this all the time. At *me*, obviously, not you. You laugh at you. I'll laugh at me.
- List what you are grateful for. Any way you want to create it, whether it's a list like one you'd take to the grocery store or visual art or you make a poem or story of it. Let it emerge however it emerges.

There is plenty to be grateful for, even when it feels like there isn't one damn thing.* Do this gratitude exercise even if you feel like you have no sense of humor and that you can't laugh. Feel gratitude for your breath, your body, and your capacity to love. Start with basic things, which so often get overlooked and taken for granted.

Here's my list from that day, in no particular order:

---

* I have felt this, this *There's fuck all to be grateful for* feeling, and I promise it's not true. There is always something. Your breath. There, that's something. That's everything, in fact. Mostly, I find that I have to pull my head from my ass, where it loves to reside, and just open my eyes. Open your eyes. See.

1. My son's sense of humor. It is sent straight from my hilarious and very dead dad and because I don't believe in heaven, let's go with Mel.
2. Best friends who bring over pizza and take me to the ER in the middle of the night for headaches and a fever that would not go down despite Tylenol and Advil on repeat and who would say *Where's the body, and where should we hide it?* No questions asked.
3. A pyrite heart filled with cracks. I carry it around, then give it to Henry when he travels, who then gives it back to me, and so on and so forth, so one of us always has it and a piece of the other's heart with us.
4. My marriage, even though it ended, or rather has altered forms (the very thing of which I was most afraid). I gained so much from it—so much love and wisdom and memories and a beautiful son. Just so, so much that is ineffable.
5. My work, despite not being able to define what I do and the fact that no one else can define what I do. How it delights me that it can't be put into a box and yet people still show up, despite often not knowing what the heck they are even showing up for besides human connection, and how this constantly reminds me that we get to create our lives and what we want. Even if we can't label it or it never existed before. We can make it so.
6. A painting I got in Paris. It was shipped to me months after I bought it because the artist added my dad's face to it after I told him I met him on July fifteenth, the anniversary of my dad's death.
7. Good olive oil. I am a condiment queen, but olive oil should be its own food group. Same with mayo. Fries *must* be eaten

with mayo, but I am not mad at ketchup, so don't come after me.
8. Waking up. In every sense. (Although I generally have a very hard time waking up in the morning and hate it.) I'm going to add a second one, a subheading, which is sense of humor. I don't care whose. Just give me some good old-fashioned sense of humor. We can even put these two together and say *Waking up with a sense of humor.* There you go, a twofer.
9. These chocolate-chip peanut butter cookies I love from a café in Ojai called Farmer and the Cook. I swear, if they sell out because you bought them all, I am going to be mad and have to ask you over to share.
10. The man I am deeply in love with named Henry. How he's shown me what was possible.

Give yourself a medal if you listed any number of things. Repeat this often. There is no downside to this repetition or to gratitude.

Spaces in Between

Gratitude creates a miraculous shift in energy and causes us to look at things differently. It often helps us see what we may have been missing. I call it being a *Human Thank You*, something I first learned to be while I was waiting tables at the Newsroom and needed a way not to poke myself in the eye with a fork. There is no exact way to be it. It's about embodying gratitude so much that you become it. You walk through the world as a breathing *Thank You*. It's taking what you've already discovered, as well as what you haven't yet, and placing it all in a box (metaphorical, but you can also use a literal one) labeled *Thank You*. Then placing that box inside your heart. Metaphorically, please.

When we are able to look at things differently and shift our perspective, whether it's from finding gratitude and listing it, your *Body Prayer*, writing, making art, putting down shame for that moment, or any of the ways that work, we can see what's really true for us.

What is the truth? That nobody is happy? That everyone is in pain? There is some truth in that, sure. It's not the entire story though. What about spaces in between? Between happy and numbness, exuberant joy and despair? The place that exists between hurt and pain? Between wanting to die and not? That filling-up station in the middle of not falling out of love exactly, but rather *between* the comfort of coexisting and falling madly in love?

These are things that interest me and why I risked what I believed would be *imminent death due to allowing change.*

Air Building

Recently, I took Charlie back East to visit family and see my dad's grave. We also went to an exhibit at The Franklin Institute in Philadelphia called *The Art of the Brick*, which I'd known nothing about beforehand except that it involved LEGO bricks. I thought maybe it would be a chance for Charlie to play and do something different.

At the exhibit, there were more than seventy sculptures and creations by Nathan Sawaya, all made entirely from LEGO bricks. It was one of the most incredible things I had ever seen. I was utterly moved, speechless at times, and delightfully tickled at the creative audacity and the artist's freedom of spirit. My hands started to move on their own, like they did that day at my table with the gratitude list. It was as if I were building something in the air. Which, of course, I was.

Every so often, we become that ballsy fucker who stops simply building in the air and makes it real.

Under Your Light We Will Grow

At my father's grave, I watched Charlie admiring the gorgeous tombstone my mom designed all those years ago, with a Jewish star and a sun engraved onto it. The sun beamed light down onto two roses, one bigger than the other, representing my sister and me.

Charlie asked if he was really down there, pointing to the earth.

No. I explained that he isn't in the ground. His body was. At one point.

He's everywhere.

Still, it's painful to be there at that Jewish cemetery, among all those last names of dead people who also aren't really there but are also everywhere.

No matter what, it needs light. I am reminded of that when I see my daddy's tombstone.

To find the will to grow, we need light.

Peripheries

No one back in Philly or New Jersey had seen Charlie since he was seven months old, and he was about to turn eight—the age I was when my dad died. Although I was in second grade at the time, I believed myself to be forty and was treated that way, too. I was overly mature and assumed I had to be tough. I also thought that toughness would keep me from drowning in sadness. When my dad died, I decided that I had to become the head of the family.

I see little me when I look at Charlie, and my heart hurts. I was his age. My little sweet boy. Yet I thought I had to be an adult. My childhood ended the day my dad died, and my son turning eight brought that to the forefront.

Can I go back? Can someone bring me back for a do-over? I want to get to be a child as free as my son is. It's a primal desire that will never, ever be satiated. I can't go back. Only forward.

It's not really my heart that hurts when I see my son now at eight. It's the peripheries of my heart, which exist everywhere and do not end with the parameters of our own physical bodies.

Hurt is shorthand for pain that is always there but has been tamed into numbness or bearability. How would one live with it otherwise?

It'll emerge like new, and we'll fumble with this *new old pain* and maybe even feel an uncontainable embarrassment when we taste the salt of snot on our lips, not realizing that we'd been crying over a bowl of chips.

What Is the Word for It?

After our trip, Charlie and I returned home.

I left as one thing and returned as another thing. Or so it seemed. Now I realize it's just that different parts had risen. Parts that weren't visible before or not ready to awaken.

I came back to an explosion of senses, packages of books, and a house that looked different—not just from changes in patterns of light that come with moving into spring but from big ways regarding our living situation and custody and other arrangements. Ways that felt uncertain and scary.

There are so many feelings that defy language, aren't there? There's got to be a word for our incessant need to name things. *Useful* or *burden*, *necessary* or *evil*—how it's got to be one thing or the other.

How about the word for the impulse to defend what's being taken, even if it's rotten? Or the complicated relationship to all the beautiful, terrible things that live in proximity to us or inside us? Is the word for that *wisdom*? I don't know that anyone can say. At times, language fails, but we have to try our best to describe our experience, even if no words can ever do it justice.

What's the word for doing something you never even imagined you could do, not even in your fantasies? Even after you've actually *done the thing* and are standing in your yard, your face in a sea of jasmine as you nod like an idiot at an invisible person, saying *It's incredible, isn't it?* Even as you nod back *Yes, it is!* you *still* can't believe you did the thing that you very much did.

What's the word for that?

Calling It In

We *are* always building something in the air.

It's up to us if we choose to take it to the page, the clay, the LEGO, the canvas, the camera, or the world. Sometimes it stays with us in a private orbit, but we are always in a state of creativity, even when it feels dormant.

The artist of the LEGO exhibit suffers from depression. He says the only thing that curbs it for him is making art (with LEGO bricks). That's *The School of Whatever Works* for you.

We always have the capacity to leave, change, begin again, and grow. We may need to find the will, but it is always there. I found it not because I am any more special than anyone else; it's just that I could no longer pretend. Once the facade was taken away, my will was right there, out in the open, waiting for me to pick it up so we could leave, change, begin again, and grow.

So I did. I left my marriage and walked into complete uncertainty. Where I still am in many ways as I write this, as I try and sort out the logistics but also avoid sorting out the logistics because it's so daunting. I'm still in a place of ambiguity in many ways as I breathe through anxiety that arises and often engulfs me when I worry that I might end up with nothing after divorce. It feels scary to share this with you, and Shame tells me not to. I am ignoring Shame and doing it anyway.

I walked into uncertainty, and although fear was in my back pocket, courage was in my front pocket, right next to trust. *Heartsight* was leading the way, and although I did not know where it was leading me, I had trust and courage so I kept following, and I still do because I am not yet out of the woods.

Are we ever *out of the woods*? I think not. It's why I keep saying we're forever *works in progress*.

It feels like I am building my life anew from scratch, but there's also something exciting about that. Embracing the unknown is intimidating, but I choose to focus on the excitement and follow that, especially on those days when I am overcome with dread and anxiety about ending up with nothing and the overwhelming logistics of it all.

Don't *Yeah, but* me like I am some kind of unicorn because I let go of something that I believed was keeping me alive.

Anyway, we are all weird unicorns.

ALLOW

YOU CAN BEGIN AGAIN

It can be terrifying to even contemplate change. Ask yourself the following:

- If I release *X* in my life, what will that look like?
- Can I look past what might be gone, missing, or lost to see what beauty might remain? If I look deeper than expected, I can discover new and unexpected things to be thankful for. What are those things, or who are those people? Is it myself, perhaps? Now, isn't that something. *Ah, there I am.*
- What would it look like to get honest about the commitments I have made to stay the same, to not change, both the conscious and unconscious ones?*
- With the willingness to really look, can I begin to see patterns emerge where I have chosen certain things to stay *safe* or because I am too afraid of change?
- What do I want to *recommit* to in my life? (I love this one because it is a reminder that we get to begin again.)
- If I make this change, who and what am I calling in?

---

* If you want to learn more about unconscious commitments—a notion that changed my life when I got clear on my own—read Katie and Gay Hendrick's books. I suggest starting with *The Big Leap*, by Gay, and *At the Speed of Life*, by both Gay and Katie.

ARE YOU READY?

After that life-changing *I am not happy* escaped my mouth, I was no longer dormant but an active volcano. I got out of the way of the hot ash, although it took me a while to move. *This hurts, and I am getting burned, but I am still not going to budge* is one of the most *human* things we do.

I had trained myself long and hard to withstand what hurts, but for the first time ever in my life, I finally got out of my own way. Ask yourself the following:

- Do I get in my own way?
- If so, am I ready to get out of the way?
- Am I willing?
- Am I still so frightened of change that it feels easier to remain standing in hot ash while pretending it doesn't burn?

It takes tenacity to identify and chutzpah to do something about it. You've got both, friend, and I got you.

To Be Spoken in a Whisper

If someone warns you of the cost of being open,
remind them the cost of living with a heart
like a closed fist behind a locked door

and how you'd give it all up and go broke from love
to avoid that, and really, it's nothing
compared to the gain,
when you realize that miracle of someone knowing when
you squint your eyes it means you're afraid,
how you only use corners of napkins,
the indentations from your fingers making small animals,
how you can shoot an arrow saying *I need help*
and within minutes, seconds perhaps, an arrow returns
saying *Help is on the way,* followed by actual help,
whatever it's disguised as, and that it's worth more than
anything is worth anything.
Here's a quiet invocation to be spoken in a whisper:
Love deeply and often and include yourself and the earth
and the ones you feel you have no common ground with.
Anyone who needs it will hear this,
even from across the universe and even the dead
because who can say what happens when we die?
Even if they don't know whose voice plays in their head
as they pull tomato plants from the other side of the earth,
or stir a pot of soup in a kitchen
barely big enough for a hot plate,
they'll hear it loud as a clap, and no,
I cannot explain the science—
can you explain the science of love?
Whether they decide it is simply their imagination,
the dead taunting, heat causing hallucinations,
possessed tomatoes—is another thing entirely.

If you shout, you're less likely to be believed and more likely
to wake the sleeping ones who, when roused,
will try and convince anyone who will listen
that the only real things are things
that can be seen and felt and touched.

CHAPTER NINE

Chasing Goats, Finding Compassion, and Ending That Lonely Life of Self-Abandonment

I MET A woman once who said she was at her best when she was escaping. I understood this in my bones. If you, too, are a master or even an apprentice escape artist, give yourself compassion for whatever it is that you are not ready to face yet. Then, equipped with that, begin to assess a *Now what?* that needs to happen so you no longer have to keep escaping.

The first step? Compassion.

Goats and Dragons

Years ago, when they still lived in Georgia, I went to visit my sister, Rachel, and my nephews, Blaise and Maddock. One morning we drove an hour to take my nephew Blaise to his karate class in Conyers. Rachel did this every single Saturday, and afterward, they went to Chick-fil-A. Like clockwork.

When we got to the restaurant, it was so busy that extra employees were standing outside to help take orders before cars got to the speaker. Two teenagers stood outside with clipboards and waved to my sister and said hi to Blaise.

Blaise said *My Angela!*

He likes to make things his. Police officers, cars, train sets, iPads. Angela, the younger girl, looked flattered.

My man! to the gentleman crossing the street. *My Officer Stevens!* once when my sister got pulled over. *My Chance* to the guy who was ringing them up at Trader Joe's.

Rituals are important. Especially for my Blaise, who has a diagnosis of autism that makes structure important for him. Blaise also has Prader-Willi syndrome, usually referred to as PWS, a rare genetic disorder in which there is a deletion, or partial deletion, of the fifteenth chromosome. This affects the hypothalamus and makes him feel like he is starving to death *all the time.*

That incessant hunger causes him to also constantly try to escape to forage for food. It's one of the dangers of being a parent of someone with PWS. They can stealthily slip away, often right before your very eyes, and magically seem to disappear as they try to self-soothe and feed a hunger that will never be satiated.

People stare. They judge his behavior, or the way he eats so quickly, or my sister's necessary firmness with him.

It is one of the great acts of compassion, both for others as well as ourselves, when we don't make up stories about what we know not. And when we know not, may we not give in to our desire to know all the facts.

Rachel herself has something called Ehlers-Danlos syndrome (EDS), an inherited connective tissue disorder that we think our father maybe had. He had major back issues and awful pain and had eleven back surgeries by a very young age. EDS causes her to be in chronic and unceasing pain.

MY SISTER IS eternally hawk-eyed in a way that would make any hawk feel shame at their poor hawk-eye skills, except on the rare occasion it all gets to be too much and she collapses on the floor in a meltdown or *I just can't do it anymore*, like any human being would do. I do not mince words. She is always in an acute stress response because that poor kid will break open a freezer and eat raw frozen meat if he could. He has. The hunger pains are demonic. You wouldn't wish this on your worst enemy. Bless that boy for the relentless torture he experiences, and yet most of the time, he still relishes the world despite it—or because of it. Who can say?

After we returned from Chick-fil-A, I caught Blaise in her car, digging under the seat, looking for food. The wild thing is that he genuinely feels hunger, despite how full his stomach actually is. I brought him back inside, where he proceeded to kick and scream and cry until he calmed down and agreed to go sit in his rocking chair with his iPad.

A little while later, I watched him go out the door and into the front yard and beyond, without closing the main gate behind him, thus letting the goats out. He was headed straight for my sister's car. Again. This time it was locked. He started to howl. The goats ran farther away.

I chased them, shouting *Come here, goats! Come here, Billy. Goats! Come back, goats!*

They did not come back. They just kept chewing grass and eating trash, in the distance, which, in actuality, was not that far away, but you try beckoning ornery goats when you are more than slightly afraid of them. The goats stayed put. Blaise sat in the dirt, crying.

I had no idea how to get goats back. (Still don't.)

Why do you even have goats? I asked my sister, flustered from chasing them. She paused and said that actually, she did not know why they had goats.

She started to cry. So did her youngest son, Maddock. Then, everyone was crying.

Blaise finally came in to eat an apple, but because it was green and not red, he threw it across the room and knocked a cup of coffee all over the clean and folded laundry. He repeatedly banged his head on the kitchen table before walking out the front door. Again.

I don't know why we have stinking goats! Rachel hollered.

The level of stress one person can handle is individual and unique to them, just like trauma, pain, and our own personal triggers. Since we can't fully grasp what it is to be in someone else's skin, having compassion, regardless of if we know veritably what it feels like for them, is the most important, and most human, thing.

I reiterate: Blanket statements do not work, and spiritual bypassing is a real thing. It's dangerous and hurtful. About my deafness, people have said *What do you think it is you are trying not to hear? What are you avoiding? If you face it, I bet your hearing would improve and your tinnitus would be gone.* Then I punch them in the eye. Kidding! It's the nose.

(Fine. I don't punch people. Ever.)

I use Blaise's hunger as an example to help us better understand that what is *fact* is not always reflected in what we tell ourselves, what we believe, or even in what we see. Consider my friendship breakup and how my friend was adamant that I had had an affair.

My nephew can turn his face red and his world upside down because he wants to sit in a parked car in a driveway and eat a red apple, not a green one. He has a hunger that we will never understand. We can only really get it if we know that particular hunger, or have known it. Most of us haven't, and hopefully never will. We maybe won't know it intimately, as he does, but we absolutely can have compassion for it.

Who Knows What It Feels Like?

The closest we can get to understanding another, let's say their pain, is by imagining what that pain might feel like in our own body.

What about anxiety, shame, heartbreak, grief, fear, or hunger? How can we know what it feels like if it is not our own? Sometimes even then we can't because we are disconnected from our bodies. Ask me how I know. (Don't ask. You already know.)

It's all relative and built upon layers of history and anatomy and fatigue and support and chemicals in the brain.

IT'S ALSO DEPENDENT ON HOW MANY GOATS YOU HAVE, IF YOU'LL PARDON THE ANALOGY:

- Sometimes you have two goats, but all you ever do is run after them. You chase them down the dirt path with a stick and try to get them back in the front yard.
- Sometimes you have three goats, but they help you. Like therapy goats or the kind you do yoga with.
- Sometimes you have a lot of goats—say five or six even—but you make goat cheese and feed your family and they (the goats) never, ever run through the gate.
- Sometimes, if you're very lucky, you have no goats and, therefore, nothing to chase.

Look, I like goats enough. One of my sister's goats was kind of mean, but Billy, the little one, was sweet. That day after karate, my sister finally chased them long enough that they came home. Blaise sat at the table, putting his beloved puzzles together. (Someone in the family is good at them.) Maddock watched *Toy Story*, and I sat on the floor wondering about my own goats.

Meaning, what stress had I piled into my front yard and then let run rampant while I chased it at the same time? What about you?

Stop *Tsk-Tsking*

We can't judge someone else's stress or pain or choices because we can never really know what it's like to be in their body. It doesn't help anything to roll our eyes at someone who has a pair of useless goats. (Even though I did. This is hindsight, remember.)

Is it really fair to *tsk-tsk* at someone who can't seem to handle their day or who leaves a marriage? It certainly isn't compassionate. After all, we are not shoveling the goat shit in their front yard. We have no idea what it's like to be the person with a son with Prader-Willi syndrome or to actually *be* the son with PWS, nor do we know what it's like to be the goat chaser or the goat itself, for that matter. We have no idea what it's like to be anyone else—not really—but we can still make room for grace. We can hold space for something even when we don't understand it.

All We Can Offer

All we can ever know is *my* life, *my* stress, *my* piles of goat shit.

All we can *do* is offer love and compassion. This goes for ourselves, too.

I don't care if you are the most compassionate goat-loving aunt if, when it comes to yourself, you've got none. We can't compartmentalize compassion like that. Use whatever it takes and whatever works to practice finding compassion incessantly, and not just for others. For yourself, too.

That means not judging someone's (including your own) crying over a green apple or running after animals in their yard, nor does it mean taking it on. It means standing by lovingly and saying *How can I support you?* It means being an *I Got You Person*. It means *Doing Love*, however and whatever that may look like.

The breath someone takes when they realize they are not alone will sound like the first breath they have ever let out. When they do finally take that breath, they will realize, as will you, that compassion is one of the only things in life we can count on to keep us going.

This is the grace and compassion inherent in someone saying *I understand you wanted the red apple*. It's not that they necessarily understand a meltdown over an apple's color; it's that they know what it's like to be in pain, or suffer, or lose something or someone, or hunger, or not get what they wanted.

It's a way of saying *I see you* and *I got you*, and who doesn't need or want that?

It doesn't matter if what they are experiencing makes sense to you or not when you have compassion. I find that what is essentially an affinity toward love is one of the most wondrous and awe-inspiring gifts of being human.

So Much Depends on So Much

Recently, my sister's pain was so unbearable that my mom took her to the ER. While they were at the hospital, I obsessed over everything. I sat in front of my fireplace, smack in the middle of the day, while the *ITG* just watched and *tsk-tsked*.

I stared at flames until my eyes unfocused, wondering *Who will take Blaise if anything happens to my sister? What if something happens to Mom or Jack? I'll die. I could not handle it. What if something happens to Charlie*—oh my God? *Why haven't I gotten dressed? What if something happens to me, or me and Robert? Who will take care of Charlie? Do we have coffee? Why do I always forget to buy coffee? Why do I forget everything?*

I stayed in my pajamas all day, googling everything about Ehlers-Danlos and *Does fair exist?, Define Prader-Willi syndrome, How do I buy a goat?,* and *Can you train goats?*

I googled *Why do some people have so much?* This is something I have spent endless time contemplating since childhood, without any answers.

There is no answer.

I looked up *What is the true definition of compassion?* and bought LEGO bricks online for my son while drinking cup after cup of coffee until my lips stuck to my teeth.

Taking the Fall

Nowadays, I try to find that compassion for myself.

At first, after I left, and while writing this book, I noticed I kept wanting to defend my good husband's innocence, so you'd be certain that he was the good guy. And that I was not. No matter what, someone would end up seeming like the bad guy. The one who did something *wrong*. Instinctively almost, I was trying to tell it in a way that would ensure that that someone would always be me.

Isn't that what women do? It's got to be *our* fault. Even if it isn't. We've learned how to absorb blame, to believe it's always our fault.

Taking the fall is the only natural recourse. Except it occurred to me that by keeping this narrative, I was not only buying into but also perpetuating the ingrained patriarchal and dangerous *Capital* B *Bullshit*, or *CBB*. (Not to be confused with CBD.)

I caught myself trying to revise everything in a way that would leave no other deduction than that fact that I just could never be satisfied. As long as I didn't make him look bad, I'd take hit after hit.

My payoff? Confirmation that I was bad.

SOMETIMES, I CAN'T find that compassion still. Some days it's not *The School of Whatever Works* but *The School of Nothing Works*.

You know those creepy Christmas trolls that people hide during the holidays? (No offense if you are an Elf on the Shelf lover.) It turns up and startles me. *You again, Elf on the Shelf?** If I am not careful, the elf takes over (not Will Ferrell because I would listen to Will), and I am back to chanting *I am a bad person and it's my fault and I do not deserve anything.*

Does it break your heart to read that as much as it breaks mine to write it?

Breaking Your Own Heart

When will we stop breaking our own hearts?

When will we stop hurting ourselves in ways that we wouldn't dare hurt someone else we love?

I have a total of four tattoos. I GOT YOU was my first. My second, on the inner part of my right forearm, is three birds embedded in an infinity sign.

---

* I'm a Jew—*Jew-ish*, as I like to say, but a Jew nonetheless. Still, we don't do this troll/elf thing and yet still it's there.

It's no secret that my favorite words are *It's going to be okay*. Once, in the van on the way to a day trip during my Italy retreat in 2018, I was telling a woman named Holly how I wanted to get those words as a tattoo. Bob Marley's "Three Little Birds" came on at the exact moment I was saying that to her. *'Cause every little thing gonna be alright.*

And there it was: Three little birds translated into *It's going to be okay*. I knew it would help to visually see those words as a tattoo in order to be consoled that every little thing would be alright, times infinity.

At the same time that I got that one, I also got my third. It says ALLOW in typewriter font on the inside of my right wrist.

My most recent one says AND SO IT IS on the inside of my left forearm in Charlie's handwriting. All of my tattoos are meaningful to me, and I'll stare at them throughout the day to prod myself into being present.

Allow stirs compassion over what I'd allowed in the past, as well as what I want to allow moving forward.

I ALLOWED MYSELF:

- To believe that my marriage not working was entirely my fault and that I should have been able to be satisfied, no matter what.
- To perpetuate the belief that I just *wanted too much*.
- To perpetuate the belief that *I* myself was too much.
- To believe every no-good, terrible, rotten thing Shame, Fear, and my *Inner Asshole* said to me as if it was gospel.

There's not one singular thing I did to break the cycle of believing this gospel. I still hear its chorus now and then. Making art was one of the biggest ways I was able to quiet it. It's something I do where I am fully present, where I am not speaking poorly to myself, and I'm hard-pressed to come up with another activity that has this same power of presence. I become fully immersed, and anything that isn't serving to help me create is not acknowledged.

Beauty Hunting helps. Also, seeing myself reflected in my *I Got You People* overrides any of the other voices. It's ever-evolving, this learning how not to buy into the Shame, Fear, and *Inner Asshole* scriptures.

Pause and consider: What are you believing to be gospel? Do you, like me, have to google *What does gospel actually mean?*

I no longer hang my head in shame over what I allowed, or still allow. I do my best to find compassion before *Now what?*ing. (I turned it into a verb. I'm allowed.)

Nourishment

For compassion to flourish, we need to nourish it.

You must nourish yourself, unapologetically, or you'll owe the *Sorry Bank*.

The more disconnected we are from our bodies, the more difficult it is to determine what we need.

Consider whether you struggle with figuring out what you need or allowing yourself to have and do what you need.

It's a privileged statement in many ways to declare *I only want to do what I want to do*. Like someone telling you to just *give yourself what you need* (like a day off work) when you have to work or the lights won't stay on.

Certain things are not feasible for everyone, *always* is not always possible, and blanket statements make me cranky. There is no one-size-fits-all for anything.

I am fortunate, grateful, and privileged. We can be those things *and* honor that we still have needs and wants. Life is a *both/and*.

Whatever *is* possible for you in terms of honoring your needs is the thing that cannot be ignored any longer, if you want to no longer abandon yourself.

Don't Hide Your Magic

Your authenticity is the magic of you. It's what makes you spectacularly you. Do not hide your magic, no matter who tells you to, or who seems threatened by it.

I wrote a letter, which I hope you'll adapt and create your own version:

> *Dear Person Feeling Threatened by Another Person Who Is Showing Up as Themselves,*
>
> *I see you. I offer you the utmost compassion. I hope that one day you will see the implicit gifts in allowing yourself to be yourself, without pretense. That's your personal magic, you know. I want that for every single one of us. What a more joyful world that would be, right?*
>
> *Can you name where in your body you feel this threat? I wonder if you can figure out what it is about someone else expressing themselves fully that causes you to feel unsafe?*
>
> *Something I say to my fiancé is* You're safe with me. *Although you may feel threatened, I promise that you, too, are safe with me.*
>
> *Check in to see where that feeling is coming from. Then, as lovingly as possible, ask it to go back to wherever it came from.*

I get that to you, I may seem more dangerous (directly inverse to how I am less dangerous to myself the more authentically me I am). I will not apologize for this. If I kick you in the head by accident, I will say Sorry bruh,* *but I will not apologize for being myself with wild abandon.*

I have found a love army out there of people who are also afraid, like me. They are afraid and doing it anyway, like me. Some days fear still wins and becomes the boss of me, which is human and par for the course.

When I say I am committed to not hiding in shame and to being utterly myself, *it's not that I am not ever afraid. It's not that I just don't care what people think at all. Again, quite the contrary. My* I Got You People *make all the difference though, especially on days when I can't see myself clearly.*

Even when I can't make out what is being said or I am having a dark night of the soul with my depression, I don't feel as lonely if I don't lie to myself, if I let myself be authentically me, if I let out my magic instead of trying to keep it bottled up.

I want that for you. You get to have this, too.

   Best,
   Jen

Sidenote: I have never in my life ended an email or letter or card with *best*. Except this one.

---

* I've actually never said *bruh*, but somehow I've channeled someone while writing this open letter who uses the moniker *bruh*. I can neither confirm nor deny that this is an alter ego of mine.

The Lonely Life of Self-Abandonment

Abandoning ourselves is some lonely business.

When we lack compassion for ourselves, we do not share or ask for help, and we certainly don't believe we are worthy to receive support. We hide our magic, and that is the thing that does us in. It becomes a never-ending cycle of shame.

When loneliness sets in, we tend to go deeper into shame, old stories, and feeling unworthy. Then, we start looking for evidence of those things. See the setup?

I recognized the loop I was in and the evidence I kept trying to seek so I decided to investigate my lack of self-compassion. I started with loneliness because I kept returning to it.

Wanting to Belong

Here's a scene: Everyone is laughing. That's the scene. For you. The end. Curtain closes.

If you closely observe this scene of apparent joy, you'd see my eyes not laughing but darting around the room, looking for clues or an escape.

I have no idea why they are laughing. I join in anyway so I don't look stupid. I hear only the frogs in throats of muted laughs. Hands over mouths, my worst nightmare. I laugh anyway.

I have no idea what you are laughing at, I never say aloud.

What is the word for laughing when you have no idea why everyone is laughing but you do it anyway? *Loneliness.*

I tucked away all of this, until recently, so I would not be a burden. You know, that whole *putting our needs and wants aside* thing.

It was an egregious lack of self-compassion.

Sometimes I return to this habit of acting like I am in on it, when I am, in no way, in on it. Especially if I am with new people or I am feeling ungrounded in some way, I'll fake my way through an evening and just nod and laugh, then succumb to feeling like the dumbest person on the planet. I try not to judge myself for reverting to hiding and instead offer compassion. What's kind of amazing is that compassion works. I do not spiral in shame.

I begin again, and mostly I now lead with the thing that caused me shame. Now, I will say *I have no idea what you are laughing at*, without shame. I can laugh and it is genuine because I am not busy faking it or trying to keep up. I will ask someone to repeat what they said, or I will decide I can just be with the energy of laughter and join in regardless of context, or I take the piss out of myself and laugh at the nonsensical things I mishear. Refusing to pretend and hide has changed my life and freed me in ways I want for us all. It's also so much less exhausting.

Come. Sit Down. Talk to Me.

- How often are you lonely? Are you right now? If so, are you willing to be with it compassionately rather than tucking it away, as I did?
- When do you feel least lonely?
- If you have been lonely, or are currently, are you willing to find any way you can to explore that with love and kindness?
- What is an actionable thing, a *Now what?* you can do today to feel less lonely, even if it seems terrifying?
- Are you lonely when you are by yourself?
- Do you have an invisible illness or disability, such as deafness, depression, anxiety, any type of neurodiversity, a genetic

disorder, trauma, a brain injury, or anything at all that's not *immediately* apparent? How does this contribute to those feelings of loneliness? Explore this until you touch on something that feels like truth or until you feel a little less alone. Or until you call one of your *I Got You People* to remind you how so not alone you are.

- What are the things/beliefs/people/places/habits that you keep returning to? I'd return to a private loneliness instead of speaking what was true, just as I returned to sameness and staying stagnant because of my fear of change, until I stopped the habit of going back by compassionately creating new choices.
- Do you see any patterns in whatever you keep returning to? What are those patterns showing you?
- Of those beliefs that you return to, which are untruths? When are the moments those beliefs seem to come back?
- Regarding any things/beliefs/people/places/habits that you find yourself returning to repeatedly, which surprise you? Which break your heart? Which do you find comfort in? As best as you can, refrain from judgment here.

The radically compassionate choice is to try to just witness, without judging, and simply sit with what you find without making it mean anything or attaching a story to it.

The most important part of compassion is to not, under any circumstances, forget yourself.

The Thing That Gets You to Ask
(and Hopefully Allow) What You Really Want

Every day, I look at my ALLOW tattoo and ask myself what I'm allowing.

I then practice radical compassion, as best as I'm able, if what I'm allowing is not intentional or if it's harmful. Then I ask *Now what?* and I'll go get some coffee or take a walk. Whatever works to get out of the bad neighborhood that is my head.

Before I recommitted to compassion, I was lonely but dared not admit that (refer to Exhibit C).

You might also know what it feels like to be among the world and also not in it. We are absolutely in the world, and we require no proof.

I felt that *in it and also not* with my deafness, being in body at a table of folks telling stories but checking out in mind because I can't follow along and it feels painful and awkward. And lonely.

I also was *in it and also not* in my marriage, how we kept our son between us, how we had separate schedules and interests, separate lives really. In body, I was going through the motions; in mind, I was nowhere to be found. Until I found me.

Whatever you discover for yourself, get interested in your own self-compassion, or lack thereof.

Some Great Advice: Never Stop Asking
What Do I Want to Get Curious About?

Note that I did not write, Never stop asking: *What do I want to hate myself for? What do I want to beat myself up for? What do I want to hide in shame over? What do I want to use as proof that I am a no-good, terrible, rotten person?*

> **HOMEWORK**
>
> *Listen, with compassion. Get lonely enough and anything is possible. What it took for me was my loneliness; it was the thing that finally got me to ask what it was that I unquestionably wanted and to listen more compassionately than I thought I was capable of.*

ALLOW

CONTEMPLATE: *WHAT DO I NEED RIGHT NOW THAT I AM ABLE TO GIVE MYSELF?*

As you do this, notice any tendencies for *very dumb reasons* to rear their heads and tell you why you cannot give yourself this, that, or the other thing.

This is about nourishing ourselves with compassion so that we may create more. Compassion begets compassion. I'm talking about nourishment in whatever form it may take. From food you eat or make, to whom you spend time with, to whom you sleep with, to how much you rest, to how often you recognize and also *do* what lights you up. Nourishment from being outside, from being creative, from playing. Nourishment from reading books, from writing them (or writing anything), from making art, from belly laughing, from sex, from masturbating, or from any kind of pleasure, self-given or otherwise. Being of service is nourishing as well; it's synonymous with being an *I Got You Person*.

By nourishing ourselves, we avoid getting depleted. When depleted, we might as well kiss the notion of compassion goodbye with pathetically parched lips.

More contemplations:

- How am I not nourishing myself?
- In what areas am I depriving myself?
- What do I need to nourish in myself right now?

The above can be the simplest and most subtle things. These inquiries are not future based, as in *Next year I'll start exercising* or *Soon I will learn to say no so that I can have more rest*, but rather actionable things for this moment in your life, the moment you are existing in right now.

Anything we do to creatively and compassionately take back the reins and start driving our own lives is a good thing. I love the idea of using whatever works because . . .

- That's the only true way I know how to do anything.
- That is what we end up doing anyway.
- No matter how or when, we do find our way.

The big (not that funny) joke is that there is no *the way*.

YOU *ARE* THE WAY

Try not to roll your eyes. Notice how that statement feels inside you when you read it or speak it. It may feel or sound like a lie or like some pseudo-spiritual sound bite from an offensive book on manifesting sitting by the register at a bookstore.

Reading *you* are *the way* might feel gross in a kind of *get that bug off me* sense until you realize that it's a ladybug and you deserve luck as much as the next person.

You deserve equality, peace, joy, freedom, nourishment, reciprocity, kindness, pleasure, rest, ease, delight, fun, support, tenderness, creativity, affection, grace, love, compassion, and potato chips as much as the next person, and you need zero proof that you deserve any of it. Zilch.

Perspective

Suppose last night our sweet server told his girlfriend
he loved her and suppose it was the first time
he's said it to anyone ever and before
he dropped our plate of arugula and smoked cheddar,
he found out from the phone he secretly tucks into his apron
that she loves him right back,
and suppose *not exactly* is *pretty good*
and that's good enough,
and suppose when he pushes his glasses up,
near the bridge of his nose, that it's code for *I love you,*

and suppose as a child you thought if you climbed
inside the hamper, it would prevent it
from happening, but suppose it still happened,
suppose he died anyway, but you didn't, and even though
you were certain you would, you didn't die,
and not only that, but you carry him with you
everywhere you are, so in a way he didn't die,
and suppose everywhere you are is your home,
and suppose your fake blue fingernail falling off
is a sign for *Good Things Await*,
like some fake fingernail fortune cookie
where *good* means *great*, and *await*:
They are already here.
Great things are here.

CHAPTER TEN

Suppose

OUR STORY CAN go so many ways, and be remembered in so many ways, including somewhere deep in our cells. Our story can also be told so many ways. Rarely is it chronologically. I find the best stories don't follow rules of chronological order. They seem to tell the *Imaginary Time Gods* to buzz off. So come with me to the sidewalk in Santa Monica in front of my apartment building, where I first physically touched Henry.

We'd only met once in person before, for twenty minutes, but we embraced like people who'd known each other forever. You know those videos someone will send with a note saying *I'm not crying, you are! Don't open at work*. It'll be two people clinging to each other at an airport and overlaid with sad and beautiful music because the two people have been reunited after one of them, the one in military fatigues—one of them is always wearing military fatigues—has returned.

We looked like the people in those videos.

I held his neck. In his ear, I whispered *Shit*.

It *was* real. Confirmation. I had the data.

I know, he said, without letting go.

We stayed like that, hugging, for a hundred hours. It felt like home. *He* felt like home to me.

It was, without a doubt, my *Heartsight*. It gave me a clarity I had never experienced before, and I chose to listen, even though I thought I knew what I knew.

It turns out, I didn't know what I thought I knew for sure. Do you know the saying *It ain't what you don't know that gets you into trouble. It's what you know for sure that just ain't so?** Well, yeah, that. It's true.

I try to live by that sentiment as often as I can now. Historically, I have been more than mildly terrible at decision-making. Except for when it came to deciding things beforehand, of course.

Some of my choice *beforehand decisions*:

- I pre-decided how hard something was going to be.
- I pre-decided that it wouldn't work out.
- I pre-decided that I'd fail or, more than likely, already had failed.
- I pre-decided that I'd always have to hustle.
- I pre-decided I'd always live in my tiny, airless apartment.
- I pre-decided I'd forever live hand-to-mouth.
- I pre-decided I wouldn't be able to fall asleep that night.
- I pre-decided something bad was going to happen.
- I pre-decided that you were mad at me. (Are you??)
- I pre-decided I'd never have enough. (Don't know exactly enough of what, but there'd never be enough of whatever it was.)
- I pre-decided that I'd be left.
- I pre-decided the other shoe . . . *blah blah*. It's so tired already, that whole *it's going to drop* thing.

---

* No one knows who said it, although some say Mark Twain.

Distinctions

Making distinctions may be more helpful than any great talent is a line by my friend, the poet Naomi Shihab Nye, from her poem "What Will Happen?"

I wouldn't ever trust myself to decide anything. Unless, of course, it had not happened yet, in which case I (arrogantly) always knew that somehow, nothing would be in my favor. I had this *selective decision-making ability* that rendered me capable of only deciding things beforehand. This propensity of mine made me think of Naomi's poem and wonder whether decisions were the same as distinctions.

I usually can't ever decide what I want off a menu. I will ask the server what I should get. Then I'll get that. Then I'll doubt my choice and change my mind. I'll run over as they are putting in my order and change it, before going back to the original order. Then as I sit and wait for my thrice-revised order to arrive, I'll obsess that I probably chose wrong again. I'll get lost in my head inside the story of how I always choose wrong and that I can never make the right decisions. Then the food comes and I'll ask to taste yours.

Because, I will explain, *I chose wrong*.

So there's that. But I can distinguish beauty as well as kindness. I can distinguish, discern, and decide exactly whom I want on my sofa sitting next to me and whom I want living inside my heart.

The distinction between a perfectly cooked salmon at a swanky fish place and the piece my friend cooked at her apartment—albeit burnt and dry—is not contestable. The latter is always better. Because love.

I can make that distinction and know it with my whole body, and no one can convince me otherwise. But man, am I bad at math, returning emails, picking colors of paint and nail polish and what I want to eat for lunch, and deciding if I should stay or leave.

Tricks Up Sleeves

I don't trust myself to choose correctly because of an old *Bullshit Story* that says I always mess it up, I always get it wrong, and I always ruin things. This makes me afraid to choose anything at all.

If I do choose, I'll go back and forth to keep trying to get it right, hoping that this time I won't wreak havoc. I have often tried to avoid making any decisions at all, as if that would make the thing disappear. (Nope.) I also thought if I did not decide, someone would decide for me, or it would decide on its own. (Also nope.)

Have mercy on us humans, for the great lengths we will go to in order to trick ourselves into the misery we think we deserve.

I can make distinctions, and I am discerning. Therefore, I decided if I am going to trick myself, so be it. I will just make it a neat trick instead, like expecting to be delighted instead of disappointed. Or laughing at my own absurd *Bullshit Stories* until my stomach hurts from laughing rather than from anxiety or starving myself.

Falling Arches

When I was a kid, I used to play this game when we'd drive over the Ben Franklin or Betsy Ross Bridges that connect South Jersey and Philadelphia. I'd imagine arches would fall on our car if we didn't drive under them quickly enough. I'd hold my breath until we made it over the bridge. Only then would I exhale.

It felt like a game of chance. I thought that the faster we went, the lower were our odds of being crushed by the falling arches. What a metaphor for life, and I was only three years old when I began this. Even then I seemed to understand, on some level, the concept of odds and luck, of fate and fortune, of likelihood and possibility.

I'D YELL *Go go go!* as we drove over the bridge. Wherever we got off, either in Philly or Jersey depending on which direction we were traveling, I'd heave a sigh so loud that the people in the front seat would whip their heads around to see if I was all right.

I was of the opinion that it was me who saved us each time. That had I not instructed the driver to speed up, we would be dead under collapsed arches.

It did look like they were coming toward us as we drove toward them, like how it feels when the moon seems to be following us. This optical illusion caused so much anxiety in my little body that each time we made it out alive, I felt relieved. And exhausted.

It was a lot of work being responsible for it all like that.

Ask yourself: How much are you making yourself responsible for? How many bridges are you trying to hold up? How many lives are you trying to save?

Panic

The word *panic* is derived from the Greek myth about the god Pan. There are a lot of stories about why Pan, the god of nature, is the origin of this word that no one enjoys embodying. It's been said that Pan sometimes caused humans to flee in absolute and yet unreasonable fear. Duh. I still hold my breath when I go over those bridges in Philly. On any other bridge in the world, I am a totally normal breather.

The body remembers. The breath, too. It holds on to patterns and habits. Lo and behold, all I have to do is *see* the words *Ben Franklin Bridge* and my breathing changes.

Deciding that you know the outcome beforehand is panic-inducing most times. Living in a state of panic is tiring, and when we are tired we have no reserves so it becomes harder to offer ourselves compassion or identify what we even want. It becomes harder to choose ourselves. We're simply too exhausted.

Don't Die with Your Music Still Inside You

Wayne Dyer warned *Don't die with your music still inside you.*

It can happen.

Early in our relationship, I went to a storage unit with Henry on a late January afternoon. He'd divorced and sold his house, and all his things were in boxes at this place in Ventura, California. Miraculously, he put together a bunch of metal slabs he'd found on craigslist. (He is wont to scour craigslist when he is in need of something, as well as when he isn't, a habit I will never judge because don't you dare peek at what I look for on the internet.)

He turned slabs into shelves with some uncanny *Bugs Bunny* speed. There was only an hour of daylight left before dark, and there were no electrical outlets in the unit in which to plug any kind of lamp. I sat on the cold pavement and watched. I swept. I read a book of poems. Mostly, I just wanted to keep him company.

Like most great epiphanies, mine came in an unexpected place: the pavement of a parking lot of a storage unit at dusk. I've also had epiphanies in sushi joints, the shower, airplanes, and nail salons. They come hard and fast and do not care in the slightest where you might be when they arrive, so try to remain steadily open to receiving their wisdom. Whether you're at the dentist's office or not.

Henry rushed to get this contraption put together before the sun set, which he did. Like a boss. The answer to my friend's text asking *How did you get the courage to change everything in your life?* then became as clear as anything I had ever seen.

How did I get the courage to change everything in my life? I had to.

Before I ran out of light.

I only understood this by watching the man I loved quickly build something, with great consideration and care, all before the light went and he could no longer see.

My Heartfelt Plea to All of Us

Don't run out of light before you fully come alive.

Brace yourself, for it can happen—the unexpected.

That flowering plant, the one you love outside your window, might entwine its roots with a tree.

It could happen you know, someone said. *One day it will grow as big as the house—bigger, possibly.*

The plant, unable to be separated from the tree lest they both die, has to go to avoid the tree taking over. We shouldn't have favorites, but come on, we all do. Still, you can admit you only cared about the flowers, not the tree.

It could happen on a day you make soup and fold underwear—the unexpected.

That plant that comforts you every time you walk in your front door is suddenly, with no warning, just gone. Someone made the decision for you—the plant had to go. *Its roots might one day intertwine with a tree,* they say, *and end up causing nothing but damage.*

It could happen—the unexpected.

You could wake in a stranger's bed in the middle of the night and decide to stay.

What Wayne Dyer cautioned—not to die with our music still inside—can happen, but it's not over for us yet. There are still so many ways our stories can go. We always get to change our story before we run out of light.

FDA Recommendations

Remember seeing signs, or memes on the internet, or maybe you even posted them yourself, like *I'll sleep when I'm dead* and *Hustle Queen*? If you don't remember, good. Trust me though, there was, and still is, often this conflation of productivity and busyness with worth. Everyone seemed to buy into the notion that we had to push to be as productive as possible in order to earn the right to rest, to earn the right to exist.

The message was that if we weren't busy, we would wither and die, or at the very least, we'd be worthless because where would our proof of life be? Then the world stopped with the pandemic, and all we wanted to do was live.

The FDA (I mean me) recommends that you ...

- Slow down.
- Spend time doing whatever it is that lights you up, including doing nothing,* and including finding out *what it is* that lights you up if you are unsure. Make it an adventure, a scavenger hunt, a daily quest to find what lights you up.
- Stop worrying what *they* are doing or thinking or saying.

---

* How I love doing nothing. Top fave. I will happily do nothing! When my son says he is *bored*, I feel jealous. Give me my nothing!

- Allow ease into your life like you get to have it. You do.
- Do not mistake productivity or your weight or your followers or your bank account, et cetera, with your worth.*
- Remember what a beautiful badass you are, and if you forget, go find your *I Got You People* to remind you, including me. Hi!

You may not currently believe any of these things, especially if your life is hard as hell right now. I know a lot of people whose lives are hard as hell right now—so hard that it's unfathomable to comprehend how it is they manage to carry on. But I promise you, whoever you are, your birthright is not stress or hardship.

In the book *Essentialism*, author Greg McKeown asks *How can I make this more effortless?*

How can I make this more effortless?

I ask myself this every day when I am not too busy making things harder for myself.

May we recommit to our willingness in releasing the belief that things have to be hard, as well as the habit of making things harder.

They lied when *they* told us it had to be hard to matter.

Grocery List of Hard

It has to be hard. Take an honest inventory of where you have bought into that lie. Whatever *it* is. Make a list, without judgment, like a grocery list, of where you may be making things harder for yourself.

We have no time for *judgy pants* unless it's Judge Judy. She's cool,

---

* This is a huge system malfunction in many humans that causes major 404 errors like when we go to our website and find it is no longer there. Go pee or have a coffee (or whatever, a tea if you must) and consider how much you've intertwined these things with your worth as you sit on the toilet or pour the coffee.

and we can make time for her. Use this grocery list thingy to *Now what?* yourself into a space of greater intention, love, grace, and, of course, self-compassion.

> **STICKY NOTE ALERT**
>
> *It does not have to be hard. Write that down now. (Do it now, or you'll pretend to forget like I did.)*
>
> *It may be hard, but it does not have to be.*
>
> *Leave room for joy and sorrow. For curiosity, delight, the unexpected, and gratitude. But do not decide beforehand how hard it'll be, how impossible it is, or that it won't work.*

Daring to Imagine

Travel back in time with me to the beginning of 2021, to the buying of my house. It is a story of finally stopping my lifelong habit of deciding beforehand that nothing would work out in my favor, an anecdote of acknowledging an unconscious commitment to not-enoughness, and replacing it with a conscious commitment to expansion and abundance. It's the tale of how I bought it. Me, who couldn't fathom moving out of my airless apartment, let alone owning a home. Not even in my wildest of dreams, which never contained that because even my subconscious knew better.

That sentence breaks my heart for younger me. Sometimes it still breaks my heart, when I catch myself not letting myself imagine. I am no longer in the business of breaking my own heart. Closed up shop. The thing to note is that I usually catch myself.

It wasn't until I read *The Big Leap* by Gay Hendricks that I dared to even fantasize of living in a house I owned.

Daring to imagine was the first *Now what?*

The subtlety of simply allowing yourself to imagine is the first step in becoming your own permission slip.

The audacity of you imagining what you never let yourself consider before is audacious and life-changing. You are doing something you'd previously believed you weren't allowed to. It's an ultimate game changer. You are changing up the rules without asking anyone if you could.

In fact, you are changing the game.

The Big Leap

I *Now what?*ed again and googled *house for sale Ojai* out of the blue one rainy January in 2021 after a call with a new friend, Kristen McGuiness. She lived in Ojai, my happy place, and asked *So why haven't you moved here yet?*

I laughed a layered laugh. I knew it would never happen, and that made me sadder than I could say. It was also hilarious that she suggested it because didn't she know that I didn't get to have that?

The minute we hung up, I reached for my loyal know-it-all pal, Google. Nothing I am consciously aware of made me type in *house for sale Ojai*. I was possessed by a force that was just bored already of my same old *Bullshit Stories*. It's similar to how I cannot claim to understand who made me speak *I am not happy* to my husband.

A house popped up that had been listed four hours prior. Just for fun, I clicked on it. *For fun!* I reassured myself.

I attached no story to it. *Look at me! I'm allowing myself to imagine!*

I wasn't into Zillow porn, nor was I fantasizing about buying a house. I was positive it was never going to happen, so it would only make me depressed to dream about it.

I clicked *More information.*

Who did you think you are to do that? a voice said. I ignored it and did anyway.

I FaceTimed my friend who lived in Ojai and said *I am going to come there and look at a house. I'm going to take a big leap. I am moving into my zone of genius.*

I was using Gay's vocabulary, having become obsessed with *The Big Leap.*

She stared at me wide-eyed. *Do you know why my hair is wet? I was just swimming at Gay and Katie Hendricks's house. They are my neighbors here.*

Shut. The. Front. Door.

I took that as a sign of synchronicity and made an appointment to go see the house in person.

THE NEXT DAY, I was in the car with my husband to go look at the house, *just for fun.*

My dear stepdad Jack* had called the day before and asked *Didn't you think I'd want to be involved in this process? Don't you want to look*

---

* Thank God for Jack. Or as Charlie and my nephews call him, Papa Jack. He held my hand through the whole process (same with my divorce), and although it was my money and my credit we were using, he handled most of it for me. He asked all the right questions that I never would have known to ask, and he helped me with everything that I never could have done on my own. He is a phenom. I tell him his only job is *do not die*. He is also the one who suggested to the agent that they throw in the furniture with my offer, to which I scoffed *Jack, that is so silly. Who would ever do that?* (Them.) I got a completely furnished home. The homeowner's son lived in another state, so it was a relief to not have to deal with clearing out his deceased mother's stuff. Eventually I replaced much of it but a lot of it I kept. It saved me thousands upon thousands of dollars and so much stress and hassle.

at other houses while you're there, since you're driving all the way to Ojai from Santa Monica?

I replied *There's been no thinking involved, nor any process, and no, I don't want to look at other houses. I am not "looking for houses."*

He said *Okay then. I'm coming.*

I Got You can look so many different ways, just like love.

Trade-Offs

It was scary to even consider leaving the freedom of having low overhead, which I had with my apartment. For years though, I had felt like it was swallowing me. I could no longer breathe in there.

When we arrived in Ojai and opened the door to the home, I loudly exclaimed *Oh!*

I walked into the front bedroom,* where I proclaimed *I am going to put in an offer.* Then, I hid behind the door so nobody would see me and whispered into my phone *Siri, what does it mean to put in an offer on a house? Also, what does* escrow *mean?*

The agent assured us that there were going to be a lot of cash offers. The woman who lived there had died, which we knew because that has to be disclosed. Her son was handling everything and lived in another state. He wanted it sold quickly, the agent explained, and so there wouldn't be a concern, like there sometimes was, whether the new owners were *the right fit* or *nice people*.

I texted friends, Is it nuts to put in an offer on the only house you've ever looked at?

They replied Yes.

---

* My office. That front bedroom is now my office. I knew it that first day.

I put in the offer.

One friend was hurt because she hadn't known I was house hunting and she thought we were close.

I was not house hunting! I had no idea before yesterday when I googled house for sale Ojai.

On a full moon in January, four days after the house was listed, and three from the day I went to see it, I put in an offer. I didn't think I would actually get a loan or the house, but that wasn't the point. It felt exciting.

Just before he put in my offer, Jack called me. *I want you to write a letter to the son. Quickly.*

You said they just want to sell and it doesn't matter if we are good people or—

He interrupted me. *Just write it.*

I wrote it in three minutes so he could send it with my offer. The next morning, he said that the son and his wife wanted me to have the house.

By living in my affordable apartment for years, I had been able to steadily save and had enough for some kind of down payment, although it would wipe out my savings, which was all I had as a kind of security blanket.

The next *Now what?*s were *How am I going to get a loan* and *How am I going to do this?* and *OH MY GOD!*

I'm not being coy when I say I still don't understand how it happened. I did not make very much money at the time, nor did I have a steady job, which banks do not dig. Plus our family had only one income, mine. But just like I say about *reasons why*, I don't care so much *how* it happened, but that it did.

I got the loan.

I kept saying *yes* even when I had no idea what I was doing, how I would do whatever I was doing, or what I was even saying *yes* to. It was, as Katie Hendricks calls it, a *full-body yes*.

I did wipe out my savings and my cushion of financial support, and although it was terrifying, it was one of the best decisions I ever made.

It was the first when I didn't let fear call the shots.

The trade-off of letting go of that freedom, which was not freedom at all, was that I finally got to live in a place where I could breathe, and with that breath, everything opened up.

None of it makes logical sense, but that the house was going to be mine is something I knew from jump. My *Heartsight* knew it was home from the moment I first opened the door.

I am home, just like with Henry.

And finally, just like with myself.

What Glinda Told Dorothy Was Not a Lie

I wanted to end this book with my wedding to the man who felt like home.*

I did shift my perspective from believing that the other shoe was always going to drop no matter what and that I did not get to have this, but I still felt apprehensive about saying too much about our relationship.

How dare I imagine a future that was not catastrophic?

What if by being excited and sharing I caused it to disappear, like a jinxing of sorts? What if it didn't work out? How dumb I'd seem.

---

* If that seems like our relationship was fast-moving, I can only say that it was. And was not. It took us a lifetime to find each other, and when we finally did, we did not want to be apart even a day. Also, we have known each other lifetimes and I never speak like that. Until now. So there's that.

How embarrassed. How foolish. (But to whom?) What if it ended up just being testimony that I, in fact, never did get to have any of it? What if it turned out that Henry was not my home after all? I'd look so foolish. (Again, to whom?)

I broke down each possible repercussion. There would be no jinxing; things don't work that way. Nor would I be punished for being excited. Our relationship would not get yanked away to teach me a lesson about the dangers of being excited and to serve as a reminder that I dare not think I get to be.

If it didn't work out, I *would* be gutted, but I would not be made dumb or foolish by it ending, just sad. If anyone thought me dumb or foolish, well, what they think of me is none of my business. If I felt that way about myself, I'd have to go deeper and tend to the pain I was really experiencing.

If it didn't work out, it would not be evidence of the fact that I do not deserve to have love or be happy. In fact, what did *work out* even mean? As I said earlier, love is never wasted.

And if it turned out that Henry was not my home after all, then guess what? I was still my own home and always would be. That, in itself, will always mean that it *worked out in the end*.

An updated question then: *How dare we continue to imagine a future that is only catastrophic?*

He proposed in Italy, while we were there for the *Mission: Impossible—Dead Reckoning* world premiere.

After the premiere in Rome, we went to Cinque Terre, where I'd dreamed of going since reading about it in one of my favorite novels, *Beautiful Ruins*. I booked us a gorgeous Airbnb overlooking the water there and then we went to Florence and stayed in an apartment next to the Duomo that felt like we were inside of it, the church bells in bed with us.

Our view from the window was the bell tower, and light poured into the bedroom, making us so sleepy and relaxed that we didn't ever want to get up. We did at times.

We sat on the balcony in our underwear and drank espresso. We took photos of the birds, the sky, the people below us on the street, the intricate architecture full of history that we knew little about. We stared in awe at the cathedral next to us—so close we could touch it—without speaking. We never had to, although sometimes we stayed up all night talking.

We drank in everything around us as we ate cherries and pecorino cheese and my leg rested on his. He placed his hand on that leg and said nothing for a while. He just left it there.

Then he asked me to marry him.

Inconceivable

According to the *Cambridge Dictionary*, *inconceivable* is an adjective meaning "impossible to imagine or think of."

It gives me chills to consider all that can show up from the choice to remain open. All that can show up from *Doing Love*, having radical compassion, playing and being creative, daring to choose ourselves, and becoming our own permission slips—all the things that aren't even in our consciousness because they were impossible to even imagine. It's exciting, if you are willing to tilt your perspective to that.

There are endless reasons why we stop ourselves from having the life we want or for continuing to cling to *Bullshit Stories* and proclivities. There's so many *I better not*s and *What will they think?*s. So many *I already know how it's going to turn out*.

I had to keep returning to *The School of Whatever Works* to remember who I was, especially without having to be defined in relation to another person.

I wanted to decide who I was *without* being someone's daughter, mother, partner, or wife. We all get to do that, to say who we are, and then we get to go be that.

It takes some real backbone, just as it does to let go of the safety net of deciding how things will be beforehand. Or the other net, where we attempt to control things to mitigate our *It's definitely going to happen* hurt.

I had to locate that backbone for both, to stop my addiction to knowing what I know when I absolutely do *not* know and my covert attempts at controlling narratives to minimize any hurt (including my own).

I know it sounds *Wizard of Oz*-y, but when Glinda, the Good Witch, told Dorothy that the power to go home was within her all along, she wasn't lying. Dorothy never needed the dang permission slip after all. She was the permission slip. As are we all.

What If?

What if you could close your eyes and make everything get really quiet? Not a scary, middle-of-the-night quiet where you suddenly fling the covers from your body to go investigate.

A kind of quiet you've experienced. Like that night on Vashon Island, Washington, when you stood by the water's edge, watching the yellow moon set. A ninety-year-old man explained to you the difference between waxing and waning, a deer ran past, and a woman yelled *Get out of here!* before announcing that *Deer are just rats with legs!*

That part wasn't quiet, not in the true sense of the word, but the way we all sucked our breath in was. We stood looking at the sliver in the sky and listening to the hoofbeats of the deer, the lapping of the water. Not that I could hear any of it with my deaf ears, but this is a kind of fairy tale, so please, if you will, imagine that kind of moon quiet.

Our Superpowers

If you are willing to not only answer but also tell the truth, you will find that you do have that kind of quiet, where the world falls away as it draws closer.

Instead of feeling like you don't matter or that you are not part of the world—as I have so often felt—you start to realize, in this space you created, that you *are* matter. You *are* the world as much as you are in it.

And it's as bedazzling as a bra decorated with hand-painted shells and small shiny objects, a hand on your shoulder when you are sure all hands have abandoned you, a song that makes you get out of your chair or off the floor or down from the side of the bridge and dance with legs that don't seem to belong to you. Except they do.

There are so many parts of us rising from the embers of old stories, from the bones of ancient hurts and buried traumas. Parts we believed were lost.

When we commit to whatever we say we are—like not deciding how impossible something is beforehand—we can actually witness transformation. To me, that's some straight-up superpower stuff.

We all have superpowers. Maybe you don't want to call them that, which I respect, as that is discernment in action. It is the doing and using what works, *for you*. It's you not choosing to abandon yourself simply to get in line with someone else telling you what is right, what you should do, what is going to happen, what something is called, or who you are.

Call it what you want and do it how you want, but pay close attention to your wants, as they are what gets ignored most of the time.

No matter where you go, those red shoes on your feet will recognize you and welcome you.

There she is, they'll say. *She is finally home.*

This Is Not an Exit

A couple months after Henry proposed, we took a road trip to Carmel and Big Sur to visit friends. I had become close with Brenda Strong, an incredible actress who played his wife on the TV show they were filming in Montreal. She and her husband, John, lived there, as did my friends Nicole and Nat and their new baby.

After years of trying to conceive, Nicole and Nat finally did. I hadn't met their baby, Canyon, yet, so we wanted a few days to spend time with all of our *I Got You People* in that area.

While at Nicole's, Henry and I got into a fight that triggered the most vulnerable and hurt places inside both of us. I started crying and couldn't stop, so I got into the shower, where I sat on the floor, water pounding down on my head. And I sobbed.

At the beginning of our trip, during a walk in Big Sur, I saw a THIS IS NOT AN EXIT sign on a cliff. I couldn't stop thinking about that sign for some reason. I wished for someone to explain why I was so fixated with it. Maybe they could see what I couldn't, like when you finally find out the answer to a riddle that you've never been able to figure out and once you hear the answer it seems so obvious. Then you wonder why you didn't see what was blatantly obvious to everyone else.

In Nicole and Nat's guest bedroom shower, I transformed into a catatonic person. I was wailing like I'd seen people do in movie scenes but never in real life. I didn't know this type of exorcism existed in the world of actual people who bit their nails and bought toilet paper, who sometimes didn't put their shopping carts back, or who never learned to parallel park.

How could something so primal and terrifying exist in the mundane world?

Easily. The terrifying and mundane and beautiful are side by side. Always.

I had not suspected my body capable of making those sounds or of withstanding relentless pounding water on my face, but the body does what it has to, instinctively and without asking permission.

We could learn a thing or two from that.

Here You Are, in the Hard Part

I wrote the following to Nicole, but read it as if it is for you, too. Because it is.

> I knew the second the bathroom door opened. I could see you in the peripheral and then suddenly, you're under the water with me. You didn't pause to talk yourself into, or out of, anything—you took off your jumpsuit and got in the shower and sat down next to me.
>
> Later, you said, "Look at my baby."
>
> You took both our hands and said, "We see this adorable baby, but the hell I went through to get him here? Those ten years of pain? We don't see that when we look at Canyon's cute chubby legs. And that's okay, but we can't forget."
>
> My love's hand in your left hand, mine in your right, you continued, "This love of yours is like a baby being born of sorts, and

people somehow forget that birth is violent and messy and hard. This is why a lot of people don't make it. You are both so brave. Because look, here you are. In the hard part."

You showed us what I Got You *means. The both of us.*

My guy, who'd rather die than let anyone fuss over him, had tears in his eyes that he was not trying to swat away, said yes when you asked if we wanted scones, and then let you actually serve us buttered ones. And coffee. In bed! I was thinking, "Well, if hell hasn't frozen over." But like I said, "I'm all in."

I'm here for this ride, and I mean it.

The tenderhearted man I intend to spend the rest of my life with said, "You're family now, even if I never see you again."

You said to him, "Whoa, buddy! If you don't ever see me again, then you're going the wrong way."

There it was. Full-on Captain Obvious holding up a THIS IS NOT AN EXIT *sign.*

You reached your hands out. As if to say, "Come, this is the way. This is not an exit."

ALLOW

JUST SUPPOSE

Hold on tight to your magnifying glass when you explore and traverse the following terrain. Look closely at what, and how often, you decide beforehand on what you know you know.

It might be shocking to register just how often you've made your mind up before you have the actual experience. Shock makes us drop things, so hold on tight to the lens as you go inward because it can be like jelly beans. You know, those games where they ask how many jelly beans are in the jar? I get anxiety and cannot even begin to fathom a guess regarding the number. *Seven jelly beans? Seven thousand? I don't know! I just know it's a lot. I just know that I hate this game!* Ask yourself:

- How many things do *you* decide beforehand?
- Can you identify when and where you do this?
- What about how "unlovable" or "broken" you are? Or any other *Bullshit Stories* you allow to inform beforehand decision-making?
- How about the old *Well it's happened before so it's going to happen again*? What about the classic *It hasn't happened yet so it's never going to happen ever*?

Check in to see what you are deciding beforehand as a *daily-ish practice*, rather than yearly or when your body gives out from carrying so much.

I'll wake up and my limiting beliefs are in bed with me, even though I kicked them out, swearing *I'll never again!* Yet there I was, *never again*-ing all over the place. All those promises, and I ended up right back on my bullshit faster than you could say *We are out of coffee*.

Have compassion for the you who thought that nothing would work out for you and that deciding that to be the case beforehand would protect you. Let yourself off the hook and have a cup of coffee, because as I said earlier, we are not out and this is not an exit.

When We Really Look

Kid's first roller-coaster ride, you know how it can be:
that rush of not dying, an immediate *Let's do it again!*
The lure of terror greater than the pain of a long line.
We eat rainbow popcorn, privately wish for someone to
make our decisions, like we pray dinner will make itself.
It never does and still, we hope.
My neck suddenly bare, crystal missing, luck's no longer there.
I search ground, hair, bra, as if I could be so charmed
and still, I hope,
like trying to find a needle in a haystack of tourists.
Employees hunt for the tiny green thing,
fingers trace bobsled veins,
Bless them, they really look, but who deserves such a miracle?
Jerry on sled seven is who! *This it?* he asks.
I reply across time, space, Mickey Mouse ears, sunburns,
Yes! *Jerry! I love you!*
And the birds, the sun, and strangers waiting their turn,
they all clap, every single one.
In line for Flying Dumbo, a little girl licks someone's face.
Sweating fools, all of us waiting for something.
My son screams *We're flying! Look!* and I do.
I really, really look.
Oh, what we'll do
when we're finally done waiting.

CHAPTER ELEVEN

Find a Way In

WHEN I CAN'T figure out where to start, I'll look for a way in—any way in. Not just with writing but with everything—writing, painting, any creative venture, hard conversations, leaving a relationship, breaking tough news to someone. A way in to starting anything that requires starting. (Everything requires starting unless you are, let's say, a circle.) A way in to connection, vulnerability, or understanding someone or ourselves. A way in to our own hearts.

IT CAN FEEL overwhelming to even *think* of quitting your job, beginning the hunt for a new place to live, starting a creative project (writing, painting, musical, or otherwise), starting to date again after a long time being single or post-breakup, starting an exercise ritual, or starting to heal. I know how lost it can make you feel. It did for me.

Beginning is usually the hardest part, but it's the essential part. We have to find an opening or some kind of portal, or else make one ourselves. If you find anything that helps you do that, grab it. Then thank it and use it gratefully, like a light that helps you find your way in.

It Might Be Weird, but It's Your Weird

For a long while after I left him, my ex and I cohabitated as cordial roommates or amicable exes who needed to keep sharing a kitchen sink might. We did this for reasons that are ours. It was weird, but it was our weird.

One day, an easel that Henry had made for me to feed my newfound painting obsession broke. Henry is a woodworker (among many other labels such as *photographer, actor,* and *fixer of things*), and I love that he thoughtfully made it for me. I asked my ex if he might be able to fix it. Again, it was *our* weird. (And it was also our wedding anniversary, even though we were not together anymore but technically still married.)

As he fixed the easel in our driveway, I realized, just as other exes maybe have, that the dynamic within our home at present was no different from what it was *before*, but like me, maybe they did not dare talk about that because it would feel too sad. Too obvious.

It began to drizzle. I stared at my ex, crouched over the broken heap of wood as he fixed my treasured apparatus, and thought of the percussion of sound.

Constraint, restraint, restrain, strain, rain, pain. Gain. Ain't. Rain-pain.

He stood the easel back up, fully repaired. He is a kind man.

I resumed painting my current partner's face right then and there in the garage, as my ex-husband—but not really ex-husband, not yet legally anyway—puttered nearby.

The pull to create can be strong, and I urge you to answer it when it calls. If you ignore it, put it off, or pretend it's not calling for you because it might not seem like the "appropriate time" to make something or because you tell yourself that you are not a *real* artist, it'll become like that broken alarm clock. The one that keeps on blaring but that you get used to. You eventually tune out creativity's call.

I urge you to answer when creativity beckons you. I promise that, if you welcome it, it will always come.

Underestimating Elephants

When it comes to language, I exist in the peripheries and edges, the in-between. A place not dissimilar to how my ex-husband (roommate?) and I remained for a long time.

I live where words fall into cracks and consonants have no discerning features.

All of it and just so much of it. For a couple years, it rained an incomprehensible amount for Southern California. We desperately needed it and yet you know how it is. *When is it going to stop? It's just too much.* Still, we knew we were in a drought. *But when will it end?*

I felt proud of the painting of my *future husband? boyfriend? dude? guy?* even though his hand didn't look like an actual real person's hand. I found it oddly beautiful anyway. I could never seem to figure out how to draw or paint hands.

I finally said to the easel *I still don't know how, but watch me.*

It turns out that I did know. We try to talk ourselves out of so much.

Am I saying I am a master and can teach a class on drawing anatomy and how to draw really good fingers? No. I am saying I made something beautiful, even if it was only beautiful to me. I made something that made me feel something, and that is what I am after. A feeling of aliveness.

During that time around my easel breaking, it *was* a strain living that way with Robert. There was this elephant who lived with us.

The day he fixed the easel also happened to be our wedding anniversary, and even though we were no longer together, we poured drinks into tumblers with ice and toasted. It was my suggestion because what else do you do when an elephant is in the room? You alchemize. You find a way in to chat with the big old clumsy tusker. You pretend you know the language and start speaking, only to realize that you do in fact know it. You pick up a paintbrush and ask it to paint with you.

Who even knew elephants could paint, with those trunks and all? We underestimate so much, don't we? I'm not just talking elephants either.

Are you underestimating elephants? How about your own self?

The Divine Creative Spirit

For a long time, I couldn't get this book started. A tale as old as time, I knew what I had to do and yet I couldn't begin. I'd find myself at the ride's entrance, unable to step on. Then, the more time that passed, the more overwhelmed I became, and the more daunting it seemed, which caused me massive anxiety. Do you, too, know this awful hell loop? (It actually sounds like a ride at a carnival.)

Anxiety renders me unable to focus or create—it immobilizes me more than depression. It feels like I'm stuck in thick mud, and I can't stop fighting to get out. Except I am only fighting myself. And rather than mud, it's my brain that I'm stuck inside of. Let me tell you though, if your brain says *This is mud*, then it is mud. Tricky things, our minds.

It doesn't matter *why* I couldn't get it going, as much as the fact that I couldn't get it going. As I so often say, I don't find the *why* to be the most important thing. I did know the *why*, and knowing *why* did not cause me to magically begin writing.

How I found my way in to writing this book that you are now reading was through painting. I kept returning to my garage, where I make art. I couldn't seem to get words down on the page, but I could seem to make painting after painting, unable to stop, as if I were consumed by a spirit. In a sense, I was. The creative spirit.

I never brought my phone with me when I made art, so I was free from distractions.

I let my imagination take the reins. I let paint drop on the canvas and then tell me what it was going to be. I painted over things. I used whatever I could find in my home, including newspaper, my son's LEGO bricks, leaves, glitter, and cut up old poems of mine. I used paintbrushes and sponges and old shirts and my fingers and fake fingernails and balloons filled with water to paint. Something opened up inside me, and I took that something to the page.

I took the freedom I discovered with painting to the medium of writing, and any time I felt myself slipping back into *What will they think?* or *But is it good?* I'd go back to the canvas, or whatever random thing I was painting on because I painted on any surface or rock or mirror that I found. Everything felt like its own example of what was possible, and I kept coming back to those examples of possibility to remind me whenever I began to feel as if there were none.

As I painted, I kept asking *What if I try this?* and *What would this feel like?* I sometimes took off my glasses so things were purposefully blurry. Then I created from that point of view so things were softer and slightly out of focus. I sat on the floor of the garage, or sometimes outside on my driveway or by the agave and angel's trumpets plants. I stood; I sat on the kitchen floor when it was too cold in the garage; I brought art supplies with me when I went away for the weekend or even just to a friend's house for the evening. I added words and lines of poetry into my paintings, sometimes obvious, sometimes not; the same with hearts. I let my hand drift to see what would happen if I did not stop my hand when I thought it was supposed to stop. I thought *What if I kept going? Who makes up the rules anyway? What if I made this thing however I want to make it, even if no one else understands it or sees the same thing?*

I took that curiosity, daringness, playfulness, and lack of attachment with me to my writing practice, and to this book, as best as I could. I took it into my relationships and mothering and cooking and teaching.

I took it into every aspect of my life.

I did not intend to paint my way in to writing, but that is what happened. The whole *life is what happens when you are busy making other plans* thing again, right? It helped me get out of the bad neighborhood of my head and let things flow. It helped me look at everything with an altered perspective.

I did not know what I was doing, not in any traditional sense or formal-training kind of way; therefore, I didn't know, or care, if I was *doing it wrong*. In fact, I decided there was no *wrong*. In this way, I let myself off the hook when I painted from having to be *good* or *get it right* or any of the things I felt pressure for in other areas.

The neatest trick that I (unintentionally) played on myself was how this spilled over into every area of my life. I'd wonder *What if I was as free with my writing, with my life, as I am with my art?* I decided to see what would happen.

Everything opened up. That's what happened.

THERE ARE SO many ways our story can go once you find *a way in*, and what you find to use as *a way in* does not have to remain. Its purpose is to give you an entry point, and once you've entered, you get to do what you want. You get to do it your way. Lest you forget, this is *The Era of You*.

It would behoove us all to remember to use the lens of *What am I trying to get right and for whom?* and to keep looking at our lives through that lens. It will help bring us back to center if we catch ourselves trying to prove something to, or get permission from, anyone besides ourselves. And let me be very clear: You've got nothing to prove to yourself. You may want to keep commitments to yourself or stay aligned with who you say you are, but in no way do you have anything to prove.

Hopefully you will realize, at least today—because who is anyone kidding, nothing works *all the time*, not our bodies, our relationships, our coffeepots, or our ability to rationalize away pain—that the antidote to feeling like it's all meaningless is creativity. So go make bad art.

Make art or consume it or dream of it or invent it or cook it or eat it or read it.

Whatever you do, treat it with reverence and curiosity. This will remind you to look up and out and through and past and farther and way beyond what you think you know for sure.

Embrace ~~Where~~ Who You Are

Recently, I jotted down *Embrace where you are* on a sticky note. Then I got a tickle and slight clamp of my vocal cords, like the beginning of a sneeze. My body was responding, so I tuned in to it—a new-ish practice I aim to do as often as I can.

It was letting me know that what I'd written down wasn't true for me, so I edited my sticky note. I hope you write it for yourself, too.

The edited, truer message: **Embrace who you are.**

We can be such destination junkies, right? *If I get there, I will be safe. If I get there, I will be happy. If I get there, I will be good.*

When we trick ourselves into believing that *there* will be better, or when we wait to begin until we are "ready" (lol), or until we think we're "good enough," or until someone else gives us permission, we end up stuck between the devil and the deep blue sea. In that in-between space, there is zero sense of humor. Even less creativity. It's as joyless as an alarm clock going off on a Sunday, the one day you have to finally sleep in. In this space, the alarm clock is broken and won't turn off, so you learn to tune it out, but only halfway. You just learn to live with it, and then eventually, you can't live without it.

Over there or *one day* or *when I am good enough* are the places or times we think we'll find what we are looking for. The truth is that in those places everything is just out of reach, and even on your tiptoes you can never seem to get to where you think you *should* be. (Should is still an asshole, by the way.)

People still hooked on a *Where are you in your life?* paradigm will ask you over coffee and their grain-free muffin, as if they'll die if they don't know the answer, *What's next? And then what? Then what will you do?*

Too busy being productive to even stop and chew, they go straight to swallow.

We create altars to made-up lands like *The Land of Better and More*. We pray to find whatever we think will make us feel that it's finally enough, that we are finally enough. We think that when we do find it, it'll be proof of our worthiness.

We hope to find wholeness in places like:

- Thinness
- Likes, followers, comments, blue checkmarks, and blessings from the algorithm gods
- Fame
- Looking younger
- More money
- Great abs
- Big houses
- Having kids, getting married, "normal adult things one's supposed to do," et cetera.

We never get *there* because *there* is ever-moving, just like *them*.

I have gotten *there* ten times over. Not once did I realize it, until I was no longer *there*.

Embrace who you are. Who who who who who who.

Make an Altar

If the thought of making anything remotely resembling "art" makes you want to run away, make something else instead. Don't try to make "art." Make a personal altar. You don't even have to show anybody.

If you did make an altar, what would go on it? You can find ideas for what to put on this altar by investigating what and who is sacred to you, what helps you remember who you are, and what you are committed to. This is just another tool to remind us who we are if we resume the worship of *I'll be happy when*.

My new altar is on my desk so when I look out the window into my front yard, then farther past that, I see the objects on my altar glimmering in the light. A matchbox from a restaurant in Virginia from 1983, a photo in which my father smokes a cigarette, and matches on the table next to his elbow. A crystal, a rock, a pen, a feather, a drawing of a robot on faded yellow paper, old hearing aids, and a candle yet unlit. A photo of my son, a locket of his hair, and a little piece of cloth I thought I'd lost.

Use anything. Your desk or dining room table or wherever might be littered with enchanted objects in the guise of disposable junk. Pick up that random Popsicle stick you blamed your son for, even though you left it on the floor.

You might still feel like you just want to get *there*, to where you think you'll be happier. You might want to crawl in bed and give up on being creative, or just being a person, generally speaking. Get in bed if you want, and when you are ready, pick up where you left off and begin again.

We are here, say the *I Got You People*, the Popsicle sticks, the gift horses, and me.

Begin by collecting all the talismans you can find. Line them up as an offering for pure, unsullied imagination, untouched by cynicism, criticism, fear, jealousy, our *Inner Asshole*, Shame, *Imaginary Time Gods*, overanalysis, or Should.

The receipts and papers and photographs and whatever else you've discovered will also serve as an altar for grace, empathy, and curiosity. Give your altar any name you like. You can call it *The Altar of Things That Don't Mean Anything to Anyone but Me*.

Keep an inventory of whatever works. Sharing your inventory is not only a way of being an *I Got You Person*, but also a way to be of service because your personal *The School of Whatever Works* could be the light someone else orients themselves toward.

It's definitely healthier and more joyful than staying in bed in the dark like I did for a long time, pillow over my face, bemoaning *See? I suck.* It's okay if you can't see your full light yet. Do you see a sliver? It's there. Look closer. Follow that. A sliver's enough.

Pseudo Facts and Miracles

One of the reasons I could not bring myself to begin this book, for a whole year, was because of how rotten and unworthy I believed myself to be. I didn't think I deserved to write it. Ew, it's so boring to read that now. I hope your *Bullshit Stories* gag you as mine do me. May we all gag on our own nonsense.

That old story—the *You're so bad* one—took hold of me, pinned me down, and put me into the proverbial mud, where I got stuck. This is why *daily-ish practices* are important, as well as whatever you find that works to help you stay grounded in who you know yourself to be, right now.

After I broke apart my family unit, I decided on what the facts were, according to me. Just like I did after my dad died in 1983.

FAKE FACT: I was bad, deserved nothing, and I'd better watch my step if I knew what was good for me.

FAKE FACT: I'd better not even so much as imagine that I could let down my guard, because I couldn't, and if I did get anything, I dare not look a gift horse in the mouth.

FAKE FACT: That gift horse would take his gift right back where it came from and drop the other shoe on my head. Yet again.

These kinds of pseudo facts think they are protecting us from future hurt, loss, heartbreak, or people we love leaving us or dying with no warning. The same way its family members, the *Inner Asshole*, Fear, the *Shame Monster,* or any of *Shame's Minions*, think they are protecting us by keeping us in check with our expectations and beliefs. Thereby helping us avoid constant disappointment.

I let go of the story that I was bad after its reemergence. I put it back to bed, where it now sleeps. Hopefully, it'll remain that way. If it does wake up, I have tools, and I have *Heartsight*, which I will never forsake for another again.

FACT: There is no guard anywhere near the premises at present. Those facts I landed on years ago were no more factual than the fact stating that the earth is flat. I took off my protective armor, and nothing happened to me, except softening.

The Alchemy

I began to play with the idea of turning things on their head as not only an act of autonomy but also an act of creativity. I like to noodle with notions of *bad* and *good*. I do a thing in my "Allow" workshops where I'll ask people this question right off the bat, then have them use it as a writing prompt.

Are you willing to be bad?

I'm really asking if they'll let themselves off the hook—rather than seek permission to be let off the hook—before we even start. Are they willing to give themselves their own consent to suck? The purpose is that there is no (or less) attachment to making something *good*, to *getting it right*, to *being perfect*. It's fascinating how much we'll struggle to be *good*, just so we will not be *bad*, even when we have no idea what that looks like.

Who is the arbiter of what *good* or *bad* is anyway? I'm not talking about obvious things like murder or inflicting intentional harm, but more in the vein of who gets to say what is a *good* poem? Who decides what makes a painting *bad*? Who knows the *right* choice regarding someone else's marriage or job or children or health? Who determines what has *value* or is *worthy*? Who sets the standard as far as *perfect* (a myth) anyway?

I stare at my ALLOW tattoo on my inner right wrist a lot. It reminds me to check in with who, and what, I am allowing to define my life. It's important to stay vigilant; giving up our autonomy and sense of self can sneak up on us. Whether it's old Shame or our *Inner Asshole* or any external voice, such as the media—whoever or whatever it may be—it is crucial to make sure we have the facts straight. And the facts are bendable in this case, meaning *we* get to decide what things mean for us.

Bendable, as in everything is changeable.

I am endlessly grateful for the *not fake news facts* I create for myself. Otherwise, I'd still be living in a land where I am a bad person who does not deserve anything and who is afraid of looking anywhere even close to the mouth of a horse, let alone its heart, and forget her own heart, that scaredy-cat.

When I ask *Are you willing to be bad?* most people get giggly and excited, exclaiming *Yes! I am willing!* Like they've been waiting for permission. There's also a few, every time, who struggle with the idea of messing up even a little bit, of coloring outside the lines, of getting it wrong, of not being great, or (gag) *perfect*.

After I ask about their willingness to suck, I offer another opportunity to dive into this idea of *badness*.

What does being bad mean?

This can throw a person for a real loop. Go ahead, ask yourself. Write about *what it means to be bad*. What you write will be illuminating.

Most people get stumped about what it means to be bad and find that they can't write much besides *You run red lights* or *You steal forks from restaurants or cars from your neighbors' driveways* or *You hurt puppies or kittens.*

This exercise may cause you to reconsider narratives you've accepted as *that's just the way it is* or *that's life*. You may recognize ways in which you are too hard on yourself or you've held yourself accountable to be *good* or to *get it right*, when in fact, it's very hard to discern what those things mean. (Can you define them?)

I find it to be an exercise in levity, too. Some of the stuff we come up with as humans is just plain funny. Also hilarious is the fact that we often can't come up with a thing to define those terms. We actually have no idea what they mean! Try laughing at yourself. It's good, cheap medicine.

Good. What does it mean to you? What have you been told it means? Dig into these questions and leave no stone unturned, because lies hide under the ones we leave unturned.

What's a *good* mom? A *good* wife? Is it someone who stays even if they are unhappy, "for the children's sake" perhaps? What's a *good* girl? What's a *good* photograph, book, bowl of soup? Play with these as creatively as you can, with as much sense of humor as you can muster.

Make Bad Art

The greatest thing I ever heard was said to me by Pietro, the sommelier who does the wine tastings at the villa where I host my Italy retreat. He's been doing it for fifty years and is excellent at entertaining people and understanding and explaining the complexities of the varietals of wine.

The greatest thing: Do you know what he says the best red wine is? *The one you like. That's the best one.*

So says the wisest sommelier I have ever known. Straight from the horse's mouth. I live by that now. I hear his lovely Italian accent in my head saying that I get to discern what I like and what I want and what makes something the *best* thing (or choice). I now live by this unapologetically.

What he's really saying is that you get to choose yourself. Boom.

Good is what you say *good* is.

You get to say, and live your life in accordance with what you say, and all without asking anyone's permission. And that is as bad as bad gets. So go and be bad. Be very, very bad. Just don't intentionally hurt yourself or anyone else.

I fell in love with someone four seconds after leaving my husband and allowed myself to finally put down the belief that I was a bad person. Instead, I chose to flip my perspective. I was not *bad*, but *brave*.

I started painting with no idea what I was doing or what kind of paint to use, and instead of worrying *Is this good?* I asked *Does this feel good?* I noticed how I felt as I made art, and that dictated to me whether anything was *good* or not. That became my gauge.

We get to flip *bad*'s meaning and decide what it can mean for us.

We are not all-powerful beings who can manifest things just with our thoughts. I said what I said. This isn't *The Secret*. We can make up our own minds as to what is meaningful and true for us, based on how things make us *feel*. We do not have to stick with old stories or lies we previously accepted because we did not believe we had any other choice.

Another thing I do in workshops is something I hope you will experiment with, too. If it is too traumatic or upsets you, find something lighter and make it all about levity. We are not here to pour salt in wounds.

Write about a time when you were bad.

Notice the sleight of hand here, how I'm using my old *bad person demons*, but I turned them into portals instead of using them to hate myself to death. I'm using my experiences and *Bullshit Stories* as a way *in* to creativity, teaching, connecting, healing, and humor. We can always alchemize. Then, we can use what we make as a way in.

I love the freedom inherent in this writing exercise. You get to decide what *bad* means, as well as how and what you want to write, or paint, if that's your jam. Sometimes that's what I do instead, or in tandem with, writing. Maybe you'll cook or bake. This is about play and discovery. The medium doesn't matter. It's creating for its own sake. Let it be whatever it emerges as.

What matters is that you are tapped in to the creative spirit, which means you are not trapped *in your head*.

And so it is.

Where the Red Fern Grows

Let's say you decide to try this *let's make bad art* thing, but then end up just staring at a wall, or staring at a book cover in the corner of the room without ever opening it. You write exactly zero words. I have done this many times. I'd stare at a book like it did something to me and I was waiting to find the perfect words to retaliate, which never come. Naturally.

Curiosity will be the first thing to go out the window when malaise or any of *Shame's Minions* start their chatter. Remain steadfast in your commitment to keeping curiosity close and choosing it over fear.

If you stare long enough at that book in the corner, you might start to remember that time you read *Where the Red Fern Grows* in fourth grade in Mrs. Murray's class after her sister died and she'd taken off those two weeks and how you'd sobbed so hard you had to shove your face into your sweatshirt, but even then you could not stop crying, and how you kept on like that. You try to recall the plot of *Where the Red Fern Grows*, but all you can see is Mrs. Murray's gray skirt and sensible pumps and how the book had very tiny writing and you're curious if the book in the corner has an adequate font size for your aging eyes, so you pick it up to see, and when you read the first sentence, you don't notice your shoulders relaxing. But they do, and you're off to the races.

Connecting to Your Humanity Instead

I asked myself what a good mom would do (or a good artist or writer or wife and on and on), but there was no singular *right* answer. I don't care anyway. I do care what a *human* would do. Notice I did not add the word *good*.

I am no longer interested in flimsy words like *good* or *bad*. Not when it comes to being creative, and not when it comes to how I choose to live. With regard to adjectives that might attempt to describe us, instead of *good* and *bad*, I want the girth of the world. And beyond.

I'm interested in the terms no one else can define, except us. This is not too much want. What are those terms for you?

If you already played around with the prompt *What would a good _____ do?* try this reframe:

- What is the choice that will have me feeling the best, whether it's about a creative endeavor or not? Investigate that rather than trying to make the *good, bad, right,* or *perfect* choice.

- How can I connect more deeply to what I want, who I am, and how I want to feel, rather than trying to be *good* for the sake of others or what I've been told?
- Am I willing to allow myself to be human when it comes to creativity and life as a whole? (Had to throw that in there to remind you.)

There's nothing more *fall-in-lovable* than a person willing to be seen, a person true to themselves and their perfectly imperfect divinely human self, rather than someone trying to be perfect, who asks the world for permission and confirmation. If the latter is you, do not fret. Trust me, it's been all of us at times. Take a breath and begin again.

ALLOW

CREATIVITY AS YOUR WAY IN

I give myself a medal for using talking horses, as well as elephants in my living room, to demonstrate how living according to *should's dumb guidelines* or those tired narratives of *good* and *bad* or the *Imaginary Time Gods* is soul crushing. I am comfortable letting my voice be whatever it may be, without contorting it so it sounds how I think *they* want it to be. This hasn't been easy. It took a while to arrive at the country of *Here I Am and If You Don't Like It, Too Bad*.

You also get to have this freedom to express yourself without pretending, without shrinking, without conforming. It's time to question ways you've been told you were bad in your life, or believed yourself to be. What were they? Alchemize them. Turn them on their heads (and leave them like that). The world's your oyster, you rotten egg, so bring us your badness.

Caveat: You must (at least try to) have fun with this. Use these creativity prompts as your way in:

- Make a list of repeating questions, all starting with *Was it bad when I* _____*?*
- Write a poem, song, or essay, or create visual art of some sort, about beautiful moments in your life and then declare them to be *bad* moments, as a way to point out the absurdity of how we do this.
- Write about how you are still bad and then share all your deviousness. Maybe you'll begin to write and have an epiphany that you hadn't actually been bad after all. And so, you begin again.
- Make a *Should List*, poking *fun* at all the things you "should" have done by now. All the ways you got it wrong, according to *them*. Tear it up, if you want, or use it as a gateway to make art. Or as a way in to healing parts of you that felt like they messed things up. Find the absurdity. Consider things you've *should*ed upon yourself and where you might still be trying to be *good*.

Life can be so hard and unfunny, so if you are not actively looking for things to lighten it up or make you laugh, you might get dragged down by the hideousness of it all.

Try any kind of creative outlet, body movement, or breathwork to see what works as a way to quiet your *Inner Asshole Shouldy Shoulderton You're So Bad* voice. Creativity helps me get my head out of my ass. Sometimes it's so far up there I've debated calling Roto-Rooter to help me get it out. Finding a way to be creative is one of my go-tos from *The School of Whatever Works* when I need a good old head-from-ass pulling.*

You can use anything at all as a *way in* to your creativity, or as a *way in* to whatever you need a way in to. Here are some ideas:

- Create your own manifesto. Feel free to use the format or the title of *What a Good Mom Would Do*, with your own thing instead of *Mom*.
- Make a how-to manual. *How to Be a Bad _____*. Poke holes in all the *Capital* B *Bullshit* and ridiculous standards you might be attempting, consciously or not, to live in accordance with. The aim here is to recognize how hard we are on ourselves and then to stop. Or at least to stop doing that *so much*.
- Create a glossary of terms for words like *good*, *bad*, *perfect*, *lost*, *stuck*, *fail*, and *right*. Be irreverent if you like or poetic or silly or nonsensical. Create new meanings for them, absurd ones (which may end up being no more absurd than the traditionally accepted definitions).

---

* I have never tried oil pulling, although I hear it's great for your gums, so say the Ayurvedic folks. I have, however, done many a head-from-ass pulling. Only my own though. You can't pull anyone's for them, which is why calling Roto-Rooter would have been a dumb idea anyway.

- Challenge your *Inner Asshole/Shame-Shouldy* voice—or any of the voices—by writing down everything you recall it has said to you, especially about how you got it *wrong* or weren't *good enough*. Try to be a *scientist-ish* and look at what you discover without judgment. Then *Now what?* to begin the shift to something different.
- Write an "Ode to Failure." Using playfulness and levity, list or write a poem about all the times and ways in which you have done it *wrong*, been *bad*, or *failed*. You can make it a poem or a painting—again, what format it may end up as is irrelevant. Flip the ideologies. Rearrange the words. Explore what they mean to you as well as what you were told they meant. To do this often, change up the ideas you are playing with, or keep using the same ones.

The more you play, the more that gets exposed as untruth, and the more you discover about yourself. You can do this with any outlet of creativity—journal entry, poem, painting, essay, or anything at all.

This is *The School of Whatever Works* so just *let it rip* like *The Bear* told us to.

So what works? This is not rhetorical.

Truthfully ask yourself: *What is working? What isn't? What am I willing to create next?*

Be very discerning, Chefs. This is your life we are talking about.

Afterbirth

Everyone shits, the nurse said when I asked *Did I, you know?*
I snorted and out he flew, born on a laugh,
like he was already in on the joke,
the son I never intended to have.
Terrified of the horror on my chest, I whispered
Is he supposed to look this way?
Other things I did not know about babies:
how to feed, swaddle, hold, mother.
The little alien was not coated in vernix caseosa,
but fondue-like ethers that caused mothers to doubt everything.
How do I know this is my baby? Are you sure? Is there proof?
I knew about giving birth
what I knew about flying planes: nothing.
But, I flew that plane anyway, despite lack of piloting skills.
A gunk-covered infant inched like a fish toward my nipple.
My God, babies are such clichés, I said as the bile rose.
*As cute as buttons, sweet as pie, bright as stars, as fresh-
blooming flowers,* vomited straight into a bucket by the bed,
but then—a miracle! This boy I never intended, latched.
Intended repeated starts to sound like nothing.
Nothing intended, intended nothing.
Ordinary as a Tuesday, meaningless as a liar's seventh *sorry.*
Repetition strips original intent to its marrow.
You must listen harder when it sounds all wrong.
It was when the only sound coming from the alien
baby on my boob, was love

that I finally understood: *Intended* was a load of crap.
All our best, all our worst, and most of it not *intended*.
How can we plan for unexpected love?
I drifted to sleep, a human kite with a drooping placenta,
until Darth Vader woke me with a stabbing.
A murder attempt can bring clarity—this was no exception.
He wasn't intended, but what is?
I silently pondered through searing pain.
What is? accidentally escaped from my lips
and the nurse said *Pitocin*.
Helps your uterus contract and prevents excess bleeding.
I felt like I was dying, not to mention deaf as a post—
no wonder I heard *It prevents excess blessing* instead.
I pleaded with the nurse, with Darth and the devil,
Give my excess blessings back!
How can we plan for what has no name, or excess blessings?
We never intended to search for someone
whom we know isn't returning,
their smell in every thread, as if their dumb photo on the wall
wasn't enough to kill us,
we never intended to cry *Where did my heart go?*
even though we know it went everywhere when it broke.
It would be impossible to recover the pieces as they once were.
We did not intend for that.
How could we have planned for *that*? Come on!
How can we plan for anything besides our next meal?
Even that is asking a lot.

CHAPTER TWELVE

Keep Bending

AFTER HENRY GOT divorced, but before he bought his current home, he was renting a small house in Ventura. There was a piece of art hanging over the bed that read BY THE SEA.

For months I read it as BE THE SEA.

I did try. I tried to be the sea. I tried to bend, flow, and merge, to remember how fluid it all is, and that there is enough.

When I finally realized that it read *By*, not *Be*, I felt relieved I no longer had to try to be like water. Don't get me wrong, I want to be like water. I was just tired. I felt I'd rather be, say, a rock.* Like a permanent and immovable boulder, incapable of change, thereby permanently safe.

The part of me that already is water knew the myths inherent in things like *permanent and immovable boulder, incapable of change.*

After I finished the painting I did of Henry, I texted him a photo of it so he could witness my love in some tangible way because he was in another country, filming a movie. He didn't reply immediately. I

---

* It is very challenging not to get Simon & Garfunkel stuck in your head when you think of being a rock. Go ahead and try not to.

resisted the urge to pick at my face or fiddle with the hands on my painting.

It was the same day my easel broke, my wedding anniversary to a man I was no longer married to—although on paper we still were. That drives me crazy. *On paper.* What does *on paper* mean? Baloney, is what. *I love you*, but on paper. Then, it must mean something, if it's on paper. If *they* gave us a paper, then it must be real.

There I was, waiting for another man, who was not my on-paper-only husband, to confirm what I knew yet sometimes felt so desperate for corroboration, because old habits die hard. It made me want to eat my own hands. On a sticky note, to settle my anxiety, I listed the things I knew to be true in that moment: *He loves me, I love him, I am listening, I am not lost, I did not die from change, I am here.*

Then I added the biggie: *And I will always be here, even if he is not.*

Henry replied the next day and said how much he loved it and me. I admitted I'd been anxious and waiting. I swore I was done waiting, too. Joke's on me, I guess.

If I take the piss out of myself though, I can be in on the joke. That way, the joke is not so much on me, as *in* me. Taking the piss out of ourselves is often hard to do. It can take vigor and force, and sometimes, I don't have it in me. (Pat, don't rub! It's piss, so use cold water!)

HAVE YOU EVER gotten angry or ashamed of yourself for being in the *wrong* lane? For staying in that lane? For having human needs? For having hunger? For feeding it? For doing things on your own timeline rather than the *ITG*'s? For wanting, for not wanting? For resting? For not knowing what to do? For staying, for leaving, for lying because you felt you had to? For your sexuality, for desire? For aging, for changing, for quitting, for slowing down? For hiding, for not staying hidden? For being utterly yourself?

If you haven't, mazel tov. Also, fear not, for we can count on *them* to consistently and creatively show us all the ways, with a sly sense of stealth that often goes undetected, that we can, and should, hate ourselves. Then we can continue counting on *them* to sell us what we need to help us stop.*

It'll never make us stop. That was never the point. That was never *their* intention.

Whatever it is will create a dependence on the thing we've been sold. It doesn't have to be an actual purchase, even though it will always cost us. We will remain hating ourselves; the only difference will be that we will be hating ourselves while also having a dependence on something we were told we needed. That something can be anything from an antiaging cream to a belief to a person to anything.

It's a scam I've fallen for time and time again. I urge you to have compassion, if you recognize you have also fallen prey. Do you chastise yourself over perceived *mistakes* or for not being "perfect"? If you do, are you willing to alchemize that into something else?

You Are Not a Perfect Robot (Thank the Gods of Robots)

Maybe you've felt this, too, in some way? A self-loathing for simply being a human with vulnerabilities. As if you should have been born a perfect robot and you resent the fact that you were not. The nerve!

---

* Imagine that if we truly accepted ourselves, how many industries would go belly up? Chilling, isn't it?

You came into the world as an imperfect, fallible, malleable, beautiful person. There are so many ways we can beautifully, subtly, and often wordlessly tap in to the dichotomy of what it means to be a person. This excites me, and it's why *Heartsight* and *Shame Loss*—and whatever it is we find that helps us be true to ourselves—are so important.

We can't get to the heart of anything if Shame is the bodyguard, if Fear is the gatekeeper, if the *Imaginary Time Gods* are the bouncers at the door telling us that we are not on the list.

You don't have to be deaf to have experienced a feeling of being on the outside, of being lonely, of not being enough or being too much, of not deserving joy. Maybe you, too, have felt confused or afraid? Maybe you've been somewhere, like an airport, or perhaps your own life or marriage or long-standing job, where you've felt (or still feel) lost? Maybe you, too, have felt a sense of betrayal? Or of not belonging?

All I can say is *Me, too*, and *I got you*.

From the Other Side

I am reporting from the other side. Sitting in my home office in Ojai, it feels as if those years I spent waitressing and weeping in the server station are someone else's memories. The years I spent all my energy wishing I was someone else, and that someone else would save me, and I begged anyone willing to tell me what it was I should be doing and who I should be.

I still sometimes wish someone would save me or tell me how and what to do. I still sometimes forget I get to put down shame, that I get to choose me. It is still the *other side* though, because I no longer feel dead inside.

I never was actually dead inside. (Nor are you.) Or lost, or stuck, or bad, or any of the things I told myself. And yet.

My greatest love-weapon is my *Heartsight*. I listen when it reminds me that I get to start over. I bend, and begin again.

You also get to do this.

Forever Begin

The longer we avoid, the more comfortable we allow ourselves to be living in *The Land of Denial*, or any of the other myriad of places we inhabit. The longer we avoid, the more we can't distinguish which voices are ours, or whose voice to listen to. The more complacent we become, the easier it is to forget we get to experience anything else besides *fine*, sameness, or misery, and the more disengaged from ourselves we become.

> **Riddle:** If one person is pretending to not see the thing and thinks/hopes that their pretending to not see the thing will make the other person/persons not see the thing and the other person/persons pretend to not see the person who's pretending to not see the thing, then who is the one actually not seeing the thing and who is the one not being seen and what actually is the thing not being seen?

We get to put down shame we've carried for all of it, every last thing. We get to let ourselves off the hook for any and all complacencies we allowed for. We get to let go and let love.

We get to have a forever chance to begin again until we die.

I always find solace in the last line of the late Brendan Kennelly's poem "Begin."

> *Though we live in a world that dreams of ending*
> *that always seems about to give in*
> *something that will not acknowledge conclusion*
> *insists that we forever begin.*

Reckoning and Adjusting

I (try to) put down my *Bullshit Stories* on the daily. I aim to lead by example, so I do my best to be someone who tells the truth, as well as someone who is true to herself, while doing her best to not harm others. That is what I want my legacy to be.

ASK YOURSELF: WHAT do I want my legacy to be? If you have no idea, no biggie. But ask yourself if you are willing to discover what it may be.

It's an infinite thing to muse. If you get hip to the fact that you aren't living in a way that reflects the legacy you say you want to create and you are willing to adjust accordingly, that is the ultimate power move. You begin to bridge the gap, day by day, breath by breath.

We reckon. We adjust.

We repeat. A lot.

I CERTAINLY HAVE some inherited things, like my father's addict blood—or his bones, his knuckle-cracking habit, his tendency toward self-loathing, his skin coloring. I inherited other things, too, like his sense of humor, a loud laugh, a love of caffeine, and a desire to connect.

Our inheritances do not mean that we can never break a cycle, let go of a fear, or do something that scares us. Sure, we often inherit pain, trauma, fears, and quirky traits, but this does not mean that we are immutable.

We inherit what is ours, as well as what isn't, but we get to decide what to do with the inheritance.

What do you feel you have inherited, and what, in the name of fixed objects in space, are you going to do with that inheritance?

I do my best to check in on a daily basis to see if I am living in alignment with what I *claim* I want my legacy to be. Some days I am full of shit and I might as well be filing an insurance claim as Flo, the Progressive girl, so it sure is a good thing that we always get to begin again, isn't it?

Contemplate your own. What legacy are you willing to create, starting now?

- What do you have to put down for that legacy to begin?
- What legacy do you want to leave behind?
- What must die or shift?

TO DO THIS *reckoning and adjusting* without beating yourself up is the true win, the truest power move of all power moves.

Reckon with what you want your legacy to actually be and then adjust your life accordingly so that you *are* living in a way that reflects that legacy, at least for today.

Try not to get overwhelmed. We are just talking about *today*. I give you all the medals for even considering doing this because it can feel overwhelming.

No one else but you gets to create your legacy though.

One Blasted Thing after Another

Once, when I was pregnant with Charlie, I woke up one morning confused as to where I was and also that I was pregnant. I had been in a deep sleep after days of not being able to because: pregnancy. The kind of sleep that leaves you disoriented when you emerge from it. It took a few minutes before I realized I was in Vancouver, Canada, on the farm of a woman named Leigh, who'd attended my Italy retreat in 2015.

As I got less groggy, things started coming back to me. I was in her guest bedroom. The night before, I'd eaten a second dinner at ten p.m. out of a paper box, with my fingers, by the light of the refrigerator. Then, I'd taken a bath in her claw-foot bathtub with the brass winged unicorns, which spied on me from the windowsill.

I kept having these anxious dreams that would startle me awake. In one, my mom and I were buying scalped concert tickets from a tiny old lady with metal braces and then we were about to be arrested. Then, I was in the Atlantic Ocean holding an expensive camera over my head so as not to ruin it as waves pummeled me. In another, I lived in the house I always dream of—the one on Madison Avenue in Cherry Hill, New Jersey.

In the dreams, time collapsed into itself. My fears looked like white foam. I got down on the ground on our old blue porch in one of them and I kissed it. Nothing made sense, and everything made sense. I was there, and I was also in water. I was with child and without.

I had that *in it and also not* feeling, even in my dreams.

In them, I offered my hands up and asked *What, what*, without lifting my voice at the end to make it into a question. What, what.

As I came to my senses that next morning, I felt my belly's new roundness. I was weaning down on my dosage of antidepressants, and it felt like I could feel layers of myself actually sloughing off me.

I went out to join Leigh in the dining room, where we drank coffee and ate yogurt with raspberries. We sat in front of her big picture window, outside the trees bare, the sky ashen, the horses waiting to be fed.

I read the obituary she wrote for her recently deceased father as she read other obituaries. She told me that she read them all the time because she liked to see how people lived and what legacy they'd left behind.

Her dad had been a blaster. He blew up things—buildings, dumps, rocks. He was quoted as saying *Life is just one blasted thing after the other.*

I'll be damned. Truer words never spoken.

I DON'T WANT to get macabre on you and ask you to write your own obituary. (Do that if you want to, by all means.) Consider though how you are living and what you are leaving behind.

I intentionally wrote *leaving behind* in present tense because you don't have to wait until you are dead to leave things behind.

You don't have to wait until you are dead to leave.

Happy Birthday, Old Fart

When I was pregnant with Charlie, albeit very close to my due date, I hosted a private retreat in San Diego. I brought my mom, just in case I went into labor there. The toilet seats were heated and the beds were made of seventeen million golden feathers and there was a beautiful Czech woman there named Sylva Dvorak who had us do an exercise that changed my life. I now do it at my Italy retreats, crediting her, of course. Who would we be without our teachers and the ones who've guided us along the way? They are all over the place if we really look. I suggest we never stop looking.

It's like this: Welcome to your one hundredth birthday party.

The assignment: Give a speech. You can also do it as if someone is giving a speech in honor of you. You get to decide; it's your party. I tell everyone coming to the retreat to pack a party outfit—whatever that means for them—whether it's a dress or a bathrobe or tiara or purple lipstick.

You are standing there in Siena with us—or in a chateau near Bergerac or your living room or wherever you feel like doing this party trick. Everyone is gathered here to celebrate you, at least in your imagination. Place yourself somewhere that feels good when you think about that place. (What is that place?)

- What will you say at this monumental event?
- Who are the people bearing witness?
- What are they eating? (Super important, duh!)
- What do you want to be able to say you did? More important, who do you want to be able to say you were? In what ways had you *Done Love* in your life up to then? Did you choose yourself, at last?
- What do you want your legacy to be?

This is different from writing your own obituary, because you aren't dead. I often need a reminder that I am indeed alive and that I get to rewrite my story at any moment. If you need it, too, here it is: *You are not dead. You are alive. You get to rewrite your story at any moment.*

The Blowout

You better believe I am making it to my hundredth birthday.

It is going to be a blowout, even if I am in diapers having a blowout myself. I want to look down at my wrinkly old tattoos and know I spent my life embodying *I Got You* and that I did not forget myself.

I want to be able to say that I chose myself and that I chose love. Even if I didn't start until my forties, when I had a child, so I could show him what that looked like—so I could be who I said I was.

I want to stand there, or sit—I will be old, give me a break!—and look out at the crowd of faces and say *Thank you for this life that I co-created with you all*. I will have high-tech hearing aids by then, and even though my hearing will be completely gone, in the future, hearing aids will be more advanced than real ears so I will hear better at one hundred than I did at ten years old.

When I am up there in my gold-spiked heels and my walker, I want to know, with that same indisputable knowing as when I listened to my *Heartsight* and allowed myself to fall in love with Henry, that I did not abandon myself. I want to hold up my I GOT YOU tattoo to the sky and declare that it was not just for other people.

I was an I Got You *for myself, too,* I want to say. I *will* say.

Had We Loved in Time

Another one of Mary Oliver's poems that gives me goosebumps is called "A Visitor." In it, she writes about what love might have done—how I love the personification of love—if it hadn't run out of time. *Doing Love*, as I call it, is I think what she is talking about when she considers what love would do. Am I *Doing Love* now, before I run out of light? Or am I waiting? Am I not expressing myself fully? Am I letting fear call the shots instead of love?

Isn't that the human ride? This pilgrimage to love, toward dying with a heart as empty of misgivings and misunderstandings as possible, rather than one full of *I am sorry*s and *I wish I did it better*s and *I wish I'd left*s and *I wish I'd stayed*s? This path to recognizing our *Heartsight* and listening to it?

Isn't this the voyage of our lives—the journey to reclaiming our heart, if we have abandoned ourself?

To think we could possibly run out of time is what causes traffic, wars, broken hearts. It can happen. Wayne Dyer knew. We can die without fully loving the things right in front of us and inside us. We must not let that happen.

I vow to love in time, before I run out of light. I vow to love and choose myself now, while I still have light—while I still am the light.

The heart the heart the heart the heart.

It really does have sight.

Reflection, Refraction, Dispersion

In 2023, I led a retreat in Rhinebeck, New York, at the Omega Institute. As my group was writing, I took the time to compose a letter to Henry. As with my letter to Nicole, this is for you, too. It's for all of us.

> *The thing I want to tell you is how crazy I am about the way my engagement ring sparkles in the light right now.*
>
> *I sit here on this stage and watch my class write, and I want to tell you how I keep moving my finger to watch it dance and that I can see why people use the verb* dance *in contexts like this.*

As if it's moving its tiny joyful body to a beat only it can hear. The way it jumps around though, it's almost like you can hear the music, too, or at least imagine a rhythm.

I bet that if someone was watching me, they'd think maybe I'd stolen it and I just couldn't quite believe what I'd gotten away with. But there it is, on my left finger. And no one is coming for me.

No one is making me take it off with a stern "You don't get to have this," so I keep rotating my finger to watch it refract, as my class writes about a food that brings them comfort, per my writing prompt.

Refraction occurs when light passes through the diamond and gets scattered.

I understand you feel scattered after all we've experienced, how much we've bounced around, how much change has occurred. I know that scattered feeling is wildly uncomfortable for you. You've told me as much. It is for me, too, and although I am known to function in chaos and you mistakenly believe I enjoy it due to the fact that I am able to exist in it, I do not enjoy feeling scattered or being in chaos. I loathe it.

When it comes to us, I do not feel scattered.

I can no longer say that I have never known clarity. You helped me find what I thought was lost: my Heartsight. And that helped me find me again.

It helped me know immediately and still know that you are my Person, and more important, that I am my Person.

I do feel scattered with how my mind works sometimes and which bills I have not paid yet and if I have an extra bed for my Italy retreat to put a body in and where I put my car keys and if Charlie has a playdate or I'm confusing days of the week. But *nothing, nothing regarding you and me leaves me feeling scattered.*

Scared at times. Not scattered.

I am still often wary and I do my best to not let it rule me, is all. Some days it does and that's okay. Especially because I have a partner who makes me feel so loved and safe and who helped me recognize that I had that safety within me already.

This makes everything feel possible. That is why Freud's "How bold one gets when one is sure of being loved" is one of my favorite quotes. Isn't it so true? I can be afraid and do it anyway, especially because of being loved by You and by Me.

Dispersion is the final component of a diamond's sparkle and is what gives the stone its rainbow effect.

I am mesmerized by this. How does something this small not only have so much complexity and so many different parts, but also have the ability to burst into a kaleidoscopic rainbow, from just the slightest change in angle? As if with only a slight shift in viewpoint it looks like, and becomes, something else entirely.

We can be like this, too. Just a slight shift in viewpoint is all it takes to suddenly feel like we have fresh eyes, a new heart, another chance to begin again.

I want that for all of us, not just you and me. A willingness to not be so rooted in "I know this to be true and so it is fact" or "THIS is the only way" or "I know how it's going to turn out already."

I want all of us to remember that we can transform on a dime if we just bend a bit. So much is made possible with a willingness to look at something a little differently and a commitment to staying open.

We have grown so much. It feels like a miracle to have allowed space for that growth, when I always thought I needed to stay safe and stagnant. If you ever doubt that miraculousness, simply remember the feeling of pain, if you can. Or the idea of it since we can't ever really recall what it felt like exactly. Think of a time like last night. How we argued and how quickly we were able to bend back.

This is an embodiment not only of I Got You *but also "I am not going anywhere."*

If needed, we apologize. We are willing to let go, to get curious, to be wrong. This resilience has allowed me to trust that my Person (you, duh) is by my side and that your love is always with me, no matter what. The biggest gift, however, is how I am able to finally recognize that my own love is always with me, no matter what, even when I forget.

Love, I still forget sometimes. And you help me remember. See how it works? What us humans get to do for each other is quite a thing.

I love you.

Keep Bending

A diamond's sparkle is caused by three things: reflection, refraction, and dispersion.

So much depends.

Just like us, so much depends on how the diamond is cut.

When light hits it, it reflects off the facets and creates the appearance of a sparkle. The word *appearance* makes me wonder if it is really there. Or do we only believe it to be there? Just like we were never really stuck or lost or bad or monsters. Yet we believed it.

It's true that we can never be lost. We may get unmoored at times, but we can come back. If we are brave enough, we can choose to begin again. The coming back won't be exactly the same as it was. Nothing ever is, and we know by now that there is no *getting it back*.

We are never the same. But we are stronger, which is to say, softer.

To bend is to allow for regeneration, which means having a willingness to accept changes inherent in regeneration. I know it's not always (or ever) easy. We know that nothing is without change, but Lord, can we stop forgetting that fact?

Nothing is without change. And everything, everything is changeable.

When light passes through a diamond, it bends. It is only when we allow ourselves to bend that the inconceivable becomes possible. We must keep bending in order to begin again.

It's All about the Rhythms

In 2024, Henry and I went to see another play in London called *The Hills of California*, again by my brilliant friend Jez Butterworth. Laura Donnelly, the lead actress, is his wife and one of my best friends, and she brought the house down and left everyone unable to articulate what they'd just witnessed. Instead, people just stood clapping and clapping, jaws agape, unable to pull themselves away from the Harold Pinter Theatre because it would mean they were leaving the world of the play, and in no way were they ready to do that. We all remained, long after the cast took their final bow and the curtain closed, standing there with our palms together like a frozen clap, like a prayer.

Tears streamed down my face despite not hearing a word. *Hear* is not the right word. I hear sounds, sometimes. They just usually have no discernible meaning to me. Speech clarification is the most challenging thing about being with other people. I rely on bodies and context and the kindness of strangers to interpret. It's how I get by in the world, and if I didn't have a sense of humor about it—especially about how I mishear everything and always manage to hear a more perverted or sexual thing than what was said—I would never leave my bed.

Despite making out only a small portion of the dialogue, I *felt* the play, even though the details of what was said and the plot were both a mystery. My energy is spent trying to parse together sounds in order to have them make some kind of sense.

Jez later said *It's all about the rhythms anyway. Dialogue doesn't matter as much as the rhythms*, he explained.

This was profound and life-changing for me, especially coming from such an adored and talented playwright, whom one might assume the *words* meant everything to.

I'd finally admitted what I had been too ashamed to tell him: that I couldn't understand *The Hills of California* because I couldn't make out the words.

What he said felt like it let me off the hook, like he was telling me that I did not need to be so hard on myself for feeling lost and not comprehending every word. Like he was telling me I could unburden myself from this load of shame I carried.

It's not at all that I needed permission, but like I said with my marriage and wanting confirmation, sometimes it's the most beautiful thing when others can help us be softer with ourselves.

I could put down shame. I could let go. I could change lanes.

It was like Jez was saying *You did get it, Jen. You didn't miss a thing. You were never lost. You weren't in the wrong lane, after all. There were never any lanes to begin with.*

Nope, Wrong Question

The day after *Ex-Anniversary Broken Easel Day*, I sat on my velvet couch after my son and ex had gone to bed. I had a fire going in my fireplace, one of my great pleasures, as I watched the finale of *True Detective* season 4. In it, Jodie Foster's character constantly reminds her officers to make sure to ask the right questions. I loved that and took note, despite not being an officer in Alaska. If the shoe fits.

Nope, wrong question. Try again, she'd say.

Then, my own voice (I *think* it was my voice, but I was watching a creepy show with implications of ghosts so who can say?) said *How did I get here?*

Nope. Wrong question. That time it was Jodie Foster's voice. I am sure.

Wrong question, try again. Okay then.

How about: Am I *here*? Where is *here*?

THE NEXT DAY I was writing when Henry called from London, where he was filming again. I said I'd call him back, that I was writing. Hours passed.

I finally texted: I am almost done. I'm trying to find an ending.

I couldn't find the ending though.

Instead, I made it a beginning.

ALLOW

FREE UP SPACE

When Jez said that it's about the rhythms rather than the words, I felt relief. Also, a sense of hope. Logically, I knew I did not have to be ashamed of my deafness, but like I say, shame is not logical. When we have support or reminders that it's safe to let go, it becomes easier to bend and then to actually let go.

Dive into the following questions—or at least get your feet wet—to identify where you can free up space by admitting *This is not mine*. Whether it was never yours or was at one point is irrelevant. We are talking *right now*.

- What do you think you get to put down versus what you don't? Are there any *Bullshit Stories* hiding out between the cracks of these things?
- Is there anything that you haven't allowed yourself to put down because you (pretended) to not know how to?
- Is there anything you were too afraid to let go of because you didn't know who you'd be without it? Can you name it/them? You don't have to go do anything drastic. Start with naming the truth. The power in that act will give you courage, which feels like freedom. It did for me.

Make a chart of ways you can remind yourself, and others if you feel called to, that you are right on time and that you are not

> in the wrong lane. (By the way, I have never in my life made a chart or a diagram or graph. Do it your way, including writing it on sticky notes or old receipts or gum wrappers.)
>
> Remind yourself in big letters: THERE AREN'T ACTUALLY ANY LANES AT ALL.

It's All Ours

No one has been here before us,
no one sat at the corner table by the window
eating roasted hatch chili salsa and stale blue corn chips,
dropping bits into impossible to reach places,
long shadows cast from the New Mexico sun so mesmerizing
that not only does it make you forget where your mouth hole is,
it makes you not care.
No one else pulled hair from the drain,
took a lukewarm bath after giving up anything
resembling hot, sat in tepid water for hours,
no one else made love in between high thread count sheets,
admired the duvet—and anything that reminds us
we get to rest and don't have to have to push so hard.
How that can feel like a luxury that doesn't belong to us.
No one but us has pressed cheek to pillow
to memorize what softness feels like,
or sat in silent naked reverie, leaning into jacuzzi jets, marveling
at moonlight.
What shatters the illusion that we're the only ones to ever
peek into the arched recesses to touch

the wooden carvings inside, as if our own hearts
were on display in the hollowed-out niches,
is the simple intimacy of a Q-tip.
A lone cotton swab under the dining room chair upon our arrival
is evidence that we aren't the only ones
to close blinds, search for forks in unfamiliar kitchens,
scrub a stain from a couch that isn't ours beyond three sleeps,
feel the hiss of old wounds opening up,
accidentally fart while laughing.
We know we aren't the only ones to discover the punch of love,
but we have to trick ourselves that we are,
so we don't succumb to the sorrow
of what's only borrowed,
or sadness of how temporary it all is.
So, we ignore the Q-tip, carry on as if everything is new,
and that it's all ours, forever.

EPILOGUE

Eat the Cake

You Get to Have This—and Eat It, Too

I love cake so I wrote a book about it, said the dental hygienist with her fingers in my mouth. Despite being with my dentist and his team for more than twenty years, I'd never met this gem of a human.

I love cake so I wrote a book about it will forever be one of the greatest sentences I have ever heard.

She also told me that she was a writer and had written a memoir called *Cake Girl*.

It's about when I first started baking cakes in my life, with my mom, and things that happened around cake.

She removed her mask, per my request, so that I could read her lips, and she spoke as she moved an electric toothbrush around my mouth.

I married myself so I could have a wedding cake. I always said that if I wasn't married by forty that I'd marry myself.

I want to eat cake with this person, I thought.

She said the wedding was held in a bar, and I asked if she'd worked on a speech, my mouth full of fluoride.

Yes! she said, as if it were a ridiculous question. *It was a wedding!*

Everything she said had exclamation points!

I had someone marry me! He was a rabbi! I had a whole script! My boyfriend doesn't show, and I go, "Well, there's a party so let's have a wedding!" I come down the aisle and say, "Well, I wanted to marry my best friend!"

The rabbi said, "Do you love yourself?" I said, "Yes!"

She put polish on my teeth and continued. *I was in the* LA Times! *I'm the first person who has ever married themselves. Look it up for yourself.*

Come on, I said. *That's not really why you did it. For cake.*

She was flossing my teeth by this point, and it was hard to talk. She gently pulled the string from between my back teeth to make it easier for me to communicate.

Yes, it is why I did it! You have no idea how much I love cake. What I'll do to get it. People watch their cakes around me.

I don't usually laugh at the dentist, but there I was, howling. She finished up and told me the last line of her book.

I may not have found my solemate, but I know a good cake when I see one.*

In that tiny office in Venice, California, I got it.

We all deserve to marry ourselves, to give a speech, to taste all the cakes. We all get to share our stories. We all get to sit over an overly nervous dentistry patient and talk about who we are as the overly nervous patient nods and reads our lips to understand, a gift à la hearing loss. We all get to remind each other how we don't have to wait for the love of our life to arrive because we are the loves of our lives.

---

* I swear that she told me it was spelled *sole* like the fish.

We can be our own best friends, if we allow it and choose ourselves.

I know it can feel weird, maybe hard, and probably kind of cheesy, to say that we can be the loves of our own lives, but look, if you can think of a better truth than *I know a good cake when I see one*, let me know. I have yet to find one, so I'm going with Cake Girl's wisdom.

I felt like I was speaking to the wisest woman in the world with my newly clean mouth, courtesy of said wisest woman in the world. I had just been shown the secret of life, which was never a secret to begin with, just like my choice to remain open being the secret to every good thing in my life was never a secret.

In the introduction, I mentioned a woman from my workshop who was taught that you show people you love them by putting all your wants and needs aside. (Cake Girl would have a field day baking a cake with that.) I hope that if you were also taught that this act of self-abandonment is a testimony of love, you're seeing the light at last.

I hope you do not put all your needs and wants aside, but rather into a huge cake.

Then I hope you shove the whole fucking thing in your mouth and enjoy every last morsel, with pleasure.

You get to have this—the cake, in this case—and eat it, too.

Forget what they told us.

Eat the cake.

Offerings

Years ago in Bali, I was at the healing waters at Tirta Empul with my friend Ceri. We prayed for people, naming them aloud to each other. I prayed for my nephew who is always starving, for all the people I love who'd passed and the ones who hadn't. I prayed for all who were hurting, all those I believed I'd hurt, and the ones who'd hurt me.

Ceri's wife had recently left her, and just before she ducked her head under a spigot, Ceri said *And this one is for me.*

I also prayed that day that I'd find my way and that I'd no longer be lost.

IT WORKED.

See? I'm right here.

I offer it all to you now, without holding back, so you will believe me when I say that you, too, get to have this. Life is just one blasted thing after another anyway, so may we keep on bending and beginning again.

That sign I'd fixated on in Big Sur was true: This is not an exit.

It is a beginning.

Remember how Charlie asked if trees stayed awake at night and my friend told him *They sleep, of course. Holding up the sky is very tiring*?

Don't forget that.

You can rest. You don't have to hold up the sky anymore.

You get to leave *fine*.

You get to choose you.

You get to let go.

You get to love.

You get to grant yourself permission to live the life you want without having to give any proof. You are the proof.

You are your proof of life.

Acknowledgments

Thank you. Yes, you. Weird, magical, wonderful you. I am so grateful we found our way to each other. I will never take it for granted that you took the time to hold my heart, by way of this book. I do believe that is what we are all here for: to hold each other's heart, as if it was our own. Or, as Ram Dass simply and eloquently puts it, *We're all just walking each other home.* So, thank you for being by my side on this walk. The courage I got just from *knowing* you were out there allowed me to keep going when I wanted to throw in the towel, which was more often than I care to admit. (This shit ain't easy.) Thing is, it's always easier when you feel supported, or *gotten*. May I also provide that same sense of *I got you* to you, when you, too, feel like *I just can't do this*. I *did* do this, as it were. That was largely due to you, dear reader. If I could name each and every one of you, I would. Alas.

It would be impossible to name everyone who helped me dream up, write, edit, publish, and promote this book. I am sure someone's feelings will be hurt because I left them out (I'm looking at you, ex-boyfriend of thirty years back, who asked why he wasn't thanked in my first book, after we hadn't spoken in fifteen years.)

Let me start with my editor, and friend, Maya Ziv. To get to work with you a second time around was like coming home. I felt loved, seen, and supported. Also nudged, in the best possible way—the way only an expert editor can, to get you to go where you didn't think you could, because they believe in you and know you can, despite what you think. To give my greatest compliment, I felt safe with this book and my heart in your hands, Maya. Those who've just finished this book know how the need to feel safe is at the core of being. Thank you for that.

Years ago, someone tagged me in a video where someone was switching out a certain president's book (rhymes with *The Cart of the Seal*) with my memoir, *On Being Human*, and I howled laughing and then tracked them down, because of course I did. That someone then became my friend for a long time before becoming became my fierce agent, whom I would follow to the end of the earth: Lynn Johnston. I will never stop kissing the ground in gratitude. Lynn, you are everything I ever dreamed of. (I am not proposing marriage, but I am eternally grateful, and full of love for you.) Another example of *I didn't think I got to have this* proven wrong. My *Inner Asshole* has been foiled, once again! I will never leave your side, lady. Be prepared.

A deep humble bow to Ella Kurki for being so lovely, and so, so on the ball. I am usually *off* the ball and you make up for that tenfold. You kept the ship on course, and with such grace. Also, the rest of the dream team at Dutton gets wrapped in a big Pastiloff hug. (I will probably get paint on you, so watch out.) Thank you to my brilliant production editors, Erica Rose and Janice Barral, and the amazing managing editor, Melissa Solis. You all put up with so many changes from me and *off-the-ballness* (thank heavens for Ella) and, well, I don't know what I would've done without you. Dominique Jones! The cover is to die for, as my mom would say in the '80s. Actually, she still says it. It is! You are a genius. Thank you to Emily Canders, my publicist, who worked her tush off and made magic happen. Isabel DaSilva, thank you for your patience with me and your kindness and, mostly, your help with the things I am the worst at: planning and scheduling. You are my savior and a marketing master. Last but not least, John Parsley, my publisher. I just love you. Having you believe in me again means everything. You will have no idea because words fail. I know this: I am the luckiest. Dutton is my family.

Thank you, Sara Carder, for your editing brilliance and your friendship. Also for teaching me what it truly means to invest in myself. I would work with you any day, if you'd have me. Ours was the most beautiful and seamless collaboration. Kristen McGuiness, ours, too; and for your endless guidance and wizardry and book proposal wizardry, I thank you until I am hoarse from *thank-yous*. I would not be here if it were not for you, KM. Also, in supporting me in getting sober, without judgment, as that brought me to the finish line with this book, with clarity and a deep sense of alignment. As always, Lidia Yuknavitch, for all the things. We don't even need words. (She knows.)

My chosen family and teachers and fairy godparents and dear friends: Katie and Gay Hendricks, thank you for supporting me in all the ways you have. Ways that bypass language even. You both are the greatest gift to me. You have helped me to become who I always was but was too afraid to be.

Thank you, Josh Brolin, for your friendship and literary inspiration, as well as also supporting my sobriety journey with love and compassion. Thank you, Anne Lamott, for seeing me, for truly getting me and my weird-ass humor and my penchant for swearing. Thank you, Maggie Smith, beloved friend and poet muse. I love how we have each other's backs. Monica Lewinsky, thank you for modeling what it looks like to *not* hide in shame and for being so connected to your integrity. You showed up when it mattered and that matters. Kiese Laymon, for giving me hope, inspiration, and your love.

Thank you, Naomi Shihab Nye and Brad Aaron Modlin, both for your generous guidance and for your friendship. I cherish you both, you glorious poets. Thank you, Mimi Feldman, for being who you are, Squid. Thank you, Ceri Conway, Stephanie Monds, Koa Warren, Kirbee Miller, and Kristin Diversi, my sisters who helped more than they know with this book here. Krista Vernoff—I hold you in the highest regard and will never stop thanking you for helping me get to where I now stand.

I have deep gratitude for my ex, Robert. Thank you for allowing our life to be one that is stable and full of love and respect, despite things not turning out like we thought they would. We are doing love and I thank you for co-creating that environment with me. And you, Charlie Mel. Everything I do is for you. Thank you for bearing with me all those days and nights I was working in my office. Thank you for being who you are in this world and inspiring me to be more free, more joyful, more loving. Thank you for choosing me to be your mommy. My own mom, of course. (She even did my author photo!) My pops, Jack, and my incredible sister, Rachel, to whom this book is dedicated. She is my hero. (Shero? Whichever.) Of course, my daddy, so long gone. Thank you for coming through my son and for encouraging me when I wanted to give up. You kept reminding me what I was made of. Love.

Thank you to my beloved, Henry Czerny. Love of my life. I would never have completed this book without you by my side. Before you, I did not know what it felt like to truly trust or let myself be seen. Armed with those capabilities, as well as your unwavering love and support, I let it rip. Somehow, through forces I will never be able to explain logically, we found each other. And we had the courage to say *yes* to risk, *yes* to not knowing, *yes* to a life bigger than fine. You are the most divine human I have ever known and I hope you feel my love oozing from the pages of this book. You showed me that nothing is impossible, that I am not unlovable or a monster, and that love can show up in the most unexpected of places. Also, your bringing me coffee in bed every morning helped a lot. Maybe more than anything. I love you, Kittridge. (He's so much nicer than a lot of the characters he plays, as you can see. He's the kindest.)

About the Author

Jennifer Pastiloff trots the globe as a public speaker and to host her retreats to Italy as well as her one-of-a-kind workshops, which she has taught to thousands of people all over the world. The author of the popular Substack, also called *Proof of Life*, she teaches writing and creativity classes called "Allow" and workshops called "Shame Loss" when she isn't painting and selling her art. She has been featured on *Good Morning America* and *Katie*; in *New York*, *People*, *Shape*, and *Health* magazines; as well as other media outlets for her authenticity and unique voice. She is deaf, reads lips, and mishears almost everything, but what she hears is usually funnier (at least she thinks so). The author of the national bestseller *On Being Human*, Pastiloff lives in Southern California with her son, Charlie Mel.